ACCIDENTALLY ADAMANT

A story of a girl who questioned convention,
broke the mold, and charted a course off map

TISHA SCHULLER

Accidentally Adamant
Copyright 2018 © Tisha Schuller

ISBN: 978-0-9993220-0-0
Library of Congress Control Number: 2018930767

for Papa Norm
1939-2016
I know you would have read it, and I hope you like it.

Foreword

by John W. Hickenlooper

I'm an extrovert at heart. Being a geologist, brewpub owner and entrepreneur, Mayor, and Governor have all been rewarding work by themselves. Most of the time.

Each time I've embarked on something new, it's always the people involved that have made my career the most fulfilling. One of the true joys of working in public service is the opportunity to collaborate with exceptional people who, despite the noise and rancor that frequently accompany the job, remain focused on doing the most good for as many people as possible.

Tisha Schuller, without question, is one of those people.

I first met Tisha Schuller as Mayor of Denver. As Governor, I had the opportunity to work closely with her on energy issues facing Coloradans during her time as the President and CEO of the Colorado Oil and Gas Association. It was reassuring to find a fellow geology nerd and eternal (and yes, maybe a tad naive) optimist working in one of the most contentious industries in Colorado, not to mention leading that industry's trade group. You can count on Tisha to always lead a thoughtful discussion on energy, while listening diligently to any counterpoints.

The progress we've made in making Colorado a great place to do business, while having the highest environmental protections, was possible because Tisha and other like minded leaders were able to have thoughtful discussions, embrace compromise, and find middle ground.

And I think Tisha has arguably the best background to give detailed advice on how to get to a place of compromise. At first blush, however, it may not seem that way. She is a former ultimate frisbee playing self described hippy who graduated from Stanford and lives eco-consciously in a cabin west of Boulder, who became the public face of oil and gas in Colorado and managed the industry first hand through five major, precedent setting, regulations.

This is usually how a fish out of water movie starts.

But as Tisha puts it, finding the middle comes down more to being dedicated and pragmatic, having an open mind, carefully taking stock of your beliefs (and regularly reexamining those beliefs), talking directly with the individuals and families your work impacts, all while having a rigorous mentor to help you identify gaps you might be missing.

With honesty and a good dose of humor, Tisha outlines how she came to these conclusions. It is a story equal parts personal narrative and a first hand account of oil and gas development in Colorado, as well as a guide for approaching controversial topics with humility and an open mind. Not to mention lessons on energy development in the 21st century on par with a university lecture.

It's worth noting, you don't have to be working in the energy sector to learn from Tisha's story and experience.

It's a story that outlines the need for each of us to be more open to discourse in our day to day lives.

Which has become an urgent need in our country.

In recent years, it's become very easy to split ourselves into teams and camps, complete with labels or monikers.

Liberal or conservative. Environmentalist or oil and gas industry representative. What news we read or listen to.

Our politics and government often appear intractably stubborn; it seems pessimistically inevitable that things will only get more divided and contentious.

Especially as listening and compromise aren't nearly as sexy when compared to having two diametrically opposed camps battling to the bitter end, hellbent on victory at any cost. As Tisha says, the loudest and most opinionated often dominate discussion.

Lincoln once said strong passions today will be our future enemies. But reason, "cold, calculating, unimpassioned reason, must furnish all the materials for our future support and defence."

Tisha's first hand experiences matter in today's environment.

We have to get back to that middle ground.

To recognize groups are not faceless monoliths, but made of people who want the best for them and their families. To be above winning and losing. To recognize that disagreement is good if done with respect. That changing your mind when presented with facts is natural and should be commended.

And most of all, to sit down and have honest discussions with one another.

For example, if you talk to both the oil and gas industry and those concerned about its development, both will want it done in the safest manner possible. Few, if any, actively want to harm our natural spaces. Once we recognize where we get along, rather than focusing on our disagreements and automatic defenses, there is a lot of great work to be done to help in the community.

In an era of Twitter, soundbites, and scoring cheap shots for political points, we need more leaders like Tisha. She is the kind of leader that makes Colorado such a great place to live and do business. She is bold, independent, and unapologetically committed to the common good.

Let's follow her lead.

Giddyup.

John W. Hickenlooper
Governor of Colorado
March 2018

Contents

Preface

April 2014

I felt sick to my stomach. I knew it was important to make eye contact, to hold my Mona Lisa smile in place, but my stomach was roiling. I was sitting in the center seat of the conference table, which was a long, glass-top oval. I had learned that this was the actual power seat at a Board table, the one in the middle of the long side. People who wanted to appear in power sat at the head, but people who wanted to wield power chose the seat I was sitting in.

Aware of every aspect of my body language, I took long, slow breaths. I kept both hands visible on the table, as if I had a gun in my pocket that I would not draw. Fingers open, relaxed. I kept the Mona Lisa smile in place while I surveyed the table, nodding, making eye contact, waiting for everyone to take their seats.

Exhaling slowly, I surveyed the scene. In a meeting, I liked to make people become quiet without saying a word: it was another way to wield power without being threatening. If you're going to be a woman in oil and gas, you must learn early not to be menacing.

I stacked my papers on the table and took up my pen, leaned forward ever so slightly, and felt all eyes on me now. "Thank you for coming. Now let's get to work." Slight smile that doesn't reach the eyes. You have to know when to include the eyes in your smile.

Twenty men representing twelve oil and gas companies sat around the table. The only other woman who normally would have been in the room was my counsel, but this was not an official meeting and she was not there.

I laid out our objectives.

"Everything we discuss today is confidential. Does everyone agree to hold our discussion entirely confidential until a deal is reached?" I looked around again slowly, one eyebrow raised. The one eyebrow is not my forte, but it has a time and a place. I had learned that when requesting confidentiality, you were never going to get it, but I liked to make sure that anyone in the room who was going to spill the beans would suffer within themselves when they did it. Like a flight attendant attending to her exit row, I waited until every single person had made eye contact and said yes or nodded.

> It had taken me a while but I had learned to appreciate awkward silences.

I did not need to reiterate to this crowd that they faced the greatest existential threat of their careers. Although everyone in the room had lived through one, if not two, oil industry boom and busts, never before had environmental activists so thoroughly threatened their livelihood. Officially, I was the head of the Colorado Oil & Gas Association (COGA) and the face of the industry. In this room, I was merely a facilitator.

> A scared facilitator.

Twelve million dollars had been raised for two statewide anti-oil and gas ballot initiatives. Although we wouldn't admit it publicly, the initiatives were cleverly crafted and polled really well. I had joined several state leaders who were working together privately to create a legislative deal that would result in funding being pulled for those initiatives. It was a sketchy prospect.

COGA represented over 300 members at the time, and here I was meeting with just 12. There is a very good reason why trade associations generally have reputations for calibrating to the lowest common denominator. That is the only way to agree on anything: aim low. Here I needed to exceed that bar if I wanted to defuse this threat.

There were congressmen, senators, state representatives, and company executives playing different parts in this drama. Today, my job was to create a legislative draft from "a subset of industry" that could get the deal done. If I failed, we faced a brutal six-month ballot initiative fight that would likely reach $50 million in spending, and which we were ultimately likely to lose.

Events in the state had been leading to this moment for years. As oil and gas development had conflicted with suburban sprawl, communities from Fort Collins to Colorado Springs had experienced an increased level of community opposition, ultimately culminating in this state-wide ballot initiative fight. If the ballot initiatives passed, it would deal a massive blow to popular support for oil and gas, and ultimately make it difficult, if not impossible, to drill in the state. The initiatives were opposed by moderate Republicans and Democrats alike, and nearly every civic and business organization that mattered. But they still polled ridiculously well.

I drew a slow breath and changed my facial expression to *let's get to work*. I spoke slowly, methodically moving my gaze around the room. I had a carefully prepared plan that I articulated well, while taking in the crossed arms, blown out breaths, and stern expressions of oil and gas CEOs and their executives around the table. This was undoubtedly the toughest meeting of my career.

Three quarters of the room wanted the ballot fight. This would have been difficult for me to understand four years earlier, but years of incessant legislative, regulatory, and local battles had turned us all into more cagey, aggressive versions of ourselves. We were all more inclined to hit first and query later. I was experiencing this first hand, and it's another reason that my total self-control was paramount. I not only had to facilitate this group to the best deal, I had to do so in a way that they *wanted* the deal. And that they felt it was *their* deal.

Under no circumstance was I to play an obvious leadership role; frankly, no one in the room liked me. I do not exaggerate. As a result of this meeting, one CEO in the room spent the next five months conspiring for my removal from COGA. All of that was irrelevant; I felt the weight of 40,000 oil and gas jobs on my shoulders.

So I had the seat in the middle of the Board table.

1

Died Chocolate

September 1990 Stanford University

I discovered protesting during my first year of college. It wasn't anything I'd planned. One day, I was passing through the common area of my co-op and saw a dozen students crowded around the tv watching air strikes. I sat down with them, mouth agape. The news coverage looked like a video game being played out, and I could not reconcile that with the reality of people being bombed. I felt a painful stirring in my gut, one that I had never experienced before. When I saw flyers papering a kiosk announcing a "protest meeting," I felt the call to action.

Today, when I think back to that day of my first student protest, it had seemed so lighthearted, more like a continuous party than a "protest" of something. We had gathered in the student union conference room armed with a bunch of chocolate bars. Using the hot plate, we festively melted the chocolate with the giddiness of twenty-year-old partiers—squirting in a few drops of red food coloring. Voila! Real-looking blood. Wary of the spoon because it would get hot sitting in the pot on the hot plate, we had drizzled the still-warm chocolate all over ourselves and our clothes.

We had drizzled and laughed, and made our bloody way out to the common area in front of the bookstore to put our preparations into action. It was the days of the Gulf War (now the *first* Gulf War), but to me, it was the War for Oil. I was headed to my first protest.

Soon I found myself face down on the concrete outside of the book-store with bikers whizzing past my head, and someone was yelling at me. My face was cold, but I was pretending to be dead, so it's not like I could switch cheeks. Especially with some woman yelling, "My brother is in Kuwait, you bitch!" at my face. I thought to myself, "My cousin is in Kuwait."

It was the first time that connection had occurred to me.

I had arrived at Stanford University in the fall of 1989 feeling like a bird freed from jail with absolutely no plan. From the first day of 8th grade, I had prepared myself to get out of Tucson with such enduring focus that, now that I had made it, the next steps seemed, well, irrelevant. I was used to taking on too much, achieving for the sake of my college application, and now that I had arrived, this girl was going to have fun.

I joined Ultimate Frisbee, took dance classes, and got a job at the Coffee House, the CoHo. A bit naive still, I hadn't thought about protesting anything at that point. I dropped my plans to be an engineer when I figured out that I couldn't make it in just four years and I had just four years of scholarship. Don't get the wrong impression, I worked my ass off. But I was woefully ill-prepared for the quality and quantity of instruction, expectations of the professors, and pure intellectual firepower of my classmates. I knew it didn't matter. I'd made it and life was now for living.

My first term paper was an exercise in humiliation.

I had asked Adam, another freshman across the hall, to give it a read. He frankly looked horrified as he read, and we spent the better part of the night rewriting it. (Maybe I should have taken the hint when I failed the AP English exam.) When I got that paper back, it had a big fat C on it, and I had cried. I'd never had a C before and I hadn't seen a B since the one I'd gotten in 7th grade when I swore I'd never get one again.

I went to see the professor during office hours and, to my horror, I cried again. She looked at me sternly from over her glasses and said, "Every year I see kids like you. You come from a mediocre public school in some town and you are *years* behind all the kids that have had a lifetime of preparation and a decent education." She took off her glasses, and softened, visibly. Maybe it was the open-mouthed look of horror on my face. *Did Stanford let me in by accident?*

Perhaps reading my mind, she said, "They don't make mistakes letting students into Stanford." I exhaled, probably visibly. Wiped my eyes, pinched my nose with my sleeve, squeezed my eyes shut then opened them wide to stop the flow. "You're going to have to work your ass off," she continued, "and it's probably going to take you the better part of two years to catch up. Go sign up for a writing class; you still have time to work it into your schedule."

That was my first encounter with a mentor, and with tough love.

And so I had spent my first two years at Stanford figuring out who I wanted to be. By the time I needed to commit to something, I'd found Earth Systems, a brand new offering. I loved the idea of being a part of a novel major focused on a field I felt drawn to—science and the environment—so I quickly quit the coffee shop and concentrated on my work-study job in the office of Career Services. But I also captained the inter-collegiate women's Ultimate Frisbee team, which allowed me to travel up and down the state of California. I was happy.

I slowly made my way from child to adult, settling more and more comfortably into what I came to realize was my hippie bent.

It wasn't a path I was funneled toward naturally. I'd made hard, unique choices along the way. I didn't rush sororities with most of my freshman dorm mates. I stuck with Ultimate Frisbee that first year even though we could hardly field a team of seven. Unsure of who I was, I took organic chemistry and feminist studies, which were both really, really hard for this (formerly) straight-A student. But I found myself increasingly among like-minded people, who expanded my thinking and my horizons.

Living unconventionally, the biggest conventional commitment I made was becoming an RA (Resident Assistant); however, I became an RA in a co-op. There were a handful of co-ops at Stanford and they were definitely known as hippie-ville. As the RA, I presided over the governance of the co-op, which collectively prepared all of its meals and cleaned the house. It was here I was taught how to bake bread, which came out of the oven every night at midnight. I also learned the process of making decisions by consensus at our monthly mandatory house meetings. Little did I know that years later I would be using this experience again in my professional life.

During those years at Stanford, I made dozens of micro-decisions that ultimately turned me into a *New York Times*-reading, elite, educated liberal. I registered to vote for the first time, not as a Democrat, but as a member of the Peace and Freedom Party. I didn't know what that was then, and I still don't today. At the time it felt the most rebellious and individualistic of paths. There wasn't a tribe, a clique, or a club, until I joined that first war protest movement.

I had gone to that first meeting of the war protest alone. You would think that, at the co-op, where every one of us embraced hippie-dom like we were in the Sixties, a big group of us would have said, "Let's go protest the war!" But in reality, at Stanford everyone is working their asses off, and there wasn't a lot of simply hanging around, let alone demonstrating. When I'd heard the news coverage of air strikes, as a newly conscious adult in the world (who had yet to vote in her first election), I'd thought it was strange that the war wasn't garnering more interest.

Was this the beginning of my Vietnam?

So, protest I did. I quickly found my first clique of do-gooding activists. Today I sigh at my naiveté. I look at activists with more empathy than they will ever recognize in my face – part of me is just like them. It had been all so exciting! We would sit around a table, first a small group strategizing, then over time growing to more than a hundred men and women! We got full-day training on participating in peaceful protests. I learned how to lock arms and sit down simultaneously, be assertive without provoking violence, and handle being arrested. We planned our first event.

Even with so much build-up, it was all pretty social and fun, and it wasn't until I found myself face down on that hard, cold concrete sidewalk that I questioned the wisdom of what I was doing. I didn't question for long.

"No blood for oil!" I chanted silently to myself. "We are in the right here! They are going about their days ignoring the fact that *people are dying.*"

"We don't need their dirty oil!"

2

A Girl, A Truck, and a Dog

April 1996

As I slowly climbed up the final rise before descending into Boulder on Highway 7, I grimaced and wiggled my right hip. My butt had fallen asleep—I'd been driving for about seven hours since leaving Salt Lake City. But the scene before me was startling for its immense beauty and I was wide awake, taking it all in…farmland on either side of the two-lane highway and, beyond them, the Rocky Mountains in all their blue and purple glory as far as the eye could see. And those shocking Flatirons, slanted reddish-brown sandstone formations, just standing there as if they had all the time in the world.

Zodi exhaled awkwardly into the air vents as she often did when the windows were closed. Zodi and I had been inseparable companions ever since I'd gone to the California shelter with the intention of checking out a "Rottweiler-mix." In actuality, Zodi was some kind of Doberman-German shepherd mix. No matter, once I saw her, I couldn't leave her there. I leaned across the cab and cracked her window, keeping my eyes on the road. Now that we were off the highway, she could take in the smells. She stood and wagged her tail, nose out the window and butt in my face. I pushed the empty Smart Food bag onto the floor and began singing.

This was a moment of adult arrival.

I had turned 24 the year before, and in classic over-achiever fashion, had felt like my life was getting away from me. Not so long ago, I'd had a decent job with a small environmental consulting firm based in California, but my romantic relationship had just ended, and I was heartbroken and emotionally adrift. After graduating from Stanford two years before, although I had planned to stay in the Bay Area, suddenly that amazing place with its perfect weather felt confining and crowded and, well, emotionally itchy. I had no Plan B.

It was on a beautiful January day, sunny and crisp, that I had been running errands over lunch at the consulting firm: picking up Zodi a new dog collar, grabbing essentials from Trader Joe's, and singing loudly to sad Alanis Morissette in the way that only the newly heartbroken can. Although it was January, the weather was perfect and the windows on my pickup were cracked open. The thrill of purchasing my first truck hadn't worn off yet, and although it had no air conditioning and absolutely no capacity for acceleration, I relished every moment in it. It was black and raised for a small truck. I had bought a matching shell to cover the bed, and, I gotta say, it looked pretty bad ass.

When I had returned to the combo office-warehouse space in Menlo Park where I worked, I'd ignored my now too-familiar office mates and headed to my desk in our large common space. I had spent the last year and a half doing fieldwork with these guys, either hand-drilling cores at oil and gas service facilities, or pushing a fancy pressure washer into big piles of dirt in a one-foot grid pattern to help clean it up. To save our per diems, we often shared cheap motel rooms while on the road. While admittedly, this is not an ideal arrangement, it had allowed me to save a good bit of money (and, voila! I bought a truck!). On the job, we traveled in a diesel pickup pulling a trailer, staying in the same hotel rooms for days and sometimes weeks at a time, and did sweaty, miserable fieldwork. I did not need to say hello when I returned from lunch.

A nod and a grunt were generally adequate.

The big boss, TJ, who had possibly one year of experience on me, called me into his office. He closed the door and I looked at him sideways, *What had I done now?* I was a surly but highly productive employee and had moved from being his administrative assistant to project manager in the last year. The economy had sucked when I graduated, and I'd had a difficult time finding any job (a Stanford degree is not particularly helpful in the Bay Area)—let alone one in the environmental field. I'd been grateful for the consulting opportunity with TJ and I worked hard. When I'd gotten the $26,000 a year salary offer, I had bought all my friends beer that night.

I was spectacularly rich!

TJ had a map spread out on his desk. Our company, Penny Environmental, had grown from 3 employees (TJ was number 3) to 40 in the last three years. We really only had one client, but it was a good one, and our primary point of contact, Linda, liked me. She was afraid to fly and so I would take the train or drive long distances with her when she needed to visit her company's field sites. Linda had called Tom, the president of the company, and said that Penny needed a Rocky Mountain field office. Through some behind-the-scene machinations, the Penny Environmental Powers That Be had decided that I should open it.

I had just won the lottery.

Three months later, here I was cruising down this two-lane highway toward my bright future. Choosing Boulder had been easy. I had written to chambers of commerce in a dozen mountain towns and they'd sent back manila envelopes full of brochures. Missoula, Sun Valley, Golden, Cheyenne. I had never been there but, trusting my gut, I knew that Boulder was the only place for me. A liberal college town with a world-class women's ultimate frisbee team. What else did I need to know?

I had flown out to Denver, rented a car, and drove north to Boulder the first week of April. I rented half of a duplex—one room I would sublet and one room for me. I planned to set up the Penny Rocky Mountain office in the living room. Three weeks later, I was driving there to move in.

I was pretty sure that I would never leave Colorado.

3

An Early Epiphany

April 1997

Just one year later, I was commuting from my new mountain cabin to a new job. The mornings were a little hectic. I would drive fast because it always took significantly longer than the ten minutes I told myself the drive required. I wound my way down to Boulder and zigzagged through neighborhood streets. I parked illegally in the Wild Oat's parking lot and ran for the bus stop. I could see the B Express coming around the curve on Broadway. Please oh please, oh please, turn light. Green! Yes. The bus pulled up, and I slowed my breathing and walked casually across the street to the bus stop as if I had all the time in the world. The door accordioned open, I flashed my Ecopass and boarded for the commute to Denver, 28 miles away.

After Penny Environmental had started showing signs of both micromanaging me and having financial issues, I had started looking around. I closed on the purchase of my mountain cabin and started that new job with PRC Environmental the same month. Penny was bankrupt three months later.

Whew—I had dodged a bullet there.

That long daily commute to work was tough, tougher than I had imagined. But I was 25 years old and working at a fun office in downtown Denver full of single, smart twenty-somethings. I also had made the premier Ultimate Frisbee team, Rare Air, which practiced in Boulder four days a week. Between working, partying, and practicing, the only challenge was getting to and from my remote cabin where Zodi was stranded during the day.

Relatively quickly, I had the good fortune of landing a large new client, a natural gas processing company with locations all over the country. One of the projects our company developed for them was a two-hour Environmental 101 course, which would be given to their oil and gas field personnel all over the country. For me, it was a dramatic step up from the field work projects I'd been doing for Penny Environmental. At Penny I had often worn coveralls and spent long, sweaty days sampling oil and gas sites to assess their contamination, or participating in their cleanup. It wasn't exactly what I had imagined an environmental career would look like. I was thrilled at this opportunity to teach environmentalism.

Teamed up with our client, we created the training and then developed a plan to give the presentation at every single one of their locations. As the project manager, I took on the lion's share of this work. I ended up giving this mandatory company training dozens of times—in the most diverse, unappreciative, often hostile sites imaginable.

In hindsight, I don't blame them for being hostile. I was insufferable.

Novice

I had come with my long straight hair and peasant skirts from Boulder, Colorado to preach the gospel of environmentalism and introduce them to the importance of environmental management practices in their operations. Here's how it would go: After a long flight and drive to a remote field location in, say, rural Georgia, I would walk into a shop, which typically smelled of grease and diesel. A skeptical field hand would open a folding table and set up two rows of cold metal chairs. I would set up my projector and laptop and cast images on a white wall, or, if I was lucky, a stand-up projector screen. With all the enthusiasm of an adolescent puppy, I would begin.

Their crossed arms and narrowed eyes stunned me.

I was hurt, embarrassed, angry, and self-righteous at the receptions I got. If only these people could understand *how important* this environment stuff was! *They needed to listen to me!*

I wish I could say that I had been motivated by mutual understanding and a desire to know people so different from me. But really, I just hated being disliked, and was desperate to find some secret sauce to successful, engaged trainings. I had a year-long contract! So I started trying different things to soften the atmosphere. Some were superficial, like bringing donuts, giving away lottery tickets as prizes, and talking about the local fishing.

These things did work.

But more importantly, I learned to begin all the trainings with questions. I asked questions, and I listened. Lord have mercy: it's obvious, I know. I asked questions about their work, what's important to them, what *environmental* means to them.

This path of inquiry led me to a light-bulb moment. I'm embarrassed to say, it was a dramatic awakening: *These employees care about their families and their community. They want to take care of them.* Clean air, clean water, proper management of waste. They got through their training requirement, and I became an effective trainer rather than a lecturer.

The key was changing the way I communicated.

By learning the language of these oil and gas workers, by listening to their stories about their work and their community, I quickly found common ground with them. That led to creating efficiencies in their work that met all the company's environmental objectives and those of the training program as well. When I started listening, the rest fell into place.

Environmentalism isn't just about the science. It is very personal, I learned. It's about family, community, the experiences of camping, hunting, and fishing. It is a powerful motivator and a broadly shared apolitical value. Tapping into those shared values and seeing the reception and warmth exuding from the groups now became more important to me than preaching "the gospel" of environmentalism.

With that, my paradigm of environmentalism shifted and was forever changed.

As I continued teaching Environment 101, I spent a lot of time thinking about what being an environmentalist meant to me. It wasn't nearly as loaded a term in the 90s as it is today, and it certainly wasn't as politicized. I hope the reader can forgive me for summarizing what environmentalism meant to me back then. It will give us a shared starting point for how much my point of view has changed.

It is easy to get wrapped around the axle on this one, so I have stuck to the basics.

- ✧ Nature and natural places have an intrinsic value aside from their economic or human value.
- ✧ Reducing the environmental footprint of human activities is a priority; environmental footprint includes impacts to land, water, air, and communities both local and far-reaching.

✧ Prosperity and its associated industrialism (and vice versa) are creating negative consequences resulting from increasing resource use, production, and waste.

✧ Population growth is increasingly draining resources like agricultural, mineral, and energy, and is resulting in more pollution and waste.

✧ Biological and environmental systems have been disrupted and permanently changed by human activities.

✧ Climate change is human caused, happening right now, and could have downright apocalyptic consequences if we don't act right away.

Over time I doubled down on my environmentalism.

✧ Industrialization has created massive negative consequences, which require turning back the clock and returning to a simpler way of life.

✧ Unchecked, humans are greedy and will consume and pollute this world to its destruction.

✧ Environmentalists have the moral high ground because we are looking out for what's best for the planet as a whole, rather than focusing on our own, personal consumption.

✧ Those who reject environmentalism in any form, including regulatory policy or climate change science, are either stupid or greedy, or both.

I believed most of these things at one time.

And some, I still do.

4

Accidentally Adamant

In my semi-secluded cabin in the mountains outside of Boulder, in mid-autumn, there were still enough leaves that you could make the dash from bedroom door to hot tub without the neighbors seeing you. Not that anyone was looking. The trick was to get the rotting, broken cover of that hot tub off quickly, before your feet froze, whip off your towel, and then hop in.

Although literally held together with duct tape, that hot tub was marvelous. Brian, my fiancé at the time, and I would soak and sigh, catching up on the week's events. You didn't want to look too closely at this hot tub. Someone had sprayed foam in its cracks and taped siding to places that had no external cover. We kept Anita, the mountain hot tub fix-it lady, busy with constant repairs. But we were 30, about to get married, and living in the mountains. By every measure, life was good.

September is an unpredictable month in the Colorado mountains. On any given day it could be hot and dry or snow a foot, sometimes both within the same day. You didn't take any weather for granted. On this day, the air was crisp and cool, the leaves were the most amazing array of golds, oranges, reds, and browns, and there was still enough foliage cover that you didn't have to stay 100 percent under water in the tub.

In a month we'd be married, and I hoped the leaves would stay on
the trees.

Brian and I had been together for four years and were very compatible.
We worked hard and started building a life together. Each morning
that Brian was in town, we commuted to the same office our company
had opened in Boulder. I had been hired into Brian's company a
year after I moved to Colorado, and we had started dating shortly
thereafter. Brian had helped me move into the house we still live in
today, and that had prompted a "thank you" dinner that exceeded
both our expectations. He moved in a year later.

The company had recently opened a Boulder office, which I ran;
Brian reported to a manager in Denver and led Navy-base restoration
projects in the San Francisco Bay Area that kept him gone Monday
through Friday most weeks. When he was in town, we usually drove
places together in that Ford F150 of mine and we'd stop at Liquor
Mart on the way home. We'd pick up a six-pack of porter, and as soon
as we hit the two-lane county road, we'd each crack one open with the
bottle opener kept in the glove box.

We don't do that anymore.

We had a renter living in the studio on the property. Kimba would
survive the upcoming winter by hula hooping to loud music on the
worst days when no sun hit our property. Kimba is still awesome at
hula hooping 15 years later. She's married now with her own daughter,
living up in nearby Gold Hill. Her kids and mine went to the two-
room elementary school together.

Making a life with someone is such a process when you are young. You
hardly know who you are, and yet you find yourself making decisions
and compromises continually. Without a lot of conscious thought, Bri-

an and I had made the transition from partying singles to a grounded couple. As we sat in the hot tub that beautiful Saturday afternoon in September, Brian and I didn't discuss environmental choices. We didn't need to. Eating organically, heating our house with wood, volunteering for the Center for Native Ecosystems were just things we did.

They were part of who we were.

We shared a strong work ethic and were naturally inclined to take personal responsibility for our environmental footprint. For us, living as close to the land as possible seemed romantic and responsible. We imagined that we were doing our part.

At that time, we were not conscious of the requisite amount of hypocrisy that this life entailed. It's only in hindsight that I calculate how living in the mountains requires a 30-minute commute. To do the incessant projects required up here, we needed a truck, so I commuted in a fuel-inefficient F150. We heated our house primarily with wood, which made us self-sufficient but huge particulate polluters. We consumed *a lot*, even if it was organic, natural, and as often as possible, locally sourced.

It's easy to live like this in Boulder County, Colorado. We were comfortable and happy among people who for the most part, looked, acted, and thought like we did. I imagine that there are enclaves like this in every college town around the country. Couples special-ordering their PBA-free water bottles and locally sourced kale. We were hard working and good intentioned, but I can see in hindsight how privileged a life this is. Everyone in our world was liberal minded and Brian and I took everything a little bit farther, feeling that we were genuinely walking the talk.

Of course I signed up for wind power.

When Xcel Energy set up a program where you could pay $2.50 per month to support development of their first wind farm, I jumped at the chance! I didn't even ask Brian. Voluntarily paying extra for wind power was exactly the kind of contribution that I knew we wanted to make to a better world.

Although my consulting work was now almost entirely for oil and gas companies, I was feeling pretty uncomfortable with this work. It would be years before I reconciled my environmental values with my oil and gas projects. I shared the view that so many people still espouse: that wind and solar are beautiful, simple, clean energy sources to which we all should switch. I was excited to be a part of this mindset in Colorado.

I had never actually seen a wind farm.

So it was interesting that it took several years before I had my first, face-to-face encounter with a giant wind farm. Ironically, that day I was permitting a gas storage facility in northeastern Colorado. A lot of the work I was doing then was new-facility permitting. Gas can be stored underground in geologic layers that will hold it. The gas companies store natural gas for when they need it, like when they need to run natural gas-fired generators to create electricity.

Permitting a gas storage facility has county, state, and federal requirements, and it takes years to get through the surveys and reports required to get the permits. And all of this permitting activity has to happen before you can start construction.

I always looked forward to going to the facility site in northeastern Colorado, about 100 miles from Boulder, because it's one of those places that has big sky as far as you can see, with gently rolling hills used for agriculture or grazing. You can easily imagine early settlers and long winters.

Hope, hardship, and beauty as far as the eye can see.

I had made several previous trips to this facility out in the prairie in the middle of nowhere. But on this particular day in 2005, after several hours of driving on rural, desolate two-lane highways, I pulled up to a shocking view. I stepped out of the car and drew a deep, gasping breath. Literally, as far as the eye could see were massive wind turbines. These were no glorified windmills. They were gigantic machines that created the effect of an army of alien robots coming to take over eastern Colorado.

I exhaled and mentally fell to my knees.

The sweet smell of grass, the cool breeze…and the *sound!* The whoosh whoosh whoosh of the turning turbines was disturbingly disorienting. I looked to the turbine-covered horizon and was surprised to find that I was dizzy. *This* is wind energy?

Yikes.

It was a strangely emotional moment. At the time, I personally was completely invested in green energy (renewable energy)—sunlight, wind, rain, plants, geothermal heat. I was truly dubious of fossil fuel energy, such as coal and gas, and absolutely committed to a fossil-fuel-free future. And yet the uncomfortable reality of this massive wind farm shocked my senses.

I turned my attention back to the natural gas facility I was permitting. One lonely acre that had already been subjected to numerous cultural and biological surveys and a forest's worth of permitting paperwork requirements. The facility wouldn't be permitted for another year and built for another two. I remember thinking, *what would its energy output be compared to this wind farm?* Which had more overall energy output? Environmental impact?

I didn't know the answers, but I knew it was time to find out.

The emotional impact of that moment sticks with me. It haunts me any time I get overconfident that I know what I'm talking about. I realized that I had been a lemming. I had taken as gospel that some energy sources were "good" and I had believed that supporting them made me virtuous. What I had not counted on is that there was a reality-on-the-ground and facts and figures on which I could and should base my opinions. I had to face my own prejudices and ignorance.

What if we aren't getting this green energy thing right?

5

Baby Food

April 2004

I peeked in the oven to check on the Mason jar of yogurt. I don't know why I peeked, I knew it would take eight hours to grow, or do what bacteria do, to turn milk into yogurt. Yup, still there. But the peek allowed a tiny waft of welcome heat to escape.

Cooking in the winter always caused ice to form on the inside of the window panes. These were old-school checkerboard single panes, so cool and funky in the summer, so terribly freezing in the winter. But I loved this kitchen, especially now that I had painted it with Caribbean colors I'd seen in Trinidad and Tobago: teal, green, and red. It made me happy, but not warmer. Cooking was the only way to stay warm.

I pulled the sweet potatoes out of the steamer and cut them into chunks to run through the hand food-mill. Carter pulled on the little hairs on the back of my neck and I grimaced. Ever since his first birthday when he'd started walking, I'd had to have him in a backpack to get anything done. I unwound his fat little hand out of those tender hairs and kissed it. Handed him a wood spoon to fill his grabby fingers with.

He whacked me on the head with it.

"Mamamamamamamama," he chanted as I winced.

Carter was my first child. I tend to approach everything in life with an overabundance of enthusiasm, so he was fed homemade yogurt, and I knew the joys of baby food thrown all over the kitchen. This was Sunday, the day I typically baked bread or made a pie. So here I was baking up a storm. I often took extras into the office on Monday.

Being this kind of mother was fairly tedious, but abundantly joyful. I relished in the self-satisfaction of all overachieving hippie mothers the days I took him to mom-and-baby African singing class and traded tips for cloth diaper enclosures. Boulder, Colorado was just 30 minutes from where we lived, and it was an enclave for this style of parenting.

It must have been an unseasonably warm spring the year that I had bought our log cabin built in 1873. I hadn't considered how the place would receive little sunlight for three months of each year. This year, in April, the snow was still piled high outside the windows, reaching up above the sills, and I could not imagine that we would see the flowers or the grass ever again.

I turned the crank on the hand mill and out came spaghetti strings of sweet potato. Putting some on my middle finger, I held it awkwardly behind my head for Carter, who immediately sucked my finger. Such an easy kid! He kicked his feet and I knew I had made a baby food winner. I started squishing the sweet potato mush with the back of a spoon into the squares of the ice cube tray for the freezer. The weekends passed like this, preparing food, feeding Carter, cleaning up the inevitable mess, changing the stinky, sopping cloth diapers, and then starting over. If you want to do everything homemade and naturally, you're going to do a lot of dishes.

Did I mention that we didn't have a dishwasher?

Winter had its saving graces. In the winter the cloth diapers weren't nearly as stinky as they would be in the summer. Most of the house was not effectively warmed by the wood stove, which had its benefits when it came to the diaper pail. Cloth diapers were as soppy and messy as you can imagine, and I was constantly hand-washing the covers that held them in place because they would inevitably get soiled too, and we only had a few of them.

I fished Carter out of his back pack and set him on the floor with a pot and the spoon to bang on it with. We had successfully kept all plastics out of our limited toy options, wanting Carter to only have wood and cloth toys. If you're rolling your eyes, you aren't alone. Parents, siblings, and cousins were half-heartedly supporting our lifestyle choices, but could barely contain their queries: *When will you get a real house? What will you do when he goes out into the real world, where there is plastic everywhere?* We persevered. Because the responsibly sourced, organic, natural toys were so expensive, it would be years before we had a decent array of toys for him to play with. But Carter was easy and carefree, happily set to banging on the pot while I finished up with the sweet potato cubes. This should be enough to get us through the week with the yogurt in the oven and the tofu I'd already put up. Tomorrow I'd be at work.

I was still working in environmental consulting, four days per week. Brian, my husband now, did the same. And we had our beloved nanny, O'Nell, take care of Carter on the other three days. When Carter was six weeks old, I had responded to an email sent to canyon residents from another babysitter offering her services. When I called to find out more, her roommate O'Nell answered. O'Nell let me know that she too was seeking a nanny position, so we set up a meeting for that very afternoon. Like a lot of new mothers, I could not face the idea of leaving my precious Carter, and I had made no plans for day care, even though returning to work full time loomed just six weeks out.

We immediately fell in love with O'Nell, who was studying child care at Naropa University in Boulder. In addition to wanting to nanny while taking her college coursework, she was seeking a new living situation. We had a former garage on our property that had been converted to a one-room studio and we rented it out to help cover the mortgage. Within a few months of meeting O'Nell, she had moved onto the property and was taking care of Carter three days a week. On this winter day, it would be another year before he would attend the Buddhist preschool in town. O'Nell fully embraced my baby food-making efforts, and I knew that the food I set aside for the week would make it at least to his high chair before he threw it on the floor. We learned parenting along with O'Nell, and she brought home lots of ideas, such as teaching all of us baby sign language.

It was fun, communal living.

But there also were challenges to living in the mountains, miles from civilization in this simple, semi-off-the-grid lifestyle. As soon as I'd gotten the baby food done that day, we needed to haul in more wood. We had a propane tank, but the truck couldn't make it up the driveway with this much snow, so we had to be very careful how much we used. The wood stove was in the living room, but ever since Carter had started walking, we had to create a huge baby fence around it, taking up 300 of our 1100 square feet.

Brian generally got the wood somewhere in the canyon for free. If free wood was available, he would section it and we would take turns splitting it. As soon as Carter could sit up, he'd ride in the wheel barrow on top of the wood while we hauled what felt like mountains of split wood into various tarp-covered stacks in the yard. We went through about five cords a year, so some part of every weekend was spent splitting, hauling, or stacking wood.

I'm an early riser anyway, so making a fire early in the morning was a ritual that I enjoyed. It was keeping the house warm overnight that we never mastered in those early years. Pine logs burn really quickly, and we couldn't afford the longer-burning oak that we would buy a few years later. Because the fire had to be stoked about every two hours, Brian was usually good for one middle-of-the-night log addition, but I inevitably got up to a house cold enough that you could see your breath. I'd put the water on for coffee, crumble up the newspaper, and start the two-hour long effort of getting the house warm.

Life was simple and good and it could have gone on like this forever.

6

Do Be Dense

As we lived our self-reliant, simple life that I felt was maximally aligned with our environmental beliefs, my thoughts returned often to that wind farm. And thus began the process of changing my mind. Or learning to change my mind, because, in fact, I have learned that changing my mind requires more effort and self-awareness than holding on to my beliefs. Holding on to my beliefs was unchallenging, simple. Life in Boulder County among friends and colleagues with whom I had so much in common—that was comfortable and easy. There hadn't seemed to be any need to think critically about the environmental values that I took for granted.

It is only in hindsight that I see the towers of self-righteousness I had built. *We* were right and *they* were wrong, and for the most part, I only had contact with the "we" characters. It has been a long, slow process of discerning between what I thought I knew and what I know now. And did I mention painful? Self-righteous confidence is such a comfortable place to stand! Questioning my beliefs, analyzing the values I took for granted, and wondering at my own ignorance has not been easy. It has been a slow evolution over years. It was not a linear process, nor a logical one.

It has been a winding mix of emotional assertions and
scientific discovery.

I looked at what was gnawing at my gut. Surely there was a way to view environmental choices scientifically and sort out the best path forward? Here is how my mind was working...I decided the first challenge in a fair assessment of environmental assertions is simply to decide to evaluate them in the first place. This is a huge step. There is this sense of righteous faith about environmental truisms, such as those laid out in Chapter 3. Take for example, climate-change science. One cannot have an intelligent conversation about the science, the models, and what we do and do not know about climate change among the faithful. Or consider recycling: recycling is good, right? Well, it's actually interesting to assess the amount of energy and materials required to recycle some goods. Can we have *that* conversation?

It feels disloyal and nearly inconceivable to question the truisms.

I believed those environmental truisms with my whole heart. Being an environmentalist was my identity, my tribe, and in many ways, my faith. It is only in hindsight that I see that that's like reading the Bible literally, without bringing a discerning heart and mind to the process.

I took that leap.

After that eye-opening day at the wind farm, I did some soul-searching. Had I been wrong? I set aside loyalty and identity, initially for just a moment, to take a good look at one aspect of energy and environment that's a cornerstone for all future contemplation. It's a given that "energy"—as compared to "environment"—makes everything we do possible, and it's an imperative part of raising and maintaining a standard of living that's, well, *livable*. Energy keeps us warm, fed, cool, moving. It doesn't have a personality, but it is energizing. How on earth could I think about energy *constructively*?

Energy is created by harnessing a fuel. There are all kinds of fuel, from dung to nuclear to wind. When you think about it, fuels have a lot of different qualities and aspects for us to consider: where do you get them, how do you move them, what kind of processing is required to get the energy out, how much do they cost, what sort of pollution do they cause? With all those questions, one quality is more important than all the others and is the best place to start...

Energy density.

This is undoubtedly an intimidating topic. Energy *what*? I have found that it's worth the effort. Not everyone is going to love this effort, so I've included just the key points, below. The details can be found in Appendix A.

To understand energy, I had to start with understanding fuel.

Fuel: Marshmallows to Uranium

Density is defined as the degree of compactness of a substance. Fuel is consumed to produce energy. I consume food to power my body. In my fireplace, we burned wood to keep our family warm through those long winters. In my car, fuel is the gasoline burned to run the engine. Okay, I think I have the gist of fuel. Sun produces electricity through solar panels, coal through a power plant, and uranium to produce nuclear energy.

But energy, it turns out, is something different. Simply understood, energy is *the capacity to do work*. So I use fuel to create energy. I eat marshmallows to power my body.

I figured out that most of the time when people are talking about energy out in the world, we are talking about the fuel that is being used to get things done, like turn on our lights or run our car. Technically, there's the fuel and there is the work it gets done, the energy.

A Science-Spiritual Awakening

So, after seeing the wind farm, I realized that I had been naïve. I needed to understand more than just fuel and the energy it produced. To assess energy and environmental issues thoughtfully, I needed a way to compare fuels to each other and the different ways power is produced. The most straightforward way to do this is to start with energy density.

We are quite comfortable with the idea of energy density in our food; we call it calorie counting! A calorie is a measure of energy, equivalent to 4.2 joules. Even though I'm a vegetarian, I know that beef is more energy dense than a tomato.

Table 6-1. Energy Density by Food Source[1][2][3]

	Calories per 100 g	Energy Density (MJ/kg)
Tomato	18	0.75
Strawberries	33	1.4
Potato	77	3.2
Ground Beef (85% Lean)	215	9.0
Corn	365	15
Sugar	387	16
Butter	717	30

It's less common to think about our transportation, electricity, and heating sources this way, but it is critically important to do so if you want to understand energy, I realized. Consider me: I heated my house with wood for 15 years, but that is a very inefficient fuel source, as you can see in Table 6-2.

Table 6-2. Energy Density by Fuel Source [4] [5] [6]

Source	Energy Density (MJ/kg)
Lithium Ion Battery	.9 – 9.7
Dung	12-22
Wood	16
Bituminous Coal	24
Biodiesel	38
Crude Oil	44
Gasoline	46
Kerosene	46
Natural Gas (methane)	55
Uranium	3,900,000

Another way to think about energy density is *how much space does the fuel literally take up compared to the energy it provides?* Learning about this aspect of energy density is where I really began to understand what a miracle fuel gasoline is! Gasoline is this ideal mix of energy: dense, lightweight, and doesn't take up too much space. Think about everything we expect from gasoline… to get us around, be completely reliable, always available, and affordable too!

Now I was starting to think in a more constructive, sophisticated way about energy, but I wasn't done yet. It's not just the fuel and the energy it creates, it's how the fuel is used to create power; this is power density.

What?

To Produce Power

We intuitively understand power as what can get accomplished from the conversion of fuel. You can think of it in these terms:

✧ How much heat does your fireplace generate?

✧ How bright is your light bulb?

✧ And, how much rev does your car have when you floor it?

Something is more powerful if it can move something bigger or faster. Of two seemingly identical cars, if one can accelerate faster, it is *more powerful*. When comparing a small car and a large pickup truck, if they can accelerate identically, the larger truck is *more powerful*.

Watt Do You Get for Your Fuel? Power Density

So what power do you get from fuel? It took some time for this to sink in, but I finally could grasp the idea that power density is the cornerstone of a thoughtful environmental approach to energy. Power density is the most universal measure of energy flux and is usually described as Watts per square meter (W/m^2). Below is a chart showing the power density of different sources of electricity; the power density varies between the low and high ranges shown depending on the quality of the fuel.

Table 6-3 Power Density by Electricity Source[7] (12)

Power Source	Power Density (Watts/m²)	
	Low	High
Natural Gas	200	2000
Coal	100	1000
Solar (PV)	4	9
Solar (CSP)	4	10
Wind	0.5	1.5
Biomass	0.5	0.6

Coming to terms with the idea of power density had the impact on me of a spiritual awakening! How much fuel is required? How large a footprint does the electricity generation have? Can I travel more than 50 miles with that fuel? Do I have room for my kids in my car? The more needs you try to address, the more important power density becomes.

When I started, I thought that fuel, energy, and power were relatively straightforward, but power density also introduces the ideas of tradeoffs. Imagine for a moment that you are responsible for finding a new electricity generation solution for your coal-fired power community? I would have started the solution with "100% wind and solar"! That could work, if I was completely unconstrained by land, weather, price, and reliability. Instead, the reality is that you will always have some constraints to work with. For example, constraints might include: the price can't go up by more than 10% of what residents are paying; the footprint needs to be comparable to the current land space; the power needs to work 100% of the time; and, the new power must be able to accommodate 2% annual growth in industrial demand.

Doomed?

At the front of his book, *Power Hungry,* Robert Bryce included a quote that captures this journey succinctly:

> "He who refuses to do arithmetic is doomed to talk nonsense."
>
> —John McCarthy
> Computer Pioneer, Stanford University

I found myself embarked upon a journey where I would let go of my pre-conceived notions about what was environmentally good and bad, and instead be open to the data. If the data demonstrated that I needed to assess a new perspective, I would.

And it was from this new outlook that I encountered two books that really affected my thinking. The first was *Power Hungry* and the second was *Sustainable Energy – Without the Hot Air* by David JC MacKay. These two authors have wildly different politics, but both have had a commitment to doing the hard work of practically and honestly assessing energy sources.

In their books, both Bryce and MacKay have provided excellent analyses of power density. David MacKay's is more complicated, and is therefore included in Appendix A. The page of *Power Hungry* that is starred and dog-eared as a result of my exploration of this topic is reproduced in Table 6-4. This was published in 2010, so undoubtedly efficiencies across the board have improved, but it effectively conveys the general idea. You can see the land required graphically in Figure 8-1.

Table 6-4. Power Density Comparison.

Energy Source	Power Density (hp per acre)	Power Density (watts per sq m)	Land Required (sq miles)
Nuclear	300	56	18.8
Ave U.S. Natural Gas Well	287.5	53	19.6
Gas Stripper Well	153.5	28	
Oil Stripper Well (10 bbls/day)	148.5	27	39
Solar PV	36	6.7	156
Wind Turbines	6.4	1.2	869
Biomass-fueled Power Plant	2.1	0.4	2606
Corn Ethanol	0.25	0.05	21,267

Source: Bryce, Robert. 2010. Power Hungry. P. 86

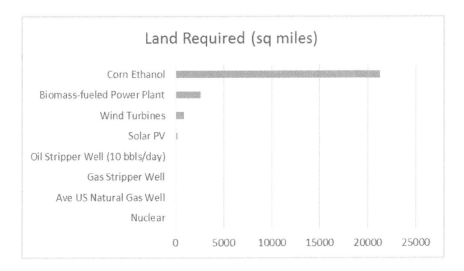

Figure 6-1. Power Density Comparison.

Looking at power density creates a shocking new paradigm for thinking about what "environmental" is. Carbon emissions are one component of an energy source's environmental impact. Other air emissions are as important, if not more important, like those that create smog and ozone, for example, and can affect people's health. Physical footprint, though, I find particularly compelling, and the data in Figure 6-1 made me really rethink the viability and scalability of sources I had taken for granted as "green."

It took several years for these realizations to infiltrate everything in my life.

7

27 Interviews

Big changes never come from expected sources, and the opportunity to become the face of Colorado's oil and gas industry was certainly unexpected. It was now 2009 and I was content working for Tetra Tech, the international environmental consulting firm where I had worked on and off for the last 15 years. In many ways, I felt that I had arrived. I'd had my second son, Alec, and Brian now stayed home full time with our boys in the cabin. I had a Vice President title, was a regional manager overseeing several offices, managed my own projects, and had plenty of responsibility.

Part of those responsibilities included a significant expectation from the company to develop business. By this point, I'd done most of my project work as a consultant to oil and gas, and I was always trying to figure out how to build new relationships with oil and gas clients. I had spent the previous decade working for companies that drill for oil and gas, the field service companies that support them, pipeline companies, and gas storage developers. I knew that the Colorado Oil & Gas Association (COGA) was having its big annual conference, and I wanted to start to build my network with this crowd. From a gas storage permitting project, I knew a lawyer who served on the COGA steering committee. I signed up for the conference.

I had an idea I wanted to pitch.

Howard Boigon and I had worked together on several projects obtaining local, state, and federal permits for new gas storage projects, and when I gave him a call, he obliged by setting up a lunch. Howard was a well-known oil and gas lawyer who not only served on the conference steering committee, but also sat on COGA's Board. I felt honored that he was willing to introduce me to Fred Julander over lunch at Ellington's at the Brown Palace, a historic Denver hotel and landmark. I had never before been to Ellington's, an exclusive meeting place for Denver's power elite.

A Start

It was truly a coup to be introduced to Fred. Fred had founded the COGA conference decades earlier, and he remains an industry visionary not afraid to raise some eyebrows. Maybe even some fists. Fred had spent most of his career swimming upstream against popular industry opinion. He believed natural gas was an important fuel years before it was recognized as such. I had attended the prior year's COGA conference, where he had embraced global warming as the central topic, creating ripples of resentment across the Rocky Mountain oil and gas industry. It would take many months for me to understand Fred's controversial role in Colorado's oil and gas industry, but at this lunch, I was excited just to get to meet him.

I remember the lunch in so much detail. My effort to take slow, deep breaths because I was nervous and didn't want my voice to shake. The maître d' pulling out my chair as I was seated. The waiter handing me my napkin when I returned from the restroom, the fancy menu, the assortment of breads. Although it was "just lunch," it changed my life.

> I still don't know all the ramifications to
> my life precipitated by that lunch.

I never could have imagined a year later the maître d' would greet me by name. That day, we had a delicious lunch while Fred told me about his vision for the conference. He liked my idea for a panel at the conference, and promised to take it to the committee for consideration. My concept was to create a panel to discuss why natural gas should be a part of the *New Energy Economy*. Colorado's governor at the time, Governor Bill Ritter, had launched Colorado on a path to being a national leader in the growth of renewable energy for electricity generation. I conveyed how I felt strongly that vision could and should include natural gas. Later Governor Ritter would make natural gas a cornerstone of his new energy economy vision that has positively impacted the nation, but at the time, it was still a novel, untested idea.

The outcome of the lunch was a success, and Fred called me a few weeks later to let me know that they had added an early morning panel to the conference schedule. That August, the panel included strangers who later would become colleagues: Kate Fay from the State; Andy Spielman, who would later sit on the commission overseeing oil and gas. We were all strangers to the oil and gas industry and provided our ideas to a packed room at that conference, with many standing at the back. The panel was controversial—as any good panel is—but successful and well received. The oil and gas industry was as skeptical about whether it wanted to be a part of the new energy economy as new energy economy proponents were dubious about their inclusion.

It was a start.

It was the beginning of so much!

For years after that lunch, I would be responsible for screening the many pitches with speakers and panels for the annual COGA conference. Working with Fred, I chaired the conference the final two. Did that conference ever again change anyone's life? I certainly hope so.

A Calling

Shortly after that 2009 conference, COGA would begin its search for a new CEO, and Fred would take me out to breakfast to suggest that I apply. We met at the Egg & I in south Boulder on a Saturday morning, I recall vividly. My boys were small, 2 and 6, and it was difficult to leave them on a Saturday morning. I listened to Fred, keeping a poker face, and told him that I would think about it. I'd immediately known that I would take the job, but I didn't tell anyone that for months.

From the moment that Fred had called me, asking me to meet him, I had felt a tug in the center of my belly. I knew something big was about to happen, even though it made no sense to me intellectually. It had been a stretch for COGA to have me—a greenie from Boulder—moderate a panel at their conference. Why on earth would they even consider me for their CEO?

I have not felt a tug like that before or sense.

I remember, at that COGA conference, I had watched the current CEO from afar. At that moment, she was staffed with a COGA employee who was communicating with staff over a radio, waiting for the Governor to arrive so she could welcome him. She seemed like a rock star: poised, confident, and on top of the world. She knew everyone at the conference and everyone knew her.

Except me.

After breakfast with Fred, I went home and talked to Brian. I started working on my resume and cover letter, which came together effortlessly, and projected a lot more confidence than I felt. I had recently started jogging a little, and over the course of the next week, I thought long and hard on my jogs about the job. Although I could not get my brain to connect the dots that would get me to the job, I knew I was going to get it.

The job called me.

The interview process, however, lasted months and was fraught with personal and professional peril. Conservatives circulated a memo around the capitol about my background and unfitness for the position. I was a capital D Democrat from Boulder, a self-proclaimed environmentalist with a questionable amount of relevant experience. (Little did they know: I had originally registered in Colorado with the green party.) I interviewed with individuals and groups from the COGA Board of forty executives all from the Rocky Mountain oil and gas industry. Many of these meetings were engaging, friendly, and inspiring. An equal number were openly caustic.

The process was exhausting. I had a very full-time job, a 30-minute commute to Boulder, two kids at home, and now I was sneaking off to Denver every other day for an interview, or a breakfast or lunch meeting set up by Fred to socialize me with key Board members. I plodded forward. It made no sense, but the job was mine and I was going to earn it.

Things were going well for me at Tetra Tech, and so there was really no reason for me to leave. Ironically, even there, I was the "greenie," running offices that focused on oil and gas work, and regularly being teased or downright harassed about my politics and positions. I chuckled to myself when I thought about my boss, colleagues, and staff hearing I was interviewing for the COGA CEO—they wouldn't have believed it if they had.

Eventually, the COGA CEO-candidate pool was narrowed down to two: a traditional candidate from Wyoming and me. We were both invited to make a presentation in Denver in the middle of the afternoon to the full Board. Driving down to that final interview, I played classical music and took deep breaths. My hands shook even as I drove. I had prepared a PowerPoint presentation introducing myself as the scientist, businesswoman, and community member that I was. Through the interview process I had come to understand that most of the Board struggled to see past my long hair, environmental background, and Boulder residence. I hoped to overcome the caricature of myself with an authentic introduction. I included pictures of myself as a volunteer firefighter, some with my kids in the mountains, and others doing field work.

> The truth is, I was a hopeless liberal, but one who wanted to represent them.

When I arrived, I was shuffled into a holding pen. The logistics were carefully orchestrated to make sure the candidates didn't meet. (To this day, I still don't know who the other candidate was.) I sat alone, feet in my brand new, stiff heels, knees pressed together. The door cracked open and a face poked in, "You're up! Good luck!" I followed her brisk steps, turning left into a room that was packed. I hadn't expected that, I figured that perhaps there would be 20 Board members there. I later learned that Board members could send or bring their staff. And who would want to miss this show?

There was no opportunity to pause or catch my breath, and my heart thumped wildly in my chest. My guide pointed to the front of the room and stood at the back. Jumping right in, I smiled, stood up straight, and strove to project confidence. I made my way along the left aisle, between the horseshoe table setup where every seat was filled and the row of occupied seats against the wall.

> That final interview was god-awful.

It took me about 40 seconds to size up the situation. Not one of my allies or supporters from the COGA Board was there, not even Fred. It turns out, they had already met me and knew how they would vote. As I started up my introduction, I looked out at a room full of stern faces and crossed arms. My smile was not returned, not once.

I proceeded, what else could I do? With all the confidence I could muster, I gave my carefully prepared and practiced 20-minute introduction. The questions were aggressive and hostile. When there were no more questions, and everyone looked at me with straight faces and raised eyebrows, I straightened my back and exited the room. I picked up my bag from the holding pen and walked out without even a goodbye.

I cried on the way home.

As it turned out, that was actually pretty good training for what was to come. As a woman who has always worked in male-dominant environments, I make it a point to NEVER cry at work. Period. But crying in the car is perfectly acceptable, especially when you're going for a job that's going to change your life. And you know you're supposed to get. But somehow no one else seems to know that yet.

A Vote

My office phone rang several days later, the caller ID telling me that it was the Chairman of the Board. The Board had convened several days after the final presentations to vote between the two candidates. The process ended in a split-even vote. *Exactly even. Seriously? ... Now what?* The chairman, who hadn't been at the final interview, sounded strangely satisfied. This made no sense to me, because I've hired lots of people, and the last thing you want is to drag out that process.

He informed me that as a result of the split vote, the Board decided to restart the process from the beginning. We hung up and I took a deep breath. It was clear that some number of people wanted to run me off. I had already been in this for two months and had had over 26 interviews and informational meetings with Board members. The next day, I called the Chairman back and let him know that I was still in, but I would only participate in one more interview, they could decide what and when that would be.

Neither logic nor an appropriate dose of self-respect informed my decision. I *knew* I was supposed to get that job.

In the same way I know I'm supposed to write this book.

An Announcement

Another month later, it was announced that I was the new President & CEO of COGA. Shock rippled through my personal and professional circles: *You are going to do what?!* That was nothing compared to the consternation and confusion that came out of the political circles in Denver: *Who? Why? How?!*

Friends, colleagues, and political pundits alike chalked up the decision to some combination of temporary insanity on the part of both COGA and me. Most people seemed to feel my selection as the CEO of COGA was incongruous at best and malignant at worst. Commentators assessed the situation with limited possible rationale:

1. COGA hired me as a liberal, environmental face to greenwash the industry. I was a tool.
2. I was embedding as a liberal do-gooder, pretending to support oil and gas, with detailed designs to undermine the industry. COGA was a tool.

3. I was a sucker.
4. COGA was a sucker.

> The truth is so relatively boring.

A Truth

For me, going to COGA was a done deal at that breakfast with Fred. I had come to love the oil and gas industry and thought they were making colossal errors in their communications with the public. In another fit of irony, I thought I knew *just what to do.* For the next five-and-a-half years I heard from endless well-meaning advisors, friends and strangers alike, on *just what I should do.*

> (Karma's a bitch.)

For the COGA Board, in my (literally) dozens of interviews (by my own count I had 27 interviews and meetings), I was ultimately selected because of my business experience and track record of getting things done. I ran operations and projects, turned failing offices profitable, juggled roles, and managed personnel. My background as an environmentalist, environmental consultant, Democrat, and Boulderite were controversial obstacles to my hire. And if anyone's intention was simply to manipulate me to provide a green face while conducting dirty work, well, duh, that wasn't going to happen.

> (because Karma is a bitch.)

I, of course, had absolutely no idea what I was getting into. I knew I'd be facing the typical challenges you'd expect in the normal course of events representing the oil and gas industry.

> But the next 5 years were not normal.

8

The First Fork in the Road

Warning signs of how difficult the journey would be began cropping up early. Why are they only visible in hindsight? I guess I did not want to see them. I had felt so clearly the tug in the middle of my gut, pulling me toward the COGA job. Nothing else seemed to matter, and so I had dismissed all the warning signs that this was crazy, that this would be difficult, maybe even impossible, and that I was getting myself and my family into something way bigger than we were. Maybe bigger than what we could handle.

But I was lighthearted about the prospects ahead. On one level, it didn't make any sense, but taking the job was what I was going to do. I knew from the first moment Fred and I had that breakfast conversation about it. It seemed crazy, but clear. As close to ordained as anything gets. The COGA president and CEO position was mine and I was supposed to get it and then take it.

So I did.

I was giddy when I was finally offered the job. Perhaps I should have thought twice when the Board chairman said, *We need you to start ASAP because the legislative session starts in a month.* And I thought, *What legislative session?* I had absolutely no political experience, and I literally did not know that Colorado's state legislature met between

January and May of each year, and that one of my key responsibilities would be to engage with this legislature.

I'll figure it out!

My World

Brian and I invited two close friends up to the house to tell them that I'd taken the job. The women are sisters and lifelong environmental activists and important to our family. I hadn't warned them that I was interviewing for the job. The news that I would be the new face of the oil and gas industry, more or less their sworn enemy, certainly must have come as a shock.

Perhaps shock is an understatement.

We stood outside of my house in an awkward spot partially on the path, leaning against a waist-high garden bed, and watched our kids play. The fall air was crisp, with the smell of slightly decaying leaves in the air. I remember clearly how beautiful and blue the sky was.

These long-time close family friends were mortified that I had taken the job.

Didn't I know that the Colorado Oil & Gas Association was evil? That the men there would try to destroy me? I couldn't stop to give that too much thought. The 27 interviews were still fresh, but I had survived, and gotten the job! And through that process, I had met several company leaders who were interesting, bold, and charismatic, and who I was excited to work with.

One statement they made I'll never forget, because it stung in a way that few things do. It still stings to this day: *They must be paying you a whole lot of money to take that job.* This was the first time anyone had ever implied that I could be bought, that I might be bought, that I had been bought. It hurt particularly because I didn't have words to articulate the calling that I felt. A calling is the opposite of taking a job for money, but how could I say, *I feel a pull in my soul to do this work?*

As it turns out, this was the first of many comments from many people suggesting that this new role was an outright sale of my soul. I had to get used to the idea, the slightly judging look of most people that I knew. *They must be paying you a whole lot of money to do that.* I never truly developed a thick skin, but I learned to look like I did.

The shock and displeasure of our close friends was the beginning of a rift. The rift was not necessarily in my relationship with them, but in my relationship with traditional ways of characterizing the energy-environment debate.

> There are good guys and bad guys, and apparently
> I had just joined the bad ones.

I have no idea what their car ride down the mountain was like, but my conversation with Brian conveyed a shock of our own. Why weren't they excited that "one of their own" was going to be working on the "other side"? Why hadn't they expressed any confidence in my ability to *do good*? Why weren't they excited to work with me? And, if we really were in a holy war, why weren't they frightened that I'd joined the other team?

> Or at least curious why?

9

The Boardroom

It was very cold that first week of January 2010. I'd been on the job for two months. I looked out over Denver from the 42nd floor of Denver's highest building. The landscape was gray, everything looked dusted with snow and frosted in ice, and steam puffed abundantly from buildings and cars. I had arrived a few minutes early for my first COGA Board meeting.

The last time I had seen most of the Board was during the hostile Board presentation during the selection process. I had attended one last interview with a small, newly formed steering committee empowered to pick the president and CEO. That meeting had gone reasonably well.

Well enough for me to be standing here, anyway.

I pushed the thought of the Board presentation out of my mind. I had designed a new PowerPoint for the Board today, outlining my plan for the first 90 days on the job. I was prepared. In my typical naively brash fashion, I thought I would tell them what I would be doing.

I shouldn't have been surprised by the room, but I was. I entered the space, which was dominated by a dark wood, oval table surrounded by high-back dark wood chairs with black leather cushions. Other than the one wall with windows, the walls were covered with dark wood bookcases whose shelves were filled with leather-bound law books. It seemed unfortunately stereotypical of where you would think an oil and gas board meeting would take place.

All that was missing were ashtrays.

At 8:30 the Board members began streaming in one by one. The meeting wouldn't start until 9 o'clock, and we had set aside this time for a meet-and-greet. I was wearing one of my new COGA president outfits: smart wool skirt, uncomfortably high but conservative heels, and a well-cut blazer. It would take some time for me to find my style. I had been working in Boulder with mining engineers for years—the fashion bar had been very low.

Of course I couldn't eat. But the Board members filled paper coffee cups and grabbed pastries. Each person greeted me warmly and shared pleasantries. Even the people I had dreaded seeing the most were kind and welcoming.

At 9 o'clock sharp, I called the meeting to order. It is extremely disconcerting to call a meeting to order with an organization that you have never seen meet before. I had asked the COGA staff whether I should sit this one out, or come in and take charge, and they had advised me to come in like I ran the place, so I did. You would have thought that the Board chair, who had typically run the meetings, would mind. If he did, he didn't let on.

I think he was actually relieved.

For some time, the meetings apparently had been something of a stream of consciousness affair, without agendas or handouts. Various consultants would report out on their activities and discussion would ensue about positions at the legislature and so forth. I had been told that meetings often ran three or more hours. I have always been a stickler for a well-run meeting, and had never run one without an agenda, so all of that was about to change.

I handed out agendas and introduced myself. I invited the meeting attendees to do a quick round of introductions. The COGA Board had a funny practice of seating Board members and general counsel at the table and consultants and other staff in seats around the table. I was busy trying to size up who was who during these introductions. With 40 Board members, it would be more than a year before I knew everyone by name.

Governor Ritter, Colorado's Democratic governor, who had promulgated and led an overhaul of the oil and gas rules over the previous two years and overseen an unsuccessful ballot initiative to tax the oil and gas industry, had just announced that morning that he would not seek a second term. In my opening presentation setting forth my plan for the first 90 days, I jokingly took credit for Governor Ritter's announcement and the cold weather that was driving up natural gas prices.

It was a pandering move, but a good one.

The room immediately lightened up as Board members and their staff laughed heartily and looked at each other with raised eyebrows. More than one sighed in relief while chuckling. The agenda, the 90-day PowerPoint presentation, the jokes indicating that I am on their side…something new is going on at COGA.

And it was clear they were going to give me a chance.

I had been warned that COGA Board meetings often ran over their monthly two-hour allotment. At 10:45, I reviewed what had been covered and the ensuing action items. I asked, with my normal brusqueness, *Is there anything else?*

Phil Clark, COGA's Board secretary, whose firm hosted the meeting, announced that for the next several months, the COGA Board would have to meet in a temporary space because this boardroom was getting redecorated. Everyone shrugged and nodded, no big deal. I smiled to myself... no more dark brown wood and black leather.

No more ghosts of ashtrays.

10

The Oil Bash

Wow! I'd exclaimed the day I first entered my new corner office overlooking the capitol on November 1, 2009, and I was moving in. My second thought was how was I going to fill all the large empty bookcases around the room?

I sat down in the grand executive chair and resisted the urge to spin around. I'd sat on an inflatable exercise ball in my small office at Tetra Tech. I had purposefully taken one of the smallest offices there when I had been promoted to regional manager, to send a signal of frugality with an absence of frills. I had had one bookcase and two squeezed-in chairs for guests. This office was at least four times that size, and had views that went all the way to the mountains in the West.

I started thumbing through the hanging files left in the desk by my predecessor. Brightly colored file folders each carefully identified with a neat, printed label. Polling. School of Mines Study. Blog. 2008 Legislature. Government Relations Committee. Even as I sat there, I thought of myself as a businesswoman first and loosely as a scientist. Now I was in a world of politics and media; it felt treacherous and I was woefully unprepared.

Take, as Exhibit A, my kickoff party disaster.

I didn't yet know what I didn't know, and so I didn't have the good sense to be scared. The idea of working for COGA was indescribably exciting for me. Sure, I'd been satisfied in my Tetra Tech job, making regular ascensions up the ladder of middle management. I had a lot of responsibilities and interesting projects, and worked with great people.

COGA had two staff members, and I was the third.

But now! Suddenly I was the face of an important Colorado industry and had access to people, places, and decisions that I hardly knew existed only one month before. My inbox filled with notes from well-wishers congratulating me on my new position. My calendar quickly filled up with introductory meetings, so many that I was scheduled from 7:30 am to 6 pm, often in 15-minute increments.

There was so much to understand! COGA's lobbyist of more than 20 years, Jim Cole, set up meetings with important legislators of both parties. Colorado's legislature runs from January to May each year, and there was no time to waste for me to get to know the House and Senate leaders of our state. We also made the rounds of some of the key regulatory bodies: the Department of Natural Resources, the Colorado Oil and Gas Conservation Commission, the Colorado Department of Health and the Environment.

COGA had dozens of members and the larger companies each wanted to provide me with their own orientation. Usually they hosted a meeting at their offices, mostly in Denver, and I'd spend a good part of my time figuring out whether to drive or walk in my new heel-and-blazer ensemble, and how to schedule meetings with enough time to make it without having to run.

I arrived at more than one meeting flustered,
calloused and out of breath.

The most surprising aspect was the many meeting requests that were simply to curry my favor. *My* favor! Future political candidates that wanted my ear, vendors to the oil and gas industry that wanted to book a presentation slot, non-profits that wanted industry support. It slowly dawned on me how important this job really was.

I set up meet-and-greets with environmental leaders, who I knew well. And started making the rounds with reporters who wanted to establish access. Some news outlets profiled me and I began the uncomfortable process of seeing myself in the news, not yet every day.

And yet each day started with a nervous stomach. I felt I had to overcome the fact that I was a Democrat, a woman, an environmentalist, and from Boulder during every meeting and throughout every day. The memo I mentioned earlier, the one that the Republicans circulated during the COGA selection process to oppose my hire, weighed constantly on my mind. I had never seen the memo, but its existence filled me with a cement-like sense of dread.

I worked with the frenzied passion of someone desperate to overcome their (my!) background. Perhaps you can imagine how determined I was to provide to the COGA members, oil and gas employees, and elected Republicans that I *was really* on their side. And at the same time, I wanted to show the environmental leaders, Democrats, and the Ritter administration that I would create change; I wanted to prove through my actions that I hadn't sold out completely.

Fortunately, I had a lot of energy.

Shortly after I came on board, my colleagues of co-workers and consultants had arranged for a kickoff party to help introduce me to this new world, and I was breathless with anticipation. I added a small list of attendees from my old life, but left the rest of the planning to them. There were so many important people to invite who I hadn't yet met…and I was excited to show off my new life to my former colleagues. In hindsight, it is embarrassing to admit how simplistic and self-centered my frame of reference was at that time.

That kickoff party disaster was the just the prelude of things to come.

It was January 2010, a gubernatorial election year, and through various proxies and connections we had invited to the party the two lead candidates representing the Democratic and Republican parties. How exciting! At my party! I didn't pay much attention to the details for a couple of reasons. First, I was very new to the job and completely overwhelmed by the schedule I had to maintain and the firehouse of information I was trying to assimilate. Second, and truly more relevant, I was completely, selfishly absorbed in the pure delight of having a party thrown for me. I was focused on what I would wear and what I would say. I was honestly enjoying this moment and how this party symbolized a milestone in my career.

The day came for the party and I ended up changing clothes in the restroom of the Sheraton where the party would be held. I put away my more conservative blazer and put on the new white blouse that tied at the front. My sparkling new silver shoes with a silver flower on the toe would give me blisters, but I didn't know that yet. Then I looked at myself in the mirror…and was horrified by the amount of cleavage that showed.

I tried to rearrange the bow, with no success.

A very nice woman, who turned out to be an executive assistant for one of my favorite executives, had volunteered to staff the welcome table. When I walked in, she looked me over and said, *If you've got it, show it! That looks great!* I nervously accepted her kindness. I didn't have a backup shirt. And my *shoes* did look great.

The party was a smashing success. It was packed both with people I knew from my career-to-date, coming to congratulate me on my success, and with notable, important people I had yet to meet. I couldn't have been happier. I floated from group to group on my stylish silver pumps enjoying the flattery, attention, and introductions.

The skilled COGA team had everything running without a hitch. Invited guests checked in at a welcome table. In the rented hotel ballroom, drinks and hors d'oeuvres were passed. The small program went off without a hitch, with one of my most influential Board members, Joe Jaggers of Bill Barret Corporation, saying some nice remarks and introducing me. My remarks were well received and all the jokes warmly applauded. At some point in the short program, the Mayor of Denver, popular, affable John Hickenlooper, who was the leading Democratic candidate for Governor, made some remarks. I was particularly struck that he put his beer on the podium: so daring! He talked about his history as a petroleum geologist in the oil and gas industry. Although that was a story I would later hear dozens of times, at the moment it was so charming, and I was dazzled. I was so delighted that a Democrat was saying nice things about the oil and gas industry. The brutal partisan divide about oil and gas was being bridged before my eyes.

I thought, *Perhaps this is all going to work out after all!*

I continued floating from person to person that evening, perhaps the happiest I had ever been, certainly in any work situation. I made small talk as I worked the room; fairly certain that I had managed to introduce myself to all of our guests.

It was only as the chairs were being stacked, and we were being ushered out by our hotel hosts, that one of my Board members took me aside and frantically told me that we had a disaster on our hands. He was so dramatic and speaking to me in a stage whisper, as if in confidence, that I was entirely confused. His warning of disaster did not comport with my happily dazzled state of mind.

In his loud whisper, he warned me that because the Democratic Governor had spoken at the event, it was the gravest offense not to have the Republican candidate speak. I let him know that that candidate, Scott McInnis, had indeed been invited, and was on the program, but he didn't arrive. I thought it was the invitation that counted and shrugged off his warnings.

But he was right, it was a mistake.

This was a serious breach of protocol. In a later forensic analysis of this event, I saw that there had been several miscommunications resulting in the no show. That analysis was important for my learning, but useless in explaining what happened. No one cared what caused the mistake.

It turned out that at the party was Colorado's senate minority leader. At least he got invited! He was someone who later would become an important colleague, but at that time he had established himself as something of a rival and a leading critic of my hire. (He was the author of the aforementioned memo alerting lawmakers to my liberal background.) I had asked my staff to alert me when he arrived so I could say hello (I knew that much), but he had by-passed the welcome table upon entry. And so I never knew he was there. He had expected to be invited to speak on behalf of the Republican gubernatorial candidate. Unfortunately, I did not divine his presence nor his wishes.

The result was an embarrassing piece in the next day's *Denver Post* with a splashy headline reading "Oil bash turns into political brouhaha [8]

I'd been on the job for a month.

Perhaps not surprisingly, this incident led to my integrity and competence being questioned by a large contingent of COGA members and interested outsiders. I fielded critical calls for days. I strove to answer them gracefully, taking full responsibility, listening to the critiques. But it was such a colossal and early error that I was deeply mortified.

Turns out, the thin ice on which I'd started the job wouldn't become solid for years.

11

Finding the Right Stuff

Every cloud does have a silver lining. That cliché would become something of a mantra for me, as the going got rough. I learned to trust that, in some future time, I would look back on any crisis and appreciate a lesson, see an opportunity that emerged, or understand how a new relationship was formed. I learned a number of lessons, many of which would not be fully appreciated for several years.

For these experiences, I am now grateful.

In taking stock of the oil bash with the benefit of hindsight, a few lessons emerged:

- ✧ Shit happens. A lot. Take a deep breath, learn, and keep going.
- ✧ Surround yourself with people different from you, with strengths you don't have.
- ✧ Nearly everyone will have advice for you. Listen to all of it respectfully; assimilate only that which meets the highest internal standards of discernment, integrity, and truth.

The oil bash and its resulting wagon-load of friendly advice made it clear in many ways that I needed to build a team of people around me who could compensate for my weaknesses and lack of experience. Ideally, it would be a team that I could trust.

Finding the right team was critical.

When I started at COGA, there were two existing employees: a Vice President of Operations, who ran the day-to-day business of the organization and the annual conference, and her assistant. The VP was very clear that she had no interest in the policy and political objectives of our organization. For that, it was time to build a team.

The first three hires at COGA stayed with me for years, and two are still there today. We hired a Director of Policy, a researcher, and a law graduate who was later to serve as Regulatory Counsel once he passed the bar. Now COGA was comprised of six people and we could really create a culture and focus on our mission.

That last paragraph made these hires sound easy. With a Board of 40 member companies and the diverse interests of over 300 member companies to represent, *nothing* was easy. More on that later.

And so I jumped in.

Consider fracking—because I was a scientist, and public concern about fracking was in its early days, I made the same mistake that the oil and gas industry makes today—I set out to *educate* our critics and the public. Sounds logical, right? My reasoning: *If only they understood more about oil and gas and fracking—they would understand how important fracking is, and how it can be developed safely.*

Fracking is simply the process of drilling down into the earth, directing a high-pressure water mixture at the rock to release the gas inside and then injecting water, sand and chemicals at high pressure, allowing the gas to flow out.

If only explaining fracking was that easy!

We would dig in, figuratively. With our new team, we would carefully review studies about oil and gas as they came out. Trade associations are infamously public relations machines for their membership; providing predictable quotes to media outlets, pushing back on unfavorable information, and providing talking points that support their industry's interests. I wanted COGA to be different. My instructions in those early days to the staff were clear: I wanted to build a robustly science-based organization and develop position papers. We would not serve as a PR shop turning out baseless talking points for the industry. We would educate ourselves and our colleagues and then, using the best information available, educate the public.

When the evidence was against us, we would say so.

The team was barely in place when those first couple of oil- and gas-related scientific papers came out in the spring of 2011 and we needed to hit the ground running. The papers were high-profile, extremely negative, gathered tons of media attention, and fed the early anti-fracking frenzy. We were still figuring out how to work together as the new COGA team when we were faced with media calls from every Colorado outlet wanting a response on these papers. The headlines were negative and alarmist, and the summaries were brusque and lacking in subtlety.

Science Daily: Methane levels 7 times higher in
water wells near hydrofracking sites[9]
Mother Jones: Natural Gas: Worse than Coal?[10]

One was Cornell's now infamous and roundly debunked paper concluding that natural gas is worse than coal.[11] That paper was discredited a dozen times, with just one early debunk referenced here for you, geeky reader after my own heart.[12] The second paper was Duke's methane in groundwater in Pennsylvania,[13] also now rigorously debunked.[14] Because of the stature of the universities, and the new popularity of the term fracking, these papers got significant media and public traction.

> Taking on institutions like Cornell and Duke was, well, intimidating.

At the time, the Cornell studies and others on the topic were accepted as accurate and given broad media credibility. COGA had no scientific credibility, and I was determined that we would build it brick by brick. I thought if we simply put together logical arguments, we could sway logical people. This was before I knew about confirmation bias, which tells us that a newspaper reader will choose to believe those stories that confirm what they already believe, particularly when those feelings are grounded in their identity. (This is discussed further in Chapter 36.)

> Thank goodness I didn't know how hard this would be.

Each new study created a crisis of information and conscience for me. It is impossible for me to overstate how stressful this commitment to science was. For example, when the Cornell study came out, I spent every hour-long drive home hashing out in my head the potential consequences: I was representing the oil and gas industry to contribute to positively changing the world, particularly by reducing carbon emissions. If natural gas was really worse than coal, as the Cornell study stated, then I was actually contributing to the problem rather than the solution. What was I going to do?

It would have been much easier to be simply
an industry spokesperson.

I decided I'd cross that bridge when I got there, and doubled down on analysis of studies as they came out. From my environmental consulting work and personal studies, I had come to understand that tradeoffs from energy development were inevitable, and I decided that these tradeoffs were acceptable to me. Like all commercial and industrial work, I concluded that there would be isolated incidents and accidents. I did not subscribe to the philosophy that the only acceptable risk is zero risk. If we all did, how would we get in our cars in the morning? From my perspective, isolated accidents were noteworthy and must be used to inform future prevention. Systemic releases, crises of pollution, however—these would be unacceptable.

During these early years at COGA, we developed robust internal standards for scientific rigor and personal integrity. If there were issues with oil and gas operations, we would admit to them. We would always strive to cite third-party sources that the public would trust. The result of these efforts was dozens of position papers and fact sheets over the first couple of years I was there. These were professional and well done and, when reviewed, were generally praised. If errors were brought to our attention, we fixed them. It was also an incessant educational process for each of us.

Later, as our COGA team grew, eventually to 13, and the public tension over oil and gas rose to a nearly unbearable crescendo, we would sit around and "call bullshit" on our own internal assessment and each other. We wanted to make sure we were being honest all around. Did we believe what we were telling our communities? Did we have all of the information we needed?

To be the face of an industry—with authenticity—
means facing a lot of demons.

Back in 2010, though, I was striving to build, brick by brick, a team and a culture of high performance and unflappable integrity. Later we attained camaraderie, and ultimately, we walked through enough fires together to garner trust and deep affection for each other. When you feel like you are taking the world on, both within your industry and without, you have got to stick together.

If you ever need to take on the world,
I hope you have a team like mine.

I wasn't the easiest person to work for, and there were plenty of hiring mistakes and ill-fitting roles that didn't work out. By the end of my time there, however, I'd had the opportunity to learn lessons about building a great team mindfully, lessons that will forever serve me.

Beware the clones. It is really tempting to surround yourself with people of temperament and capabilities similar to your own. Those teams are like a rowboat with too many people on one side. Distribute the weight of personality types, skill sets, and intellectual gifts. You'll likely have more conflict, but it will be constructive, creative conflict. You'll also have better results.

Embrace young talent. It was only after my right-hand man, Doug, pointed out that I was the technological equivalent of a 65-year-old that I decided to embrace technology. For all the genuine miseries of managing the young, talented, and over-eager, there are more benefits. Young talent keeps conversations challenging, work plans fresh, and leaders on their toes. Without young people on your team, no one will know how to connect the printer.

Create your culture. A workplace's culture will never emerge strong and resilient by accident. I focused on love, taking calculated risks, self-reflection, and excellence.

Invest in progress. Every manager faces the daily grind of petty conflicts and grievances among team members, but the wise leader invests time and energy in the people and efforts that move the organization forward. I learned over time to starve drama of my attention and lavish creative time and energy on the team members and projects that kept us growing.

12

Et Tu, Oil?

I'd managed to survive those first few weeks. My hour-plus commute, 2- and 6-year-old boys at home, and the punishing schedule at work didn't allow much time for wallowing. The legislative session was underway, and the small COGA team got busy putting together an Oil and Gas 101 training for legislators. It was a non-partisan event, but largely aimed at helping Democrats understand the importance of Colorado's natural gas industry.

Unfortunately, over the previous few years, oil and gas had become a partisan issue both nationally and in Colorado. As a Democrat myself, I had to overcome the traditional partisan bias against our industry. Oil and gas was one of those unspoken platform issues where a good Democrat was expected to oppose future development in favor of switching to renewables. In the coming few years, Republicans would also struggle with their party's expectations to support, without question, oil and gas development, particularly when it bumped up against the concerns of their local constituents.

In early 2010, it was fashionable to be a certain kind of forward-thinking environmentalist. I was just such an environmentalist. In this context, one could support natural gas as a *bridge fuel*, spanning the transition to a renewable energy future. The calculus was relatively straightforward. Forty-five percent of U.S. electricity production was provided by coal with about 25 percent provided by natural gas.[15] Climate change was just picking up a head of steam as a topic of political and public interest. Natural gas had a much better environmental footprint than coal.[16]

Furthermore, natural gas as a potential transportation fuel was just garnering local and national interest. As a fuel for cars and trucks, natural gas was not only cheaper, but provided significant opportunities to reduce the air pollution caused by traditional gasoline and diesel fuel vehicles.

I learned a lot while preparing that Oil and Gas 101 presentation, and I began the juggling process entailed in being both an environmentalist and the primary spokesperson for Colorado's oil and gas industry. Because of the benefits of natural gas, there was no clash here. I could be a dyed-in-the-wool environmentalist and support it. Hell, Sierra Club even accepted $26 million from Chesapeake Energy, the country's largest producer of natural gas.[17]

Sierra Club loves loved natural gas?

At the time, 85 percent of Colorado's oil and gas production was natural gas. So I focused my educational materials for COGA on the benefits of natural gas, often over the benefits of oil products such as gasoline and diesel.

One of the main reasons I had taken the President & CEO job for COGA was to ensure that natural gas could be a viable, responsible, and accepted part of the solution to climate change. I was overt and unapologetic about this stance, although it was not particularly popular on either side of the fossil fuel debate. One of the few areas of solid common ground was reducing air pollution, both fuel-switching from coal to natural gas in electricity generation, and in promoting natural gas as an alternate transportation fuel. In both cases, natural gas provides enormous air quality benefits.

During this short window of peace in the valley, I contemplated how COGA could best position itself in the role I imagined for it: providing clean electricity and better transportation fuel. I evaluated changing the name of our organization to the *Colorado Natural Gas Association*. This was neither as original nor clever an idea as I had anticipated; later that year, a group of natural gas producers started *America's Natural Gas Alliance* to distinguish themselves from *the oil* in "oil and gas."

> Oh how sweet the ring of Colorado Natural Gas Association would have been to my ears.

COGA had just completed a rebranding the previous year, so the idea was dismissed outright. As it turned out, that was fortunate for the organization and for me.

This idea of promoting natural gas in Colorado at the expense of oil was not without controversy itself. It was the first of many rifts I would have to navigate among COGA's diverse members. In this case, COGA had Colorado's two oil refineries as members, and they didn't take kindly to being thrown under the public-relations bus. Additionally, COGA had many small, oil-producing members, who were not about to sit on the sidelines while I rebranded the industry.

> It turned out not to matter for long.

Sierra Club's ongoing *Beyond Coal* campaign had effectively shut down and shuttered new permitting efforts for coal-fired electricity generation. This effort had the potential to benefit natural gas electricity generation and therefore created a muted acceptance from industry.

The "natural gas is cool" détente only lasted about a year. The reasons for the end of the truce varied, depending on your political perspective. For those that oppose natural gas now, the détente ended because fracking picked up, creating a world of controversy. For those folks, certain studies, now robustly debunked, articulated a case that natural gas was actually worse for climate change than coal. These studies allowed environmental groups to dramatically shift and take anti-natural gas positions. The Sierra Club was the most dramatic example of this shift.

Soon after, they began their *Beyond Natural Gas* campaign.

If you supported oil and gas, the narrative looked very different. Exploration and production techniques in the U.S. were so wildly successful that we ended up with a massive oversupply of natural gas. So much so that gas became cheap. Incredibly cheap. So cheap that it displaced coal in electricity production without any policy incentives. So much so that carbon dioxide levels in the U.S. dropped to their lowest levels since 1996.[18] And these market forces both increased the amount of drilling happening around the country and the world, and called into question the economic viability of wind and solar for electricity production.

This girl suddenly had a situation on her hands.

The price of natural gas fell precipitously. As a result, natural gas exploration in Colorado came to a halt, seemingly overnight. Environmentalists about-faced and opposed natural gas under the narrative of opposing fracking. Drilling rigs shut down and companies began laying off their employees. For a few months, I wondered if I'd have any Colorado oil and gas industry left to represent.

Then, it felt very sudden; the same techniques that had been so successful for developing natural gas were used to develop oil. Rigs drilling for natural gas moved to new basins and started drilling for oil. Places in western and southern Colorado that were once busy with natural gas development were relatively quiet. Areas that were once historic oil development basins, like northwest and northeast Colorado, were seeing new interest, focused on oil. Seemingly overnight, Colorado went from a natural gas producing state to an oil producing state.

Oil is, well, oily.

And this girl was very uncomfortable. I was now representing oil development in what I thought was a natural gas producing state. Any environmental allies COGA or I'd had a few months earlier were long gone. Along with the new oil-focused rigs came new protests about fracking. My life was about to change dramatically.

It was a little late for second thoughts.

13

Rebate

Early fall was the time to start thinking about member dues for the following calendar year. I had never run a non-profit before, and my instincts were to run operations like a business. In my first nine months I had cut expenses dramatically and made several hires, and still we had a surplus of cash. Although most people viewed me as a political operative with an agenda, I knew that the Board had ultimately hired me because of my business acumen. And I wanted to deliver.

I proposed that we return funds to the membership. My small staff was not happy. It was time for me to assert myself. I proposed that we take my proposal for a membership refund to the Board and let them decide.

The Board was understandably shocked; in all the various oil and gas trade associations to which they belonged, no one had ever proposed returning money. They asked good questions... *Shouldn't we put it in a reserve?* I articulated that I already had a plan to build up a reserve over three years. *Shouldn't we just hire more help?* I wanted to demonstrate to the membership that we were and would operate efficiently, and that I wasn't here to build an empire.

Ultimately the rebate was approved.

Like pretty much everything I did at COGA that I thought would be a groundbreaking big deal, the rebate was just another thing that we did there that happened and then was over and never thought of again. Nevertheless, I'm proud of that rebate. We offered members the opportunity to apply the rebate to the 2011 dues or donate it to one of our funds. The vast majority took the rebate and applied it to their next year's dues. A few members expressed surprise, or relayed gratitude to me, but largely it was a non-event.

The reason that the rebate ultimately mattered was because over the next few years I would return to the Board, and ultimately the membership, again and again, for fundraising. Within five years we had grown the staff from 3 to 13 and hired teams of consultants to run outreach, educational, and political campaigns. I had no idea then how difficult and contentious the future of COGA would be. I was thankful and more than a little lucky that I gave that rebate when the opportunity presented itself...so when I returned to ask for money, the membership was confident that we really needed it.

Oh boy, we sure did.

14

Fire!

Immersed in COGA issues, I'd had no time to catch my breath when the worst fire in Colorado history started one mile from my home. It was 2010, my first summer on the job and the first year I toured all of the state's oil and gas basins. I love the Raton Basin, which surrounds Trinidad and Walsenburg, Colorado—a few hours' drive south of Denver. It's some of the most beautiful country that you will find anywhere. Rolling hills and dramatic plateaus. High desert landscapes converging with mountain forests.

After my meetings, introductions to the regional county commissioners, and field tours, my extended family had stayed for the long Labor Day weekend in a rustic cabin on Colorado State Highway 12: the Scenic Highway of Legends. It was Labor Day and we'd spent the morning at the Trinidad rodeo. In addition to Brian and my boys, my sister-in-law Wendy and her family had joined us.

> Overall, that was a highly memorable day, and my boys still talk about the wild horse racing.

As we drove home on I-25, it was so windy that we felt unaccountably nervous, worried about things like RV's tipping over on us. My family was in one car, and Wendy's in theirs, with my son Carter riding with his cousin Matthew as always.

As we cruised through Colorado Springs, due south of Denver about 70 miles, I kept noticing the number 100. It seemed so odd. For one, we'd passed a 100-mile marker and then I looked down and saw us roll through 100 on the odometer. Then 100 on billboards as part of phone numbers, and I also saw a 100 on a license plate. It was odd enough that I thought, *What does that mean?*

I still couldn't really tell you, but I never forgot that portent.

Heading north, we took a planned detour in Castle Rock to Brian's sister Dawn's house. The Schuller clan is vast, and we operate as one big extended family. Dawn's family had our dog for the long weekend, and we all stopped by for lunch. It's always joyous and very loud among the Schullers. We dug in to make sandwiches and catch up with our usual zeal.

I didn't think anything of it when the phone rang.

The call came from Brian's third sister, Ali, who knew we were all gathering. She told Dawn to turn on the news, which she immediately did. My brain couldn't put the pieces together fast enough. An odd hush came over us. There was a fire. In Fourmile Canyon. An address was listed on the TV screen. I felt like I knew that address. Yes I did. That address was one mile west of us. Well that's pretty far. No it isn't! Oh my God, look how big that plume of smoke is. Oh my God, our house has burned down. Oh my God, our friend's house has burned down…

Everyone started talking at once.

I have this eerie other personality that emerges in any kind of emergency. I know it well from my time as a volunteer firefighter and the occasions my kids choked or got really hurt. I got to know it very well over the years at COGA. Every sense shuts down and I get a kind of very clear tunnel vision. All the noise becomes dull and distant and my brain starts functioning like an old-school computer, showing me only the certain bits of information that require immediate action.

"We have got to go," I heard myself saying. "Brian, I'll drive." I put my hands out for the keys. "You get Sasha and her food." "Wendy, Carter is going to ride with us." "Dawn, can you pack the boys some sandwiches for the car?"

When I go into that mode, people do what I say, and we were soon driving north in silence. The five of us gaping at the massive plume of smoke ahead that was consuming our community of the last 14 years. Well, four of us anyway. Sasha was just glad to be back with her nuclear family.

Adrenaline was coursing through all our veins, and we knew we needed a few moments to gather ourselves, get practical. All of Brian's fire gear was at the house, so we made our first stop at the evacuation center housed at the West Boulder Rec Center. All of Boulder was smoky. We quickly found neighbors and acquaintances we knew vaguely from the canyon in our general area, but no one had much information. People described driving out through flames. A renter from the house directly above us, with which we share a driveway, ran over to us as soon as we arrived and said hysterically, "It's gone! It's all gone!"

I closed my eyes and took a deep breath.

Standing in the Rec Center parking lot, I thought, *Everything we now own is in our car?* The neighbor was hysterical enough that I heard myself telling Brian, "Let's not have any opinion about our house until we see it for ourselves." Robot Tisha was still in control. A few minutes later, another neighbor pulled in, his white van blackened with smoke. He stopped in the middle of the parking lot, got out, and hugged his girlfriend, who had left the mountain earlier. He had stayed to chain-saw down trees between the fire and his house. He left when the fire began to overtake him, driving through flames on the way down. He said, "It's gotta all be gone."

I started thinking that it probably was.

Pretty quickly the situation went from full adrenaline to anxious boredom. New information on a fire generally comes about once every 8 or 12 hours, so there's a lot of waiting. We decided it was time to figure out how to get Brian on the fire line.

It's a faux pas to show up at any emergency incident without your gear. Brian keeps two sets of fire gear in his car at all times: wildland and structure gear. This situation was unusual because of our trip… he had taken the gear out of the car, and now it was sitting six miles up the canyon. Or possibly in a pile of ashes.

We dropped the kids off at Wendy's house. Then I drove Brian to the bottom of Boulder Canyon. There were sheriff cars with lights on blocking the road, and the entire canyon was so filled with smoke that you could barely see the huge flashing road sign that said "Closed for Fire."

We pulled a U-turn and drove over to the Boulder justice center, which was serving as the command center. The fire later got so close to Boulder that they had to move the command center farther into town. As soon as we pulled into the parking lot, we saw one of our neighbors, a long-time friend and professional fire fighter, in his truck. Rod looked at Brian and said, "Where's your gear?" Brian said, "At the house." Rod said, "Get in." Brian looked back at me briefly, and got out of the car without a word. I saw him get into Rod's truck as Rod threw an extra wildland shirt at him. They sped off up the canyon.

And I started to cry.

I pulled into a parking spot, put my face in my hands and wept. What if I had just sent Brian off to his death? I hadn't even said good-bye, or I love you, or be careful. Brian and Rod had been on some really scary fires together in the past, but nothing even in the same family as this.

There is significant debate as to how the fire got started. In the end, the fire investigation identified a fire pit that had gotten stirred up by very fierce winds. What is clear when you go to the fire source, and I run by there now nearly every day, is the fire moved in five directions at once. It spread out like a star where still-blackened trees stand. The firefighter's house where it started was destroyed within the hour. By the end of the fire, 169 homes were destroyed in three canyons, and for a time there was an evacuation order in parts of the city of Boulder.

But I didn't know any of that yet.

Personally, I prefer a good crisis requiring action to this phase of an emergency, where I was stuck waiting and watching for days. I went back to Wendy's tiny condo, where we were invited to stay. I felt nearly psychotic with waiting and worry, and it manifested into a kind of claustrophobia. Unless I was outside, I felt like the walls were closing in on me. I'm a woman of action, but there was not really anything to do.

I gathered the kids and took our weekend trip belongings over to a hotel that would accommodate us and our dog. They had an indoor pool, which was great for the kids, but added to my overwhelming sense of claustrophobia. I couldn't breathe. I couldn't even worry. And tomorrow I was supposed to go to work.

One of my girlfriends brought over a six-pack of beer and we watched the kids play in the pool. The hotel and pool were filled with people evacuated from the fire. I couldn't really talk to them. On some level, I was shutting down. Everything felt chaotic, claustrophobic, and lacking adequate oxygen.

I now know that, under stressful domestic situations, when Brian isn't around me, I can't really think clearly. It's a goofy trait for a powerful, professional woman and it took me years to admit it. Having him on the fire felt like one of my organs was out in the world exposed. I was now functioning at a very low level.

Very late in the night, Brian came to the hotel and I let him in. There was just one room, one bed with the kids, the dog, and me. So we sat on the edge of the bed and whispered. Early in the fire, fire fighters had evacuated Wall Street, the area where our home was located. No one knew what was left. Brian had stayed with Rod, gotten some gear, and managed some home protection teams. Unfortunately, Rod had deployed all of the teams on other homes, and he watched the fire approach and then ultimately consume his beautiful home. Brian sat awkwardly next to Rod when he had to call his wife and tell her that everything was gone.

Brian slept a few hours and we dropped him back off for a full day shift the next morning.

I called in and reported that I'd be working from Boulder. The boys and I spent the day at Wendy's. Still claustrophobic, I sat at her little outside table and tried to get work done. It was Tuesday and I had my first Board retreat on Thursday. In the middle of that afternoon, Rod texted me a picture of my house. It was still standing.

I still have that picture.

That second night we stayed in the hotel again, and in the morning, I packed up the kids and Max to take them to the park to where there would be an informational meeting for evacuees. We pulled out of the hotel parking lot onto 28th Street, and I looked back at Alec, who was 3 and sitting in his toddler car seat. His eyes were wide—and he was turning blue. I put on my hazards in the middle lane of 28th Street and stopped the car. I ran around the car, unfastened the buckles, pulled him out, and swept his mouth with my finger. Nothing. I flipped him upside down over my knee, cars honking (are you serious, people?) and hit his back with the heel of my hand. A red and white striped candy hit the asphalt below me.

Someone stopped behind me and got out, asking, "Are you okay?" I sighed. Smiled. Yes, we're okay. Alec threw up. And I started crying again. Some well-meaning person near the hotel desk at checkout had given Alec the candy, feeling sorry for the evacuated kid. He had opened it surreptitiously, knowing I wouldn't allow it. My kids still talk about all the candy and presents you get when you're evacuated.

This turned out not to be the last time for that.

We made our way to the evacuee meeting at beautiful Chautauqua Park in Boulder. Brian and I had been married at Chautauqua in 2001 and knew it well. There were hundreds of people, most of whom we knew. Many had lost their homes, many didn't know. The fire was completely uncontained and nearly every face was streaked with tears. Sheriff Pellee has always been wonderful at meetings like this, a balance between professional and compassionate. He told us to prepare to be out of our homes for a minimum of six weeks. Tens of miles of phone and electrical infrastructure were destroyed and would have to be rebuilt before we could return.

I arranged for a basement for us to live in. A very kind woman, a friend of my acupuncturist, had put out a message on her Board offering this space for evacuees. I snapped it up. Although being in a basement did not help my continuing claustrophobia, I was desperate to get out of that hotel room.

As the fire transitioned from local to federal, the Four Mile fire fighters got released one by one. Brian had managed to stop by our house and grab a few things and my fire gear. He knew I was going to want to see the house, and that was the only way I would be able to.

He was right.

I put on my wildland fire gear, which mercifully still fit. I hadn't worn it since I had found out I was pregnant with Carter. I grabbed my ID and jumped in our truck, giving me what I hoped was the most fire-fighter credibility. For anyone who knows me, this little expedition overplaying my role as a firefighter so I could go see my house is extremely out of character. I am a rule follower, and I have deep respect for emergency response, sheriff, and police personnel.

When I reflect back on that time, I saw I had been driven by something so deep, so fundamental, that it took me months to name it. When I was young, my parents had divorced when I was seven. From that age through high school, I moved back and forth between my parents' houses about every two weeks. In college, I had lived somewhere different every year and then every summer. When I moved to Boulder in 1996, I lived for one year in a house in north Boulder. When I bought our cabin in the mountains, it was my last stop. I had now lived there for 13 years, and for the first time in my entire life I had put down roots.

But now I had to talk my way through two sheriff's roadblocks, showing my (dusty) fire fighter ID that miraculously wasn't expired. I believe the second sheriff knew I didn't have a legit reason, but let me through, looking down her nose and sternly saying, "20 minutes."

"Yes, ma'am."

The drive to our house was shocking. Half the landscape was burned to a char. Smoke drifted up in spirals everywhere I looked. The land was unrecognizable. As I pulled into Wall Street, I gasped. The Cole's house was smoking rubble. They had had a huge shed of ammo, which had apparently gone off for hours. All of Ed's unique historic, restored army vehicles sat in unrecognizable lumps.

Richard's cool house that was built back into a mineshaft and was filled with exotic birds flying around the living room was a melted roof over debris. The cute two-house rental across the street from us was two piles of bizarre, burned stuff. Strangely, a white claw-foot bathtub that I'd never seen before stood alone outside on the hillside.

I turned left up our driveway, over the bridge, and then right into our parking area. My brain did not go into its efficient, emergency mode. It turned as slowly as molasses. I dragged my feet out of the truck with the large Tupperware container Brian had given me to grab stuff with, and stared at the miracle of our still-standing house. I was immediately struck by all the small animals in our yard. It seemed like dozens, or maybe hundreds of squirrels and mice and rabbits.

For a moment, I felt like Snow White.

Our town of Wall Street had burned on every side, and so the parts that didn't burn had created a little oasis for animals. By the time we returned a few weeks later, that had eaten through everything that had been left outside.

I went in the house. We never locked the house and didn't even have a lock on the door at that time. Ironically, conditions at COGA down the road would change that. I fast walked straight to my jewelry box to grab the one item that had been torturing me since the fire first began: my beloved engagement ring. I slipped it on with a happy sigh. I grabbed the big Tupperware bin of photo albums that we had assembled a couple of years earlier during the then worst blaze in Colorado's history, the Hayman fire, and threw it in the back seat of the truck. I guess my excuse not to complete the boys' baby albums was gone.

I returned to the house, proceeding to pack the most nonsensical hodge-podge of items. Knives. Underwear. Dog food. Later when I returned to our temporary housing in a finished Boulder basement to unpack, Brian just said, "I see you didn't make a list." Since then I have had many opportunities to talk to people evacuated from other fires who get to run back to grab a few things.

"You'll be out of your mind. Make a list."

Three nights into our fire evacuation, I drove alone the two-and-a-half hours down to the Broadmoor Hotel in Colorado Springs to oversee our first-ever Board retreat. Interestingly, as much as I could not get my head on straight at home, I have an entire other brain that functions for work. I was effective, efficient, and the meeting went very well. My small staff was supportive, but if anyone knew about my evacuation, they didn't say anything to me.

Several weeks later we returned home to a community that would never be the same again. Many of our fire fighters and friends had lost their homes and were living elsewhere. Many families that we knew and loved never returned. I ended up serving on the community foundation's Board to give away money raised for fire victims as a representative of our fire department and broader community. $1.6 million in the end was woefully inadequate, and the process to decide who got what was extremely painful and difficult for all of us involved.

I began to come to terms with how important my home was to me. And to understand how fickle life is and how transient such an important place truly is. I also began to look at Brian, my boys, and our extended Schuller clan differently—as my foundation and the heartbeat that keeps me going. It was a sudden event, but it took years to process, this understanding that the only thing that really mattered to me was this family, this home, this community.

I also knew that it could all disappear in an instant.

I started experiencing anxiety and sleeplessness. I smelled smoke even when I was in Denver. I was simultaneously relieved at my circumstances, grateful for my good fortune, sad about the changes in my community, and anxious about what could happen in the future. In our community, everyone had the eyes of a ghost.

The Denver Business Journal ran a story about how my home had been spared, and people that I met in Denver congratulated me on my good fortune. I felt that I couldn't share how massively devastated I'd felt, how much things had changed both within me and without, how crushed my community was, how terrified I was for the future and the unknown terrors that could suddenly befall my family.

It was another year before I faced that anxiety head on.

15

Gremlins

I had called and invited him out for a drink, but he had declined. Instead I found myself awkwardly standing by his desk in his office in the middle of the morning on a holiday. He hadn't invited me to sit, and I hadn't taken a seat, which was probably for the best because this was going to be awkward. Standing there silently, I could see that Chance was handsome once, but he had grown a bit puffy and pasty with the stresses of work and life.

A month earlier, I had embarked upon making my first hire—for a Director of Government Affairs. After my oil bash disaster, it was easy to justify to the Board the need for someone to anticipate issues and who would have known who to invite. What I hadn't anticipated is what a hot spot this hire would be for people who wanted to control COGA and keep an eye on me.

I did a little research into the prior person who'd held this position. He was a Republican, well respected, working under the prior COGA President, who was also a woman from Boulder. He had lasted in the position at COGA exactly one month before he resigned. No one would say why, including him, when I invited him in for coffee and asked him if he'd consider re-applying. He very politely declined and wished me luck. He was the picture of poise, grace, and respect.

His silence made me nervous.

When I started at COGA, the association had one committee that was still meeting, the GAC. Say GAC out loud; this is not a pretty acronym. The Government Affairs Committee was run by Richard, a prominent Government Affairs company representative, possibly the most powerful and influential in my circles for years. I later would come to have a grudging respect for him, but only after he had suffered through a miserable divorce, which seemed to somewhat level the playing field between us.

Richard ran the committee well.

There were a handful of regulars on the weekly committee phone meetings, and I sat in without participating for those first few weeks, to get the lay of the land and an understanding of the personalities. When it was time to announce that we would be hiring for this position, the GAC naturally was the first stop after the Board.

I invited anyone who wanted to participate to sit on the hiring committee. I knew that process was going to be key, although I didn't know exactly how to manage it. I hadn't yet learned the imperative of counting votes before calling a vote, but I had good instincts for this kind of thing.

The committee weighed in on the job description, referred candidates, and participated in the selection of candidates for interviews. This hire was the first test of both my ability to bring my critics into the fold and to make a hire that would not undermine me.

That would be a very narrow path.

Chance, the man who had turned down that drink and left me standing in his office, worked for one of my most important member companies; he was also their Government Affairs lead. Gracious to a fault, he had an interesting way of sending his lobbyist, Melissa, to most meetings, so he could observe from afar, keep his distance, and preserve his power for when he needed it. It was an effective strategy that I was later to copy for many of my own important efforts.

The selection committee worked well together, meeting periodically, refining the list of candidates, and conducting phone interviews. I did not participate in any of the early in-person or phone interviews, letting the selection committee take the lead. The process went smoothly and the candidate pool was reduced to two candidates for final consideration. I interviewed both: one was local, and we met in my office. The other was in Texas, and we conducted his interview over the phone.

I actually liked both candidates equally, and felt that this presented a good opportunity to empower the selection committee to make a final decision, so I brought them together to discuss the candidates. Interestingly, both Chance and Richard came in person to this meeting. Melissa too.

As we were discussing both the local and the Texas candidate, something strange happened. Both Chance and Richard acted as if they were hearing about the Texas candidate for the first time, asking basic questions about his whereabouts and experience. This was particularly odd because that candidate had described to me in some detail his prior work experience with Chance, the fact that Chance had recruited him to apply for the position, and the earlier "phone interview" he had had with both of them.

So I asked, "Has anyone here had any prior experience with either of these candidates?" And everyone shook their head *no*. I paused, confused. I had never been baldly lied to before, and I thought it was strange, especially when the truth was so blatantly obvious. I said nothing at that point.

My silence in this situation was not some Machiavellian impulse.

I just didn't want to embarrass Richard and Chance in front of their peers. It was such an unnecessary, transparent, and easily discovered lie that I couldn't understand what could possibly motivate it. So I continued to gather feedback and then said, "Okay, thank you very much. I will give this some thought and make my decision."

"Wait!" Richard said, "Aren't we going to vote?" In fact, I had been planning to let the group decide on the candidate, but I hadn't articulated that, and the strange turn of events had given me pause. I looked around the table and realized that Chance, Richard, and Melissa made up three of five votes. They had intended to make this decision for me.

"No," I said, and with a big smile and a decisive stacking of my papers on the table before putting them in my carefully labeled manila folder, added, "Thank you all so much for your efforts here." I stood up and waited for everyone to leave the room, ensuring I was the last to leave and no additional discussion would ensue, at least not here.

At this early point at COGA, I did not have anyone I could discuss this with. I took my drive home slowly. *Why would Chance and Richard lie about knowing, recommending, and speaking with the candidate?* They could have stated their experience and opinion and gotten their choice if they hadn't lied to me. *What were they trying to accomplish?*

I thought about my conversations with both candidates.

Doug had good experience and was very personable. Most importantly, he had the right Republican pedigree that would make my members feel comfortable that I wasn't building some left-wing organizational structure. In our interview, he had made a point of saying that he valued loyalty to his boss very highly. He said that he knew I was in a tough position and, if I hired him, I could trust him.

Tough position? At the time, I had thought that comment was strange.

Loyalty is something that is earned, and trust is built over time. Why was this person that I had just met promising me both?

Turns out that Doug's extensive political experience had given him a read on my situation at COGA that I could not yet see. I needed a loyal lieutenant to help me navigate the treacherous political path I was on. He had read about the Oil Bash disaster in the paper; he knew what his conservative peers were saying about me.

Doug knew I needed him before I knew I needed him.

I decided to sleep on the Chance and Richard mystery. The next morning I decided to call and invite them both out for a drink and just ask them what was going on. In voicemail tag, they both declined, saying they were unavailable. I pressed both, until finally, Chance agreed to meet me at 10 am at his office the following Monday, which was a holiday. In hindsight, it seems rather obvious that he didn't expect me to make the hour drive to Denver.

I made the hour drive to Denver.

And that was how I found myself standing awkwardly in his office chatting about our children. *Hmmm, how to do this? Just jump in, I guess...*

"Chance. I know that you know our candidate from Texas, he told me about your work together. Why did you say in our meeting that you didn't know him?" I fussed with my fingers, then put them awkwardly by my sides, trying to project as much openness and confidence as I could.

He held my gaze without flinching.
"I don't know him. I've never met him before."

This was not the response I expected. An entire weekend of preparation and I had never anticipated this. Doubling down? I had imagined several scenarios, my favorite of which was him congratulating me on my forthrightness and then the two of us agreeing that we are on the same team. But this? *Now what?* I bumbled forward awkwardly, of course, what else?

"But that's so strange. He told me he worked with you and you recruited him to apply?" I could hear my voice get higher, my fingers twisting together, unable to stay confidently by my side.

"No. I've never met him before." Long, straight, unflinching stare.

If the meeting lasted a full seven minutes, I would be surprised. "Okay," I said, "have a good holiday," as I turned and put my hand on the door handle. Then I turned back and looked at Chance again and I just knew that surprise, naiveté, and even pain were in my expression.

"Goodbye, Tisha," he said, no smile, no explanation.

I slowly walked to the elevator. I knew I had made a truly terrible mistake, although I didn't know what it was. I was in a new world and the rules were different. I was scared, confused, and I felt an unfamiliar nervous flutter in my stomach. That flutter was the beginning of anger.

It probably won't surprise you that Richard never returned my calls. Clearly they had decided that Chance had this one handled.

And so, I hired Doug.

He was true to his word, and gave me loyalty and trust, before I earned it. I like to think that I earned and rewarded that trust through our five years together. Now I had a right-hand man to run these crises by. He was cynical, experienced, and skeptical therefore provided me realistic counsel on the challenges we faced. We walked through some fires together and forged an enduring bond that will last both of our lives.

It was several years before I told Doug the story of his hire, and how close he had come to being the first runner up. In my mind, I named Chance and Richard "the gremlins." For years they conspired together, wreaking havoc. Being straight-up lied to became a familiar experience in the political world I now found myself entrenched in.

It became familiar, but never comfortable.

16

My Three-Question Test

It's one thing to question your basic assumptions in the privacy of your own home. It's another entirely to engage in this process when you are the very public face of an industry. This required a kind of compartmentalization and self-review that I hadn't yet developed.

I had a long commute home each day, and I never knew if it would require one hour or several. Some combination of weather and traffic would determine my fate. In those early COGA years, my schedule was so demanding, that when I got in my car, I took the drive home in silence. I was eager to get home to Brian, Carter, and Alec, and I needed that transition. My body hummed with adrenaline and stress, and my mind raced as if too many streams of thought were competing for my conscious attention.

I would take this time on the road to be relentlessly honest with myself. Each day was packed with meetings and decisions that felt frantic and largely out of my control, and it wasn't easy to reflect upon the day and ask myself if I'd acted carefully, with integrity, and in line with my values. There were so many moments of fear, of confusion, of uncertainty, and I had to be honest when I was too chameleon-like, or too wishy-washy. Later, when I got my feet under me, my mistakes tended to come from over-confidence, anger, or ego. But early on, I was mostly groping blindly for the right path forward with very little time, experience, or help.

During the interview process for the job, I had decided privately that at any point that I had to take a position within COGA with which I disagreed, I would lobby to change the action, and if I couldn't, I would resign. This plan B—resign rather than act in contradiction to my conscience—was not intended to be dramatic and defiant, but to be quiet, thoughtful, and consistent. From the beginning of my tenure at COGA, I did assume that the day would come when I would be faced with this choice. The very nature of the job meant presiding over a lot of difficult and controversial decision-making processes.

I prepared for that day mentally, emotionally, and financially.

I followed the taillights on Highway 36 weaving through the non-stop construction diversions, sometimes blissfully; sometimes uncomfortably fast if traffic was moving. *How*, I asked myself, *would I know* if I was presiding over a decision with which I disagreed? Often I was facing so many opinions, a plethora of disagreeing data, and the need to *act fast* to respond, that there was little time to develop an opinion of my own. Legislative hearings, media inquiries, and company requests were an incessant, hourly assault. That was the price of being a relevant and responsive organization, and it never let up.

A Process

And so I kept my car within the flow of traffic, while my mind experimented with developing a test to apply to my activities and decisions made at COGA. It may sound outrageous, but at first it was simply an experiment designed to keep myself fully engaged in evaluating COGA's internal and external positions: Run every decision through three questions. If the solution didn't successfully pass the three-question test, I would have to seek a new resolution.

I wasn't sure if this idea to turn to a three-question test to assess right and wrong would work. I quickly found that the world goes from black and white to shades of gray really fast when you are working on emotionally charged, political questions that affect a lot of people. My three-question test was:

> **Is this good for most people affected?**
> **Is this good for Colorado?**
> **Is this good for Colorado's oil and gas industry?**

In that order.

This was a personal and private process. The three-question test allowed me to acknowledge how difficult and painful my work was on a daily basis. It gave me a framework to take a hard look at my decisions and honestly assess all of the people affected. Small companies risked being pushed out of business by the positions of large ones. Rural natural gas basins had competing, conflicting interests with urban ones. Charged community conflicts had elected officials, small business owners, and homeowners expressing wildly different needs. There was no way to make everyone happy.

There wasn't even a way to keep someone from becoming furious.

It was only later, when I'd determined the robust nature of the three-question test that I began to share it with my staff as we evaluated our positions. In the beginning, it was a systematic way for me to think through the onslaught of challenges. Later, it began a process by which we evaluated our positions as a team.

An Extended Test

On the topic of Colorado's oil development, the three-question test could not be answered overnight. As the "Niobrara play" came into full development I was faced with the collision of simultaneous residential and oil and gas expansion. It would take me some time to fully answer the three questions in this case.

The rock formation is called the Niobrara, and it is located in an area known as the Denver-Julesburg (DJ) basin about 180 miles northeast of Denver. The Niobrara rock in the DJ basin is known as the Niobrara play, and issues surrounding it would dominate the rest of my time at COGA. In oil and gas lexicon, a play is an area where oil and gas exists and can be developed. From the pure perspective of an oil and gas geologist, the emergence of a new play is one of the most exciting things that you can participate in. An area that was once just a place now has unknown, untapped potential: a play!

It seemed a very sudden transition for me indeed. Instead of presiding over an industry largely producing the then-popular natural gas, now my job was more about a massive growth in Colorado oil production in growing urban and suburban areas.

There were numerous interesting dynamics.

First, natural gas prices were undergoing a dramatic collapse. Between July 2008 and September 2009, the price of natural gas dropped from over $13.50 per million British thermal unit (MMBtu) to $2.50. That's a drop of more than 80 percent! Two factors contributed to this price collapse. The first was reduced demand from the recession that began in the autumn of 2008. But the enduring factor, that has kept the price of natural gas under $2.00 to this writing in 2016, was the overwhelming supply. This once-scarce resource became so available, so cost-effective to produce, that as a country we were able to produce it so abundantly that the supply completely outpaced demand.

It was unthinkable that the same phenomenon that created an abundance of natural gas in 2010 would affect oil prices as dramatically five years later.

By then I would be gone.

In July of 2008, a year before I took the COGA job, the U.S. had about 1,800 drilling rigs, about 80 percent of which were drilling for natural gas. By September 2009, there were only about 1,000 rigs and around 70 percent were drilling for natural gas. The same pattern was happening in Colorado, only more dramatically because of our relative abundance of natural gas. Over the same two years, rigs drilling for natural gas would decline and the number drilling for oil would grow. This continued until January of 2014 when for the first time in contemporary memory, the 33 rigs drilling for oil in Colorado surpassed the 28 drilling for natural gas.

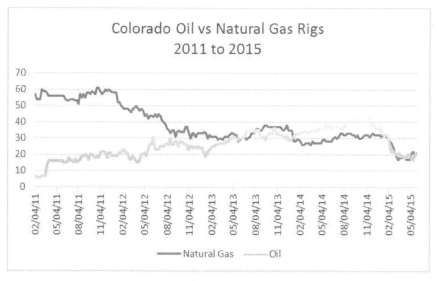

Figure 16-1: Colorado Oil and Gas Rigs (2011-2015)[19]

Back to school

I had come to COGA to help natural gas gain prominence as a solution for climate change. Now I was leading an organization representing oil production. The issue weighing heavily on my mind was:

> Did I still have a part to play in the solution,
> or was I part of the problem?

And so began the extended exploration of the three-question test.

Question 1: What's best for the most people concerned?

I had to begin with the basics, which I'm embarrassed to say, I didn't have a clue about when I first sat in my new corner office. What are petroleum products, where are they used, how are they used, and what suitable replacements exist?

Which brings us to Petroleum 101.

When a well is drilled for oil and gas, it produces a variety of products. Some underground formations consist mostly of oil, some produce dry gas, and every variation in between is possible. To simplify for the purposes of Petroleum 101, there are three main products produced during oil and gas drilling:

- ✧ Natural gas
- ✧ Oil
- ✧ Hydrocarbon vapors

Natural gas is mostly methane; it is what makes the blue flame on a gas stove. Oil refers to crude oil and makes the fuels you are familiar with, like gasoline and diesel. Hydrocarbon vapors are gases that are heavier than methane; these contain everything from condensate to propane. Condensate is a natural gas liquid (or NGL) composed of heavier hydrocarbon chains, which can be refined into oil, and various other products including propane.

Virtually all oil wells will produce some amount of natural gas and hydrocarbon vapors. Natural gas wells may be completely dry or can produce some condensate as well. So you've produced yourself some oil, natural gas, and hydrocarbon vapors.

Now what?

Natural gas processing

From the well, these products are either piped to a processing facility or transported by truck or train.
Natural gas and the associated hydrocarbon vapors are sent to a natural gas processing plant, where:

- ✧ Condensate is separated out and sent to an oil refinery
- ✧ The natural gas is cleaned of any contaminants such as water and hydrogen sulfide (H_2S)
- ✧ Then, the natural gas is broken up, or fractionated, into separate streams:
  CH_4 – Methane
  C_2H_6 – Ethane
  C_3H_8 – Propane
  C_4H_{10} – Butane
  C_5H_{12} – Petane
- ✧ Anything heavier than pentane, referred to as C5+, is about as heavy as condensate and can be sent to a refinery for further processing.

<u>Oil refining</u>

The oil pumped out of the ground is referred to as crude oil and it contains aliphatic hydrocarbons, which just means the molecules are composed of nothing but hydrogen (H) and carbon (C). Just like with the natural gas products described above, the carbon atoms link together in chains of different lengths. Crude oil is sent to a refinery so it can be separated into various useful products, such as gasoline and diesel fuel. The crude oil that arrives at the refinery can be characterized as either sweet or sour, based on the sulfur content.

✧ Sweet crude has less than 0.5% sulfur; most of Colorado's oil is sweet.
✧ Sour crude has greater than 0.5% sulfur content; sour crude tends to be from the Gulf of Mexico, South America, and Canada

Refineries produce the products we use every day, and some that are used in more industrial processes. These include:

✧ Gasoline
✧ Diesel
✧ Kerosene (from which jet fuel is derived)
✧ Lubricating oil
✧ Liquefied Petroleum Gas (LPG), often referred to as propane
✧ Residuals:
      Petroleum coke
      Asphalt and tar
      Waxes

<u>Petroleum products</u>

So you've refined your oil and natural gas. What can you do with those products? Turns out nearly everything you're wearing, sitting on, or holding in your hands are made from petroleum product. In addition to the fuels produced, ethane is a feedstock for the production of plastics. Among other things, you get all of the products are listed in Table 16-1.

Table 16-1: A few products made from petroleum[20]

Auto	Bathroom	Clothing	Yard	Kitchen
Tires	Cologne	Rubber Boots	Paint	Sponge
Motor Oil	Shampoo	Umbrellas	Asphalt	Cooking utensils
Oil filters	Nail Polish	Yoga Pants	Shingles	Blender
Speakers	Aspirin	Sunglasses	Pesticides	Trash bags
Drive Belts	Hair conditioner	Polar Fleece	Vinyl Siding	Coffee maker
Door Handles	Toothpaste	Panty Hose	Pool Liners	Kid cups
Wipers	Lip Balm	Polyester	Glue	Dishwasher
Coolant	Mascara	Velcro	Tape	Non-stick pan
Anti-Freeze	Contacts	Fake Fur	Beach balls	Fridge shelves

In my quest to understand the role of oil, I figured out that I was surrounded by petroleum products, but in many ways that is the least of our interdependence on fossil fuels. The network by which we move people, goods, and services to school, to work, and, indeed, around the world is completely fueled by the products of oil, including gasoline, diesel, and jet fuel.

Think for a moment just about what you might buy on a monthly trip to Target. All those goods are transported to the store from around the world, then across the country to your neighborhood. All of these people and products are moving around the world to bring things to your community, and often directly to your door! These everyday items are transported overwhelmingly by fossil fuels (see Figures 16-2 and 16-3).

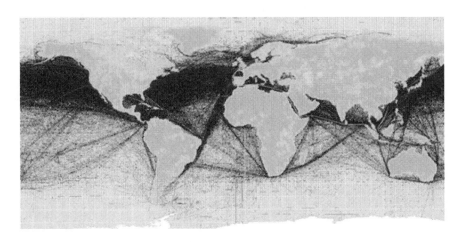

Figure 16-2. Shipping Lane Traffic

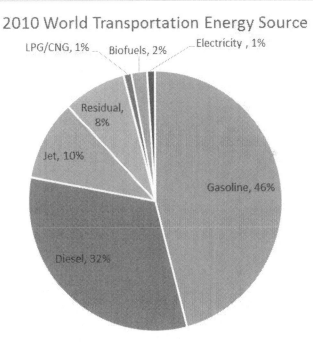

Figure 16-3. World Transportation by Energy Source[21]

It was both enlightening and embarrassing to realize how completely fundamental petroleum is to our lives, in every possible way. This made me wonder about the assumptions I had made about alternatives, from biofuels to bamboo clothing, being more desirable.

This is a query that has not ended.

So that took care of question 1: Is *this good for most people concerned?* Even if there exist better alternatives to petroleum products, there is a massive reality to be faced! Right now there is a huge, urgent demand for petroleum and the resulting products and services it provides. Without these products and the transportation network moving them around the world, our life would change dramatically.

With an eye to that "three-question test," and with a contented sigh, I recognized that I could comfortably continue to be the face of oil production in Colorado.

Question 2: What's best for Colorado?

At first this was an easy question. The economy of Colorado was barely beginning the climb out of the Great Recession that began in 2008. Many were crediting the oil and gas industry for Colorado's quicker-than-average recovery[22]. Unconventional production of natural gas was driving thriving economies in the Piceance Basin of western Colorado, the Raton Basin of southern Colorado, the San Juan basin in southwest Colorado, and the Denver-Julesburg (DJ) Basin in northeast Colorado. By 2012, oil and gas production was responsible for about 9 percent of the state's economy[23].

I'll give you some other numbers from 2012 that show the importance of oil and gas to Colorado's economy.

✧ $1.58 billion was paid to state and local governments as taxes[24].

✧ $9.35 billion generated for the Colorado General Fund in fiscal year?[25], which was 16.8%.

✧ 8.66% of all property taxes in Colorado came from the oil and gas industry[26].

✧ Colorado's oil and gas jobs were and are almost double the average Colorado wage[27], with about 40,000 jobs in the state.

As natural gas prices collapsed, and natural gas rigs stopped drilling, there were a few months where I wondered if I'd have any job to do at COGA. Suddenly, it seemed like a gift from God that drilling started picking up in nearly perfect response to the natural gas decline, this time for oil in the DJ basin. The unconventional drilling techniques that had become both famous and infamous for creating the massive natural gas supply were now being applied to oil, and in a few short years, a second technological revolution was underway.

There were plenty of early warnings that this new opportunity to produce oil domestically would be controversial. Ultimately, it would require many visits to the three questions. But for now, the answer was clear: oil development was important for Colorado.

Question 3: What's best for Colorado's oil and gas industry?

The purpose of this question was to ensure that my personal, philosophical perspective did not undermine the job I had to do. I might make peace with a task or political position, but that was irrelevant if it did not serve COGA's member companies. The three-question test ultimately was designed to challenge my thinking and make certain that I aligned my personal philosophy with my professional obligations.

Here Colorado's industry was making the shift from natural gas to oil, from economic recession to recovery, and now I had to ask myself if my representing the industry was best for the industry. Answer?

Indeed, yes. It was important to have someone like me put the best foot forward for the industry. I was empathetic to concerns, cared about environmental issues, and could communicate scientific material to lay audiences. I *was* the right woman for the task ahead.

No change is easy, and as the challenges of the next four years piled on, rifts began to develop between the philosophies of COGA's diverse members. Navigating these sides dominated my remaining four years. There were large philosophical questions, such as:

- ✧ Should the organization prioritize keeping small, family-owned businesses viable?
- ✧ Or, was the priority to conscientiously raise standards across the industry?
- ✧ As legislative and regulatory challenges piled on, should the industry fight, engage, or flee?

Philosophically, I resolved the inherent conflicts of the three-question test by landing on the idea that my job was to both bring out the best in the industry and to put the best foot forward on our collective behalf. This approach combined with the three-question test provided me guide rails for the next five years.

I was comfortable, but was Colorado?

I had made peace with the path ahead. The best place to start at this point was with how we, the industry, work with the public. I was appalled by the misinformation I heard about oil and gas development. To exacerbate the problem, most of the industry-created educational materials out there looked and sounded like oil and gas propaganda. This propaganda could easily be dismissed by both activists and a concerned public.

As drilling activity picked up, communities across Colorado became increasingly alarmed. I had to invoke the three-question test weekly, sometimes daily.

The outcome of consistent application of the three-question test was that I would organize COGA to focus on educating the public. We built the COGA team, we focused on creating honest, third-party sourced educational materials, and we committed to building rapport and dialogue between our organization and others.

Turns out, even that was a naïve path.

17

A Family Affair

All projects are easy when planning them in a conference room looking at maps. When you take that plan into the field, you are suddenly confronted with hills, roads, vegetation, houses, and other pesky three-dimensional objects like people who make the project much more challenging. I concluded that, in reality, oil and gas development was a lot more complicated outside of the walls of my COGA office as well. So each of my years at COGA, I toured Colorado's oil and gas basins.

Initially my objective was to see the places I knew from my oil and gas research. There are a lot of places in Colorado with funny names like "The Piceance," pronounced "pee-onts," and I wanted to *know* each place, not just how to pronounce it correctly. I wanted to know more than just the companies and the controversies written about in the papers. I wanted to see for myself the landscape, topography, types of wells—and get the feel for the community. I intuited that each community was different, and understanding this—firsthand— would help me in my work.

Getting to know and understand each community was very worthwhile. I quickly came to understand that any time the "headquarters" of anything is in Denver, you're going to experience an understandable rural resentment. And so, my second objective became simply to learn, listen, and understand. I had to overcome my Denver view of the world to see the world from the eyes of these communities. I strove to build relationships through those visits that would allow me and COGA to better represent the rural parts of Colorado, even though I was "headquartered" in Denver.

While a lot of these communities had some group of people that opposed oil and gas development, the vast majority of my time was spent coming to understand how much oil and gas made up the lifeblood of rural Colorado. Most people I met had a multi-generational relationship to both Colorado and with oil and gas. In some cases, it was because oil and gas wells were on their family's ranch, in others because half a dozen people in their extended family worked in the industry.

It was easy for me to understand why they resented and mistrusted me, an environmentalist from Denver, making an annual trip to represent the industry. What could be more annoying?

I got it.

Those trips were never comfortable or easy. They were always fraught with that "otherness" that my white collar, environmental Denver-ness came with. But they were the best part of my job nonetheless.

On most trips I brought the whole family.

It was a huge learning experience and a broadening of horizons for us all. The kids grew up over the course of five years of these road trips. When we first started, they were 3 and 7, and by the last one they were 8 and 12. We went from coloring books and potty stops every two hours to iPads with headphones and one stop for gas and donuts. I think we've seen every small town coal-history museum that Colorado has to offer, and I am pretty certain we have traveled every single two-lane highway. We have absolutely been to every fish hatchery (thank you, Brian) and probably to every hot springs.

Even the nudey ones.

We took our role as the family-face of oil and gas seriously. Our operators and communities always welcomed us warmly and made sure to shake both kids' hands and comment on how much they had grown. The boys sat through presentations and meetings, and played cards on the floor at countless potlucks. We learned *a lot* about Colorado.

Before we started touring the state, we knew our slice of mountain rural, had a good handle on Boulder, and spent enough time in Denver to *get* Colorado's big city. What our travels exposed us to were the historic, the quirky, and the truly rural. When the kids were small, we had to stop so frequently, we would make an adventure out of each stop. Most small town diners are sleepy, and diners would stare as we came in and took our seats. Waitresses were brusque and friendly, and served soda in huge plastic glasses with fine ice you almost never see anymore.

The mining history around Colorado is intense! We came to have a deeper understanding of how mining created life-transforming opportunities for individuals whose names now identify streets and towns all over the state. Some of what we learned was brutal, talking about the hardships and dangers, and even wars between management and labor.

One time we spent a night in Colorado's only drive-in movie motel, which you watched out your window and had a speaker in your room. We drove two-lane highways through breathtaking mountain passes, like the one between Durango and Ouray. How had I never known this part of the state was so magical? We found hippie, muraled coffee shops where you'd least expect them, and kindness when the kids ran annoying laps around other diners at roadside hamburger stands.

David Ludlam, executive director of the West Slope COGA in Grand Junction, an affiliate chapter of the Denver COGA, taught me about the phenomenon of "up valley" and "down valley" communities. The up valley exclusive ski resorts and playgrounds of the rich can be anti-oil and gas in spite of their huge energy consumption footprint. They fly private jets (not powered by bio-fuels, I have come to understand), keep extra SUVs at extra 10,000-square foot houses. Meanwhile, the working communities down valley provide the work force, and incidentally, the oil and gas and other natural resources that keep those homes warm and well lit.

> I saw this up-valley and down-valley
> idea play out all over the state.

During my trips, I came to an understanding of Colorado that is vastly different from the one I started with. Although the voting population resides on the Front Range and can often be forgetful about the rest of the state, I feel more comfortable in the other areas.

18

The Hickenlooper Bus

The 2010 October Board meeting was being held in a different venue this time. The long table was set up with awkward pillars that partially blocked my view. Board members could sit back, and I couldn't see everyone. If they were talking to their neighbor, rolling their eyes, or taking a snooze, I had no idea. Not ideal.

I'm not generally one to sit at the head of a table, but I was still experimenting with how to best project power, so that day I took the seat at the head. I knew it was important where I sat, and the room setup was so strange that I figured I should take the traditional power seat. There are two heads to every table, and, in this case, I took the one opposite of the entry doors, so I could see who was coming and going without having to awkwardly turn my head. This meeting was going to be a doozy, and I needed all the help I could get.

Lots had to happen at this Board meeting, not the least of which was for me to regain some semblance of dignity or respect after the latest brouhaha. In many ways, it felt like my last chance. It was, however, my eighth Board meeting and it was 9 am on the dot.

I was comfortable calling the meeting to order.

At about 8:00 that morning, one of my Board members had called my cell phone to tell me that half a dozen Board members were planning to ambush me at the meeting. There had been rumors making their way around conservative and oil and gas circles, those bands of brothers who kept each other informed of political developments. In these rumors, I was riding on Democratic gubernatorial candidate, John Hickenlooper's campaign bus while it toured southern Colorado. I had heard these rumors the previous week, but dismissed them outright, because, well, I hadn't been riding on the campaign bus. Nor had I been in southern Colorado. It was a completely baseless rumor, and I hadn't given it a second thought.

Somehow this rumor had developed a head of steam, and I was informed that my Board members were furious, and wanted a full accounting and reckoning of why I had been on that bus, what I was doing conspiring with a Democratic candidate for Governor, and what I planned to do to regain their trust. The warning call came as I was completing final preparations for the meeting, so I didn't have time to consult my staff or any trusted advisors to develop a plan.

Instead, I developed one in my head.

I opened the meeting, went through the normal round of introductions, and completed regular business. I was always on high alert during these stressful meetings. We had a packed house, with at least 30 Board members at the table and another dozen staff and contractors at the seats surrounding the room. Under the best of circumstances, a Board meeting felt high stakes and high pressure, but the tension in this room could be cut with a knife.

I figured I could not wait any longer.

"Before we go on to the next order of business…" I said, leaning forward with a stern but I hoped, confident expression on my face. "it has come to my attention that several of the members of this Board believe that I have been participating in the campaign of Mayor Hickenlooper, including riding on a campaign bus and advising his campaign. It has also come to my attention that you are upset about this and would like to have a reckoning at this meeting."

Suddenly, heads popped out from behind pillars, leaning onto crossed arms on the table, with wide eyes. I had everyone's attention. It was clear that they had meant to surprise me, but instead, I had surprised them. I paused to give everyone a chance to process what was happening.

And to catch my breath.

From the looks around the table, at least half the room had been in on the ambush. I have young boys, I know that look.

"First of all, I have done no such thing. I will be happy to give you an accounting of my whereabouts, but I shouldn't have to. Second of all, if members of this Board have any question about my professional responsibilities or actions, I suggest that you *ask me*. It would save a lot of the time and energy of this Board if, instead of talking amongst yourselves, you simply *asked me* about my engagement in the campaign or anything else you are curious about." Deep breath. Pause. Stern eye contact around the table.

"Any questions?"

The opened-mouthed stares looking back at me were a mix of chagrin, confusion, and respect. The question hung in the air for a good thirty seconds. Heads retreated back behind pillars. "Okay then. Moving on to the next order of business."

My heart was racing, my palms were sweating, and I did not allow myself so much as a micro-smile. I soldiered on through the rest of that two-hour meeting without a backward glance. As the meeting wrapped up, everyone, including myself, acted perfectly normal. I neatly stacked my papers, put them in my briefcase, and nodded good-byes to the meeting participants.

The Association's lobbyist, Jim Cole, who had worked for COGA for more than 20 years, looked at me sternly. I knew I should have run the situation, the conflict, and my response by him, but there had been no time. He had been initially skeptical of my hire, but jumped into the job of preparing me for situations such as this with wisdom and a passion I was lucky to be the recipient of. I looked down, sheepish, with no good excuse to offer him. He leaned forward and said softly in my ear, "You have balls the size of cantaloupes."

That, my friends, was a good day.

19

A Purple Jog Bra

Both times that I'd had a meeting with Roxane White, the Governor's Chief of Staff, I'd forgotten something critical. The first time was my shoes. We were meeting on a freezing Saturday during their transition to the Governorship. I had had to be very brave to request this meeting, and Roxane had replied immediately in the affirmative. The oil and gas industry's relationship with the previous Governor had been strained, to say the least, and I wanted to start this one off on the right foot.

Right foot, indeed.

It was hard enough to commute to Denver five days a week, but making the hour-long drive on a Saturday to the Capitol was brutal. I made the best of it by going to a swim workout on the way downtown from the hills. I'd brought my dress clothes, changed after my workout, and made my way to Denver. I parked on the street outside of the Wells Fargo building, and went to grab my heels. Shit! I tore the car inside out, about to be late, and realized I'd left the little grocery bag with my shoes at home. Sorel's were going to have to do.

Knowing Roxane as I now do, I could have attended this meeting in jeans and tennies, as long as I was prepared and had something interesting and relevant to say (and as long as it didn't take more than 15 minutes to say it). But at this moment, heading into Denver's second tallest building in my dress, tights, and winter boots, I felt my life was about to end.

With good form, I never mentioned my shoes, and if Roxane noticed, she never said anything. And so it was with ironic glee that one month later I watched Governor Hickenlooper get sworn in on a frigid January day *wearing Sorels*. That day I was freezing in dress boots.

This was no normal Administration.

That day in my boots, Roxane and I'd had an excellent, brief meeting. We immediately recognized in each other efficient, effective managers who don't need to waste time with pleasantries. Mission accomplished. We'd agreed to quarterly meetings to check in and keep the communication channels open.

The second time I forgot my bra and underwear.

By reputation and in reality, Roxane is an ass-kicker. You never go to a meeting unprepared, and anyone with half a brain, which I have, essentially prepares for the meeting as if you report to her. You know what you want to say, and if you have an ask, you'd better get to it. For our second quarterly meeting, I was wearing a stylish brown, sleeveless dress. I ran through my list. She asked thoughtful, appropriate questions, made no promises, and we concluded. As I got up to leave, Rox said, "I just want you to know, you look really beautiful and put together today."

I laughed, and on a whim, put my thumb under my purple jog bra, pulled it out, snapped it to my shoulder and said, "That's because you can't see the sweaty jog bra and underwear that I did a spin class in this morning." We both laughed and I told her the story. My house is

40 minutes from the gym, so when I forget something, I have to run to Target. This meeting with Rox did not allow time for a Target run. "Thank goodness it isn't Tuesday when I swim, or I'd be sitting here commando right now."

We had a good laugh and Rox told me about the previous week when she'd had to safety pin a blazer over her bra because she'd forgotten a shirt after biking to work.

And a friendship was born.

One of the greatest personal challenges of jobs like those Roxane and I had is that you have no idea what relationships are real and enduring, and which are born of necessity and mutual convenience. In truth, there is no way to know while you are in the job. Rox and I needed to have a high functioning, trust-based relationship to successfully accomplish our jobs, but there was no way of knowing if this translated into real friendship. We never discussed it; we didn't have to. We both knew we couldn't prioritize our personal needs over the roles we played and the people we served…in her case, the entire state of Colorado.

While at COGA, there were a half a dozen people who I came to know and love, including Rox. I strove always to maintain internal clarity about how I felt as a person, and the boundaries I had to maintain as part of my job. I also had to know that these "friendships" might not last after the job. For someone like me, who prizes loyalty above almost anything else, it's a very difficult situation to be in.

Over the next five years of working in our respective roles, Rox and I regularly found some solace in each other's company. We were both targets of violent threats; we were both mothers. We were both ass-kickers who intimidated and alienated a good many people who couldn't handle us.

The greatest gift that came out of this relationship is that eventually we both left our roles, and I told Brian it would be interesting to see if there was any there there. Could we be friends without needing something from each other, without the weight of our roles propelling us toward the other? Thankfully, the answer is yes.

> And we now have a friendship unburdened by
> our job descriptions.

Only a handful of relationships endured after I left COGA, and Rox is one of the most important.

20

Inherently Evil?

What I'd thought was my open-minded view of energy got decimated once I'd been at COGA a while. I realized that I had as many incorrect notions about energy as the people I was tasked with "educating." I had to deconstruct my political views from my understanding of energy and build it all back up from scratch.

From the beginning, we'd grown our staff quickly as I transitioned money out of consulting budgets and into a salary bucket. The committees all needed to become formalized, and well run, with good leadership and efficient decision-making processes. There was the daily grind of state rulemakings, legislative hearings, and media requests. And then there was always a crisis, such as a company running into an urgent regulatory hurdle, or a negative hit in the media.

There was never really time to catch my breath, so I was inevitably trying to get a handle on the underlying energy-environmental questions on the fly, while engaged in a rulemaking, or a hostile newspaper interview.

First, I had to face my own demons.

It took me a long time to understand that I had been anthropo-morphizing energy, giving different fuels personas and good or evil intentions. When I had first seen that huge wind farm, part of the shock was realizing that the wind mills didn't look benign, they looked like recently landed alien robots! Among my pre-COGA circle of friends, it had been easy and acceptable to start from the premise that "fossil fuels are bad." My worldview, social group, and inherent sensibilities made this a statement that I could make without much introspection.

It has taken time to come to terms with the simple fact that fossil fuels are just carbon atoms organized into rocks, liquids, and gases. They don't have personalities, intentions, or even actions. I now recognize that it is what we do with fossil fuels that matters. Daily, I encountered the real conflicts, big and small, that come with producing, *or not producing,* energy.

What is particularly painful for me to admit is that I now understand that my over-simplified, silly worldview had consequences. Creating an unintended caricature of energy sources, where some are angelic and some are devilish (well, not literally), polarizes important energy policy discussions and blinds us to the reality of energy tradeoffs. I didn't understand this until, as COGA head, I began to see the prejudices and preconceived notions that *others* were bringing to these conversations.

I saw that an over-simplistic approach leads us to make energy decisions that can and sometimes do hurt the environment, the nearby community, and its people. Our prejudices can blind us to the real energy tradeoffs that we must discuss and work through, in good faith.

Now I strive to cultivate an agnostic approach to energy.

Additionally, when people say "all of the above," it often sounds like a generic cliché of someone who can't make up his mind. Now I think of "all of the above" differently. All the sources of energy are tools in the toolbox: hydrogen, nuclear, natural gas, bio fuels, oil, coal, wood, dung. We have the opportunity to consider the tradeoffs of each.

Take for example, oil. Oil is not inherently evil. It's not inherently anything.

It is liquid and energy dense.

It is perhaps understandable that we can imagine wind and solar as coming to us from the heavens. I love sunshine on my face and a cool breeze in my hair! This perspective can be summed up in a popular Boulder bumper sticker: *A solar spill is just another beautiful day.* Well, tell that to the neighbors of a Chinese solar plant's hydrofluoric acid spill into the Mujiaqiao River in 2011, which killed hundreds of fish and resulted in the death of farmers' pigs.[28]

Every source of energy requires mining of the materials, manufacturing of its parts, construction of its infrastructure, and ongoing maintenance. The source of fuel is just one component of an energy's lifecycle environmental footprint.

Thinking agnostically is not easy; it requires acknowledging the tradeoffs inherent in all of our energy consumption. Is wind holy if you are a decapitated bat or bird? Is oil evil if you are driving your first car to your first job? I would argue that nuclear energy is holy if reducing greenhouse gas emissions is your bible. Hydro is counted as renewable; but it is only angelic as long as you are the fish on the right side of the dam.

I landed on an agnostic approach to energy because it drops the useless judgment of energy sources and instead considers how those energy sources are engineered, implemented, and used. As a result of my soul-searching to determine what really matters when considering the tradeoffs inherent in the life-cycle of all energy sources, here is what I landed on.

Efficiency: Dense energy sources are important because we use so much energy and should make good choices. Dense energy requires less space and provides more power. Efficient use will make our energy go farther. Energy density was covered in Chapter 6.

Thoughtful Development: Life cycle development from the mine to the consumer must continue to improve. There is no form of energy, when considered in its entirety, that is perfect. Life cycle development that accounts for stakeholders' priorities such as water protection, air emissions, and interface with communities is critical. Thoughtful development of energy is discussed in Chapter 32.

Access: We know that access to energy can dramatically improve quality of life. Access to diverse forms of energy that incorporates transportability, energy security, and availability is critical to societies. The importance of energy access is in the next chapter, Chapter 21.

Affordability: Energy policy must be cognizant of energy cost, especially as it relates to our most vulnerable citizens. This is covered later in this chapter.

Energy Tradeoffs

Which brings us to the second part of the question of driving to alternatives... will it actually help? It turns out that both beauty and environmental improvement may be in the eye of the beholder. There are lots of ways to measure environmental impacts—and carbon emissions is just one of hundreds.

To get a fuller picture, the subject is worth revisiting. Instead of anthropomorphizing, here is what I came up with. There are many considerations when looking at fuels. Every new solar field requires a footprint and infrastructure. Every electrical transmission line that connects a new solar field to the grid requires a right of way, through public lands or somebody's private property. Every new source of energy entails mining for the materials, construction activities, and ongoing maintenance to install it and keep it working.

Every form of energy requires tradeoffs.

Energy Transitions

These tradeoffs are even starker when you are talking about replacing massive amounts of existing infrastructure with new infrastructure. If, for example, you decommission a natural gas turbine and build a new solar field to replace it, the change in fuel (natural gas to sun) may be the least relevant environmental component in this project. It's much healthier to look at the lifecycle needs, costs, and benefits of various fuel sources in their actual context.

Energy transitions will happen, and frankly there will be winners and losers along the way. Although this kind of market change is inevitable, it represents another real factor in the consideration of energy choices and environmental projects—and was something I thought about daily. In Colorado, the 2010 bill creating the transition from coal to natural gas-fired electricity generation was considered both an environmental coup and a win for the natural gas industry. But it devastated entire regions of Colorado, with very real impacts to the people, schools, and communities that depended upon both coal mining and coal-fired power plants.

Tradeoffs, sigh.

I thought about these touchy and difficult people issues with a similar approach to the one I used to manage personnel. I strove to be honest with myself, taking stock of the real impacts and how they would affect not only the individual, but their family, even their community. I put myself in their shoes and imagined what it felt like, and crafted real empathy for their circumstances. I always want to really see people, and understand their worldview. And then I would take my perspective to 30,000 feet, distance myself from my desire to prevent difficult consequences, and ask myself, *what's the best overall outcome?* To care about people broadly, you often have to make decisions that negatively affect smaller groups of people. I am willing to live with that tradeoff, I just don't want to lie to myself and pretend that someone isn't suffering. They are.

Simply put, you upset the apple cart when you take one type of energy and convert it to another. The result is a community that has lost jobs and is left with infrastructure that needs to be decommissioned. In the developing world, these transitions have ramifications even when the benefits are overwhelmingly positive. For example, LPG cook stoves reduce indoor air pollution and dramatically improve families' health outcomes, but the entire network of people who sell charcoal gets upended.

The ripples matter and must be considered.

These kinds of transitions happen all over this country every day in evolving economies: manufacturing, technology, and even urban renewal. Transitions are possible and do happen, but aren't simple, and are always messy. And it's important to understand that there is a cost. The cost includes the entire infrastructure that must be mined, constructed, transported, installed, and maintained. The cost includes whoever has lost their job, or whatever company must decommission their now useless infrastructure. And all of this takes a toll on the environment in mining, use of resources, emissions, waste, and physical space.

Importing Energy

I looked into the idea of zero-carbon emission economies, and those moving in that direction. California and some EU countries were leading the way toward a decarbonized energy future. It wasn't long into my investigation that I realized that these solutions are often oversimplified in their description. A community that imports energy does not have a zero footprint or zero emissions; they are simply outsourcing their environmental footprint.

Importing energy requires other tradeoffs as well.

Importing energy or transmitting it is costly, resource intensive, and energy inefficient. It can be a great win-win solution, such as California importing 33 percent of its electricity from other states.[29] In 2013, the European Union imported more than half of its primary energy from non-member countries, and no EU member state was a net exporter of energy.[30] So it can work, but those tradeoffs are still in play. The environmental footprint sits elsewhere, the transportation of energy is inefficient, and the total process can be very expensive.

Contemplating tradeoffs was a daily event at COGA.

These questions quickly got complicated, so it was important for me to start at some simple ideas. Day after day, in my office and on the way to work and home again, I thought about energy and best solutions. Like the pieces in a big puzzle, I looked at how electricity is generated in the U.S.: the diverse sources all have their own tradeoffs. Figure 20-1 graphically illustrates this mix and the relative capacity of the various sources, which is a good way to begin to understand the complexity of just one component of the energy mix. From this figure, it is clear that energy challenges are immensely greater in areas of dense population because the demands are higher, but the available land for energy production, storage, and transmission is much smaller.

Plant capacity by power source in megawatts

Figure 20-1: Electricity Power Sources across the U.S.[31]

As I contemplated the amount of land taken up by various sources of electricity production, I really began to understand the tradeoffs of fuel, and to see power density as the cornerstone of that consideration. In the abstract, the idea of transitioning existing power sources to fossil-free fuel sources sounded fabulous (and easy!).

One has to do the math to honestly assess energy tradeoffs.

One study looked at what infrastructure would be required to transition one-third of energy demand in the United Kingdom (UK) off of fossil fuels to low-carbon electricity.[32] The study found that it would, indeed, be theoretically possible with either wind or nuclear. To provide adequate nuclear resources, 40 gigawatts would be required with a land area of 290 square kilometers (112 square miles); this is one-tenth of 1 per cent of the UK's land area. Wind would require either 130 GW offshore or 150 GW onshore (because of wind's intermittency) requiring approximately 16,000 square kilometers (6,200 square miles) or 6.5 percent of UK land area. These land areas are compared to the size of New York City in Figure 20-2. Imagining the political and public relations hurdles of implementing either of these new, clean energy options is enough to give one pause.

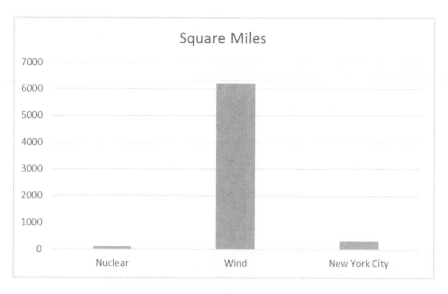

Figure 20-2. Comparative Land Required Nuclear vs Wind, with New York City for Reference[33]

Food, Heat, or Medicine?

The demands of a dense urban population, the resources available, and the land footprint accessible are only the beginning of the considerations for providing energy. How about the cost of energy? Indeed, even in the United States, one of the richest countries in the world, we have to think about the cost.

I was shocked to learn that, even in prosperous Colorado, 15 percent of the population lives in poverty.[34] For those who live with income below the poverty line, they spend between 10 and 50 percent of their monthly income on energy.[35] So these families have to regularly choose between the cost of keeping the house warm or putting food on the table, commuting to work or buying needed medicines.

> The cost matters—particularly to the most economically vulnerable among us.

Price Sensitive

Even though the cost of energy disproportionately affects the poor, probably everyone you know is very sensitive to changes in energy prices. How much does a gallon of gasoline cost? How much to you pay for your winter electricity bill (or summer bill if you live in Arizona or California)? We all know these things, more or less, even if they aren't the source of deep stress or daily tradeoffs.

We take our energy for granted and we want it free of charge, or at least as close to free as possible. This could be a tenable position in the U.S. in this age of massive, domestic energy abundance. Except it is not because we also want our energy to meet all sorts of other priorities, such as being free of carbon. In the assessment of energy tradeoffs, price is a very important consideration.

Let's look at costs of electricity generation. There are lots of different ways that you can generate electricity, and many of these are listed on the left-hand side of Table 20-1. The capacity factor is the percent of the time you can expect it to run. The next four columns are the different costs that go into building and running power plants, resulting in total costs. This table allows you to compare different types of power and the costs associated with them.

Table 20-1. Comparable Costs for New Electricity Generation[36]

Table 1. Estimated levelized cost of electricity (LCOE) for new generation resources, 2020

U.S. average levelized costs (2013 $/MWh) for plants entering service in 2020[1]

Plant type	Capacity factor (%)	Levelized capital cost	Fixed O&M	Variable O&M (including fuel)	Transmission investment	Total system LCOE	Subsidy[2]	Total LCOE including Subsidy
Dispatchable Technologies								
Conventional Coal	85	60.4	4.2	29.4	1.2	95.1		
Advanced Coal	85	76.9	6.9	30.7	1.2	115.7		
Advanced Coal with CCS	85	97.3	9.8	36.1	1.2	144.4		
Natural Gas-fired								
Conventional Combined Cycle	87	14.4	1.7	57.8	1.2	75.2		
Advanced Combined Cycle	87	15.9	2.0	53.6	1.2	72.6		
Advanced CC with CCS	87	30.1	4.2	64.7	1.2	100.2		
Conventional Combustion Turbine	30	40.7	2.8	94.6	3.5	141.5		
Advanced Combustion Turbine	30	27.8	2.7	79.6	3.5	113.5		
Advanced Nuclear	90	70.1	11.8	12.2	1.1	95.2		
Geothermal	92	34.1	12.3	0.0	1.4	47.8	-3.4	44.4
Biomass	83	47.1	14.5	37.6	1.2	100.5		
Non-Dispatchable Technologies								
Wind	36	57.7	12.8	0.0	3.1	73.6		
Wind – Offshore	38	168.6	22.5	0.0	5.8	196.9		
Solar PV[3]	25	109.8	11.4	0.0	4.1	125.3	-11.0	114.3
Solar Thermal	20	191.6	42.1	0.0	6.0	239.7	-19.2	220.6
Hydroelectric[4]	54	70.7	3.9	7.0	2.0	83.5		

Energy Travels

Finally, when considering tradeoffs, getting your energy where it needs to go is no small task. We move electricity in the form of power lines. A massive pipeline infrastructure allows each of us to refuel our personal cars. We also move every form of goods and nearly every kind of service in trucks, trains, cargo ships and airplanes powered by petroleum fuels. How we move both energy and goods around matters.

Getting electricity from the raw fuel to my house is infamously in-efficient.[37] In Colorado, my electricity is generated from a combination of coal, natural gas, and wind. Even if someone could produce enough solar power in Arizona to power all of Colorado, they would have to get that power to the people that need it in population centers hundreds of miles away. On average, just the transmission and distribution of electricity on power lines causes about a six percent loss of energy.[38] There's more on transportation tradeoffs in Appendix B.

In Praise of Atoms

I don't always do the math myself. But now I do bring a more thoughtful, even skeptical mind to questions of energy and the environment. I can dismiss over-simplifications quickly, and seek to understand what are the key questions.

I look for where the real tradeoffs lie.

Energy comes from fuels and that fuel is simply made up of atoms. Fuels, the way they are converted to power, and how we use that power, is all in the hands of humans. Bringing a thoughtful detachment to our analysis of energy, without aggressors, saviors, or victims, allows us to understand the various tradeoffs that all forms of energy have.

In the end, with my COGA hat on, I decided I'd consider energy—and the way we use it—as tools in the toolbox. This would allow me to bring my passion, my emotions, and my engagement to the questions of how we can make the best choices. We need energy. If as a society we could acknowledge the tradeoffs inherent in all forms of energy production, we could have productive conversations about energy development.

21

The Belly of the Beast

Throughout much of my adult life, I have strived to make environmental living a top priority. I bought our log cabin in the mountains, maintained my vegetarianism through all that field work in Texas, carted reusable coffee cups and water bottles when traveling around the world, and paid the premium required for organic everything.

I don't know that addressing climate change was ever my top environmental concern. In 2010, there were still abundant priorities shared by environmentalists: clean air, water quality, wildlife, riparian corridors, protecting special natural places.

At the helm of COGA, I kept all this up. I subscribed to the downtown Denver shared bicycle program, making a point of showing up to my meetings in sweaty disarray with my pink helmet. I continued to pay annual dues to environmental organizations. I became the sole vegetarian at many an industry conference. Not that any of that is tied to true environmental values, but it was important to me to maintain my connection to my environmental self.

One day, Carter came home from sixth grade with a series of assignments focused on the hero's journey.

"What's that?" I queried, anticipating an eye roll.

With my obsession for math and science in my own education, I'd somehow missed the whole concept of *The Hero's Journey*. Carter didn't roll his eyes. Instead, he excitedly sat down on the couch, his elbows on his long legs and bony knees. Leaning toward me, he said, "Mom, it's so cool! Basically, every story you have ever read or any adventure movie you watch is based on the hero's journey. The main character has to have a crisis, leave home, have some adventures, have some more crises, learn some stuff, and then come home."

Because I'm *that Mom*, I did a little Internet research to verify that this universal story line actually existed and justified a mid-week movie.

He pretty much got it right.

If you have a better memory than I do, you might remember *The Odyssey*, the classic hero's tale. Personally, I'm more inclined to reflect upon *The Lord of the Rings*, and my son on *Star Wars*. Joseph Campbell made the observation that nearly all classical myths followed a similar pattern, with some variations.

It was so encouraging to become acquainted with the Hero's Journey just as I was trying to make sense of my own journey in COGA, as an environmentalist, and as a person.

The hero's journey is generally described in 12 stages.

1. Ordinary World: This is the hero's normal life before the adventure begins.
2. Call to Adventure: A challenge or problem causes the hero to begin the adventure.
3. Refusal of the Call: The hero would like to avoid the journey.
4. Meeting with the Mentor: The hero encounters an advisor who helps with the adventure.

5. Crossing the First Threshold: The hero leaves the ordinary world for adventure.
6. Tests, Allies, Enemies: The hero must endure tests of will, meet friends, and face foes.
7. Approach: Setbacks occur, causing the hero to try new approaches and ideas.
8. Ordeal: The major hurdle or obstacle, such as a life or death crisis, is faced.
9. Reward: The hero accomplishes his or her goal.
10. The Road Back: The return back to ordinary life begins.
11. Resurrection: The hero must face a final test using all that has been learned.
12. Return with Elixir: The hero brings the knowledge gained back to the ordinary world.

If all felt...familiar.

One of my personal fundamental operating principles, which I have relied on for most of my adult life, is that *everyone is doing the best they can given what they know.* And I'm also pretty sure that nearly everyone, even the delusional, imagine that they are *Doing Good.* They are doing good in the world, or at least doing the best they can. By assuming everyone is doing the best they can, and acknowledging that they believe they are doing good, I could continue to navigate this path through oil and gas and environmentalism.

There was just one problem: Who's the bad guy?

We currently live in a world, and I live in a country, where you are expected to take a side on issues of importance. In energy-and-environmental issues, it is far too easy to lay out the sides, each described in hostile terms by the opposition. We see this with a lot of social problems where dogma, polarity, and gridlock have shut down progress toward shared goals.

So a key principle of *my* hero's journey was deciding that *there are no bad guys*. But that doesn't make everyone a hero. The hero's journey follows the predictable path from call to crisis, adventure and a return home. So far, my journey had taken me to the belly of the beast serving as the face of Colorado's oil and gas industry.

My return home had yet to happen.

Within a couple of years into my tenure at COGA, climate change had begun to dominate and consume all other environmental-related conversations. I had come to the conclusion that the topic was too hot, too divisive to use to seek common ground between industry and environmentalists, Republicans and Democrats. I had to find other ways to think and talk about energy and the environment that were accurate, but also emotionally engaging. I consciously began to explore different angles on both energy and the environment, to both push my own understanding and seek common ground with others.

I sought out broader sources of understanding and motivation.

We live on a planet of 7 billion people. Every day that someone turns the pages of this book that number rises by more than 220,000 people per day.[39] Among these 7 billion live more than 1.2 billion who do not have access to electricity.[40] More than double that number (2.7 billion) do not have clean cooking facilities[41] These numbers are almost unimaginable, with the population of New York City (8.4 million) dwarfed by the worldwide populations without access to energy (Figure 21-1). This is staggering for a number of reasons. First, access to energy is the most basic building block of a decent quality of life. Consider your current situation with no light, heating, cooling, means of cooking or means of transportation.

You are suddenly sitting on a dirt floor, cold, in the dark. And hungry, too.

> My early married years of chopping wood
> were wildly privileged by comparison.

The United Nations has identified raising people out of energy poverty as the single most important action that will raise quality of life.[42] And in fact, the results are extraordinary. When provided with access to energy, birth rates decline, life expectancy increases, and all sorts of amazing benefits become manifest, like increasing income, education, and health.[43] Figure 23-2 provides just one metric, life expectancy, demonstrating the dramatic correlation between energy access and longer lives.

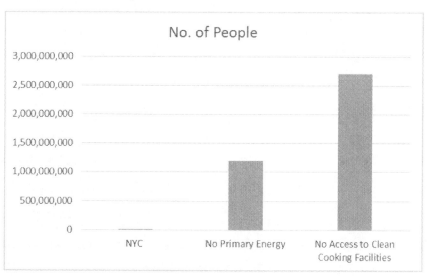

Figure 21-1. Population without Access to Energy

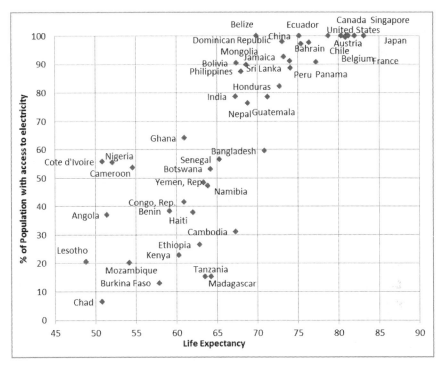

Figure 21-2. Energy Access Drives Life Expectancy[44]

Consider just this one statistic: 4.3 million lives could be saved annually simply by changing out dangerous coal or dung cook stoves for something cleaner-burning like natural gas.[45]

4 million lives saved annually, with one fuel change.

I was delighted during my writing of this chapter to hear an environmental organization executive say, *1.2 billion people need to gain access to energy, and we should not do anything that will get in their way.* I couldn't agree more. The global middle class is going to grow astronomically over the next couple of decades, and that means that people in developing countries will be gaining access to energy. In India alone, the middle class is projected to expand from 50 million

to 583 million by 2025[46]. And people with minimal access to energy
will consume more natural resources as they power their lives.

> And thank heavens, because energy access is the cornerstone of
> prosperity.

All of this means that demands for energy are going to grow, and
interestingly, nearly all of that growth is going to be in the developing
world.[47] Check out Figure 21-3 and the astonishing energy demand
that is projected in the developing world; these are shown as the
green, non-OECD (Organization for Economic Cooperation and
Development) components. This projection is all the more startling
when compared with the flat projections for the developed world
(shown in blue and labeled OECD).

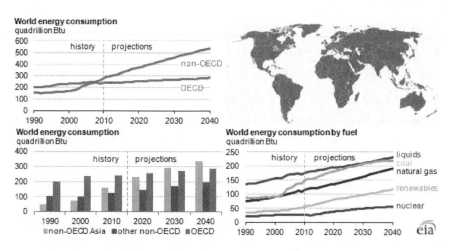

Figure 21-3. World Energy Consumption[48]

And while this projected energy demand is very dramatic on paper,
it's even more dramatic in the real world where the tremendous
migration of families to cities means that millions move from rural,
subsistence farming to densely packed urban neighborhoods. The
expansion of the middle class results in tens of thousands of energy

construction projects from coal-fired electricity generation to natural gas pipelines.

It is this demand for energy that resets my compass to a true north.

Although I have found the science of climate change very compelling, I find the opportunity to help lift over a billion people out of devastating poverty much more so. I will explore climate science and a changing climate later, but for now here's a thought. A changing climate is big and abstract, with significant unknown consequences. It looms heavily. Yet human suffering around the world is here now, and we have opportunities to help people better their lives and improve the lives of succeeding generations as well.

Let's get them access to energy.

I began committed to changing the world through a combination of personal persuasion and personal sacrifice. The place I have arrived in is in a different philosophical zip code entirely. Along the way, I have had to look closely at every preconceived notion I had about the characteristics of people, the stereotypes of cultures, the science of environmental issues, and the priorities that matter.

The facts about the planet, the climate, species, and humans are dense and subject to interpretation. Digging them up, they didn't always take me where I wanted to go. But they did allow me to approach these environmental issues optimistically and realistically, something I was so hungry for. At that point, I got excited about a path to a vibrant planet with a prosperous humanity.

I'm still excited.

22

Where's Your Army?

Those first 18 months at COGA had been eye opening, causing me to participate more actively in determining my future fate. I was quickly concluding that I could not succeed in this work without creating a network of support. Thus, I focused on recruiting my second Chairman of the Board to the position. Three people became crucial mentors to me over my five years and this is the story of one of them.

I met Scott Moore when I was seated next to him at my very first black-tie event. Brian and I had been so excited to attend. Our first of probably many black-tie events! The crowd was intimidating; the foyer and then later the ballroom were packed with beautifully dressed people. The decorations were blue and white, and reminded me, incongruously, of my junior high dances. We had been invited to sit at Scott's company's table by their COGA board member, who I adored.

Scott and I introduced ourselves interruptedly through an unmemorable program. I knew he was smart and tough, and I liked and respected him immediately. When the program was over, I tried to continue the conversation, but he said, "Go. You need to work this crowd."

So I did.

About six months after I met Scott, the current representative of his company decided to retire. At the time, COGA didn't have a clear succession process. The previous year, I had watched, open-mouthed, as my current chairman, who was not exactly openly hostile to me, was nominated and voted to receive a second one-year term before I had even had the opportunity to rearrange my face into a respectable grimace. I would not make that mistake again.

I had been planning to ask my now-retiring Board member to serve as Chairman. Yikes. The obvious replacement for the Board from his company, the regional operations vice president, was uninterested in sitting on the COGA Board. The company was a critical COGA member, and getting the right Board member was essential. I set my eyes on Scott. Not just for the Board, but to be the Chairman of the Board.

It was a real long shot.

We didn't have a succession planning process, but we did have a lot of Board members (remember, there were 40 of them) who would love to serve as Board chair. Recruiting Scott was my first challenge. He intuitively understood my situation and COGA's, but he wasn't comfortable with being fast-tracked into a leadership position for a Board to which he was a stranger. Then there was the fact that he was already incredibly busy with a full-time job that had him traveling constantly.

Yet, we had some great challenges before us, and I needed a really strong Board chair. I talked to some other Board leaders, and they agreed, Scott's leadership strengths spoke for themselves. We needed him.

In the end, he was easily nominated and elected to the Board. He attended one Board meeting before he was nominated and elected

Chairman. But, to complicate matters, Scott received a big promotion at his company during the election process. Fortunately, he didn't know about the impending promotion or I'm sure he never would have agreed to accept the COGA Board chairmanship. His new job became effective the same day he was elected Board chair. He was going to be busy, ridiculously busy by most people's standards, but he was up for it. Phew! Our working relationship over the next two years turned out to be one of the most significant of my life.

That said, it wasn't long before I regretted recruiting Scott.

I neglected to get to know Scott's working style before engaging him. How did I not notice how tough he was, how hard he worked, how thoroughly organized he always was?

I met with Scott at least monthly through his two-year tenure. I have never before or since prepared so thoroughly for any meeting. Scott was not only one of the smartest people I've ever had the pleasure and pain of working with, he prepared for every meeting mercilessly. He read everything I sent him, highlighted sections of interest, and came armed with questions. Tough questions ranging from 30,000-foot strategy to minutiae.

Frankly, I had been used to skating through meetings with bosses throughout my career, being habitually more prepared than my peers or managers. Now I had met my match. Scott was an intimidating force of nature in the form of the boss I had hand-selected for the toughest job I'd ever had.

In hindsight, I can articulate my gratitude for those two years because in every possible way Scott made me a better leader and a more sophisticated manager. Although I sighed in relief when he passed on the gavel, I have never before or since been so creatively and comprehensively engaged in any work. Having a rigorous, smart boss is a gift from the heavens. I aspire to be such a boss.

If Scott found me competent or even successful in my work, he never lessened his comprehensive analysis of what could be done better. I shouldn't make him sound so exacting. Scott also had the rare gift of giving limited but lavish praise to both me and my team when we deserved it. Because the praise was so hard earned, I remember those moments of recognition to this day.

How to give praise was not what I learned from this chairman.

"Look back, Tisha. Where is your army?" Scott asked one day. He had a habit of stacking his papers, and then fixing the corners with his pinkies. Leaving his head down, he would look up at me with a scowl. "Where is your army?" he would say. I would sigh, scrunch up my eyes, and take a deep breath. It would actually be years before I fully understood the import of this question, which Scott queried frequently.

An army of one, I was ceaselessly proposing some massive new program or another for COGA to pursue or suggesting an extremely detailed position regarding a regulation for the Board to adopt. The COGA Board's 40 members had wildly varying interests, dispositions, and positions on issues. The fact that I was consistently met with hostility from some quarter or other didn't dissuade my enthusiasm for cultivating radical culture change. I might spend months and dozens of meetings developing a position. I would then present it to the Board.

More often than not I'd be met with stunned silence.

Scott would sit with me in the boardroom after everyone left. He would stack his papers and look up at me with a furrowed brow. "You are leading the charge two hills ahead of your army. You need to know where they are. You need to know where your army is and bring them along."

At the time, I was more interested in my destination as a leader than the disposition of my army. In hindsight, I am shocked and grateful for Scott's patience because every one of my lavish propositions reflected upon him. To external observers, the COGA Board chairman was ultimately responsible for everything accomplished, or not accomplished, by the staff. Quotes in the paper, discussions in the Board meetings, and positions taken on draft regulation were all discussed publicly and privately, with dozens of divergent opinions. My previous Chairman was constantly fielding calls from upset Board members, and then calling me to tell me what they were upset about. It was about as productive as junior high student council.

Scott never conveyed such a call to me.

Scott was teaching me the iterative process of leading significant change. There is a difficult balance to navigate between providing the leadership your organization desires and providing the leadership that you believe is necessary. I would learn that a very skillful leader, which I wasn't yet, pushes the boundaries of what the organization can handle, for the good of the organization, not for the satisfaction of their ego.

I had decided to craft a strategy of bringing out the best in the industry, engaging bold ideas in changing the culture in which they had operated for decades. My diverse and often difficult Board had not empowered me with this strategy and wouldn't have agreed with my objective if I had asked.

My naiveté served me well; I would not be so bold today.

My counterpart at the major Colorado environmental organization, whom I met with periodically, had a similar situation with his Board. However, he seemed more inclined to further entrench in the fights of the moment than seek new paths. In our monthly coffees, he often articulated to me the limits on what he could accomplish as what his Board would tolerate. I rebelled against such limits and imagined that in his shoes, I would be much more forceful. I felt it was my obligation to push the Board beyond their current vision and perhaps even their capabilities. Privately, I scorned what I viewed as his lack of true leadership. He ran a successful organization, but not one that would change any environmental paradigms.

Scott, on the other hand, suffered no such delusions and taught me the skill of iteration. Lead, come back and bring your army to the first hill. Retrench, perhaps move backwards. Lead again. I learned that leadership progress doesn't follow a straight line but happens in fits and spurts. I'm proud of the work we did at COGA and everything we learned. We had five years of massive culture change and five national precedent-setting rules and programs. We often teamed up with diverse groups to create new oil and gas rules. The most lasting impact of these efforts was to provide some great models for successful compromise and outreach.

The major lesson I learned from Scott was the importance of creating a process. An integrative process requires bringing along a lot of people. In some rulemakings, we would have 50 committee members, representing different companies, sitting around a table developing positions.

COGA made decisions by consensus.

This is not easy stuff.

As a result of so much collaboration and iteration, I learned a genuine humility that has allowed me to trust that a group can come up with a better solution than any individual. Even when that individual was me. Where early on I had thought my job was to pick a path and convince a majority to follow it, I quickly learned that those hard-won victories were short-lived. Although I might be able to use charisma and logic to win a group over with my arguments, those successes would not survive the dispersal of the meeting.

If people could not argue the case for themselves to each other, to their colleagues, the hard-won decisions quickly disintegrated. And so I learned to not only know where the army is, but to incorporate their point of view into creating the best path forward.

Two years later, when Scott passed the gavel, and I stupidly sighed in relief, we went out for a drink. I asked him, only half joking, "So how many calls have you taken in the last two years over my antics?"

"Not one. They knew I had your back."

23

Disenchanted with Environmental

Nearly every day I got up at 4:30 am. Even in the summer it's dark at 4:30 am. I'd meditate for 10 minutes, grab my pre-packed gym bag and hanger of clothes, and try to get in the car before my brain could kick in.

Whenever possible, I attended a 6 am class. Working out on my own isn't my forte. I can do it, but I do much better under instruction. At least two days a week, I attended a master's swim class in the outdoor pool. When you swim year-round outdoors, you develop a camaraderie with your lane mates. For more than a decade now, I've been swimming with more or less the same people.

I considered my time at the gym my sole Me Time. It was the only thing I did just for myself, and it was a critical part of my mental, emotional, and physical well-being. Unfortunately, as things started heating up in the oil and gas wars, my gym time became an extension of my public persona.

The 6 am crowd all recognizes each other, even if we do different activities. One gym member, Millie, was consistently supportive. "I grew up in Texas, you go get 'em, Tisha!"

Most were not.

I tried not to talk about my work at the gym. First, it was pre-dawn when I'd arrive and I was not at my best. Second, I really needed a break. I lived at the limits of stress that a person could handle, and working out was my best tool to manage it. I stopped making eye contact. I stopped initiating conversation. I answered with as few words as possible. It was painful because I was very conscious of my role as the face of Colorado's oil and gas industry.

And I was at my limit.

Any illusion of a safe space was shattered one morning when one of my swimming mates shouted over the noisy hair dryer. She was getting dressed and I was standing in my bra and underwear, blow dryer in hand. I shut it off and smiled at her, "What did you say?"

"You're a mother. Surely you don't mean the things you say in the paper about fracking. How can you live with yourself?"

How do I live with myself, was right.

My Identification

For several years while at COGA I stopped calling myself an environmentalist. It has been a long, torturous process to untangle feelings, sort out what is my true identity, and try to do so with some semblance of rational thought. I'm not sure I'm done yet. Even as I write this book, I am constantly clarifying who I am and what I think.

Traditional environmental identification is a pretty straightforward process. If you are going along in your liberal urban life, taking the kids to school and getting through your workday, the environmental truisms are clear cut: Recycling good. SUVs bad, but necessary. Wind energy good. Fracking bad. Nuclear bad. GMOs bad. Solar panels good. Natural gas—mostly a necessary evil. Light rail good, but not always practical. There's not a lot of debate or discussion, just an overwhelming consensus of what is good.

And what is not.

I don't want to be hasty in my caricature of the environmental movement. It actually cannot be easily summarized: it is diverse; different groups are focused on a spectrum of issues. The people who work within and support the environmental movement are themselves creative, thoughtful individuals with their own interests, divergent perspectives, and priorities that sometimes conflict with each other's. But there are some commonalities that I became familiar with, first as a supporter and later as an advisor. Now I consider myself a critical observer.

A critical observer who loves many people environmentalists.

It's easier now, in hindsight, to unwind my complex relationship with environmentalism and environmentalists. I'm no longer a target of constant criticism, for one, and I have the mental leisure to dissect my own unfair prejudices and blanket assumptions.

It was much harder in the middle of my COGA tenure. I stopped calling myself an environmentalist because I was so frustrated with the misinformation and combativeness of the anti-fracking movement. For a short while, I even embodied the anti-environmental fervor you will find common among conservatives. (We can and should talk more about this anti-environmental fervor, because it is, in itself, counterproductive. And it takes two to dance that tango…so, more on that later.)

It got so bad, I practically had to spit whenever I said "environmental". I was so disillusioned and angry with the movement I had until recently passionately embodied in my life for the two decades since college. Later, as I reflected more and allowed myself to chart my own path at COGA, I became passionate about reclaiming the term, and not ceding it to people and organizations with whom I have very little in common. I *am* an environmentalist.

It's okay if you have to spit when you read that.

At the risk of alienating you, reader, I admit that this book started essentially as an anti-environmental-establishment tirade. After five years of doing battle over energy-environment issues with the goal of making the best energy-environment decisions, I had become completely frustrated with the lack of a worthy, engaging opponent. With the benefit of a year of space from the fight, I've only indulged myself in one chapter on the topic.

I will redeem myself by then going on an anti-anti-environmental tirade of my own.

Why so angry?

I have many perfectly lovely, committed environmental friends who do not share the characteristics that I'm about to describe. Yet, I still think this depiction of the environmental movement is fair. I don't write it in the hopes that anyone will change, just that clear-thinking people who really care about environmental progress will think twice before adopting these as their own internal norms.

I have two primary beefs with the environmental movement general-ly. I'll be brave here and speak directly to you, environmental activist.

   (1) You are more committed to fighting than you are to crafting solutions, and

(2) You are so aspirational as to miss the many opportunities for change that are right in front of you, embodying "perfection is the enemy of the good."

At the continued risk of alienating you, reader, I will also state my gripes with the generally liberal, do-good public who weigh in on these energy-environment topics:

(1) Stop acting like lemmings, believing what any Hollywood type tells you about fracking or climate change, and
(2) You are ridiculously hypocritical driving around in your SUV and then condemning fossil fuels over cocktails.

During my time at COGA, I came to understand that, like me, people are mostly lazy about their political positions. My understanding of health care positions, for example, is simplistic and guided by my general impressions and politics. Same with education policy. This is how most people are engaging in energy.

Fine, but then know your limits.

The environmental movement of today has made climate change the central mobilizing issue. And yet, the environmental movement has a lot of other responsibilities that are being massively neglected and critically underfunded: riparian health and wildlife, to name just two. I think the hyper-focus on climate as the only environmental force to be reckoned with is very counterproductive and short sighted (for reasons I'll go into further in Chapter 28). Secondly, even where environmentalists have focused successfully on projects motivated by climate change, such as the Keystone pipeline and energy transitions, they have taken such a hard line to leave many viable solutions unaddressed.

Understandably, this political work does require a left flank, which I appreciate, but it also requires a pragmatic middle. Far too often, environmental organizations, funders, and supporters act like the Tea Party of the left, encouraging a culture of partisan and political extremism that is unpalatable, impractical, dogmatic, and lazy. This has two unfortunate results: the public adopts these positions as mainstream and it alienates half of the country unnecessarily.

And for that, there is a price to be paid.

The price is the loss of incremental, practical improvements to policies and projects that could actually make a difference on the ground in real life right now. Examples include reasonable fossil fuel regulation rather than this nonsensical obsession with "leave it in the ground."

In my COGA time, I was limited in what I could accomplish with the two environmental organizations that were willing to work collaboratively. Why don't I name them here? Because environmentalists shun and abuse these two when they are called out for successful, pragmatic compromises.

That is certainly a pity.

Anti-environmental fervor

I have literally never met anyone who hates nature.

I came to have a first-hand understanding of the anti-environmental fervor that pervades most political conservatism. It has a few roots:

   (1) Being blamed for climate change: nobody likes being the villain, whether they buy the storyline or not.

(2) Absence of options: environmentalism came to mean this hyper-partisan political movement without room for all the people who love the outdoors.

I encourage all former anti-environmentalists to join me in reclaiming the word. No one gets to corner the market on loving the outdoors, wanting to protect special places, and taking solace and refreshment in nature. No one hates nature. In fact, in the oil and gas business, there is an unusual over-representation of outdoorsy men and women who were attracted to the business as biologists, geologists, and engineers because of its cool, earthy work.

Vilifying environmentalists is no way to live.

Here's the kicker: doing so reinforces the stereotypes of oil and gas workers and conservatives by allowing all of us to be painted with that anti-environmental brush.

If you can't hug an enviro, at least hug a tree.

Seeking pragmatic allies

It took a while, but I navigated my way through frustration with the environmental movement, rejecting it completely, and then finding my way home. I was left seeking an environmental philosophy and an approach that is realistic, passionate, pragmatic, and caring.

But first I had to have a bit of a breakdown.

24

Full Buckets

It was another late evening in Denver. I was on stage with an interesting cast of characters, including former Colorado Senator Tim Wirth and Randy Udall, who I was fortunate to meet before he passed away just a couple of years later. The year was 2010. I was the sole representative of the oil and gas industry in a discussion of the energy future. The parking lot was filled with Subaru's when I arrived, and the gray-haired crowd struck me as polite, but not particularly friendly to my point of view.

It was an all-star cast who I had only begun to get to know. Patty Limerick, Colorado's State Historian, among other accolades, provided opening remarks. I had been enamored with Patty from the first moment I had met her a couple of years earlier when she spoke to a Leadership Group, 50 for Colorado, of which I was a member. Patty has and continues to be a significant contributor to my thinking. The evening was moderated by Kirk Johnson, who several years later as the Director of the Smithsonian Natural History Museum would become the single best keynote speaker ever at the Rocky Mountain Energy Summit Conference. Former Senator Tim Wirth would introduce me to the great work of the United Nations Foundation. And the evening featured the president of the World Watch Institute, Christopher Flavin. The topic was, *Where will our energy come from in 25 years?*[49]

I had prepared my 10 minutes of remarks, but revised them on the spot as I took in the conversation. This was a more emotional presentation than I expected, in some ways, more poetic than its title should have allowed.

It was the first time I allowed myself the luxury of going off script and speaking from the heart.

I talked about what the world looked like from the perspective of the oil and gas industry. My thoughts were only half-baked, because I was still in the process of trying to understand why my COGA members were so angry, so entrenched in fighting. It was also half-baked because I had jotted down three lines on the back of my original notes and was speaking without knowing exactly what I would say.

Stream-of-consciousness presentations are generally not a good idea.

I hadn't yet really gotten to know the diverse, multi-dimensional employees who made up the worker bees and future leaders of the companies I represented. Rather, I was thinking of the baby boomers, all men, who were leading companies and with whom I interacted every day. These were guys who grew up in the 1950's and 60's and had participated in the miracle of energizing the United States. They had seen the expansion of the national network of highways, gas stations, and motels. They had come of age when heating oil, propane, and natural gas had just transformed dwellings from smoky, cold hovels to warm, cozy homes.

Then the world had altered, and now people were talking about energy in terms that were completely unfamiliar to them. They weren't greedy fat cats; they weren't big oil. They were people trying to come to terms with a society that no longer appreciated what they provided. And, in fact, blamed them for doing their job and providing the energy that we all require.

> As I spoke, I felt that wonderful flow when
> your remarks are full of grace.

The audience, apparently, did not. I received polite applause when I took my seat. I sighed and furrowed my brow. At that time, I was still really hard on myself. I wanted to reach people and deeply transform their thinking, and I thought I could do that if I just worked harder, tried harder, got it right.

I was absorbed in my self-critical thoughts, and so could never have imagined that when COGA organized a public education evening with the Museum of Nature and Science, it would plant the seed for one of my most important professional relationships.

A fine measure of the quality of one's talk is the line that forms to greet you as a speaker after the event. I did not have a line. So I quietly gathered my belongings, strove to make eye contact and nod at each of my co-presenters, who were each occupied with fans, and slip up the aisle to the exit at the back. Perhaps I could slip out without having to network through dessert. It was an hour and fifteen-minute drive home to my kids. I had already missed bedtime, but if I was lucky, I could get there before 10 and watch them sleep for a bit.

And there in that aisle I was stopped by George. I did not know who George Sparks was, although I now know what a huge oversight *that* was. No matter, George is always a picture of humility and grace, and he introduced himself as the President and CEO of the Denver Museum of Nature and Science, or the DMNS. The idea of someone presiding over the massive dinosaur skeletons that for me define the DMNS was incongruent.

How could there be a President & CEO of the DMNS?

When I was a child, starting as young as I can remember, my sister, Marcy, and I would fly out to Denver by ourselves and be met at the airport by Mama and Grandpa. We'd go to their modest tri-level in Denver, which to me, seemed like a mansion. My grandmother had decorated every room in a different shade of green. Some were scary, barfy colors of green. We made this trip every summer until I was 12, when they moved to Tucson to be closer to us.

The basement was the real place of wonder where Mama had kept all of my mom's childhood dolls. Each summer we picked two and took them to the doll hospital where they were carefully repaired. My grandmother had been a school teacher during the depression, and she had an old school desk and old school books, which I loved to play teacher with. Over these summers, Mama taught me to sew. We played endless rounds of Yahtzee.

I vowed I would move to Colorado when I grew up.

During each summer visit, we always made a trek to the DMNS. I only knew it as "The Museum" and hadn't connected the dots until I had first taken my children there and seen the huge dinosaur skeletons that had stood so intimidatingly over me as a child. *Oh my gosh*, I thought, *I've been here before!*

As a result, I always enter *The Museum* with a child's awe and wonder. And now I was standing with the king of this wonder, incongruously called the President and CEO.

George complimented my remarks, noting my authenticity, and saying, not once but twice, something that really struck me.

"I think you and I have a lot in common."

Now that I have known George for some years, and wondered at his charisma and interpersonal genius, I imagine that that compliment was standard George fare. He appreciates and values people, and finds a way to connect with everyone. I doubt that I stood out particularly for George, but it didn't matter.

I thought that I did.

My evening was saved. I felt articulate and special, and I had made a new friend.

Embracing Technology

It wasn't my idea to have George speak at our annual meeting. My first COGA annual meeting was a big deal, like everything that first year. In years past, the Board chair had given a speech of varying effectiveness. Instead, this year, I gave a State of COGA presentation, our Board Chair made brief remarks, and George spoke about the role of embracing technology and change.

George was the perfect emissary to our audience: he was a baby boomer with backgrounds similar to our Board, and yet he embraced change. He talked about the importance of taking up technology in order to engage with their employees, their public, and even their own children.

It was a great motivational talk, and he had obviously put a lot of thought into it.

Although his talk was aimed at COGA's audience, which was overwhelmingly dominated by white, middle-age oil and gas executives, his talk struck a chord with me. As part of Brian's and my personal environmental philosophy, we had self-identified as Luddites. We didn't have television reception at our house, we refused to buy the latest phones and gadgets, and we generally eschewed the latest developments. For different reasons, the COGA members rejected texting and social media. COGA members were overwhelmingly baby boomer men; their wives hadn't yet made them get on Facebook to see the grandkids!

My avoidant relationship with technology was notably in contrast with that of my small staff. In a recent office meeting, Doug had announced that he had taken a quiz, and he was technologically 25. He said that I didn't need to take the quiz, I was obviously technologically 65. I chuckled self-consciously. I honestly didn't even know how to text (never mind tweet), and Doug taught me on the spot.

So as I sat in the audience, listening to George's talk, I used my new skill and texted him, while he was still on stage, from my Blackberry. (It was several more months before I was willing to try an iPhone.) While I was new to texting, he was not. He replied before the meeting was over, "Of course."

My text had simply said, "Will you mentor me?"

Reading Assignments

I still meet with George periodically at his office at The Museum, and it continues to always be thrilling for me. That first meeting was not what I had expected. As a massively over-achieving workaholic, I expected my new mentor to advise me to "find balance," "smell the roses," and "prioritize my family." I couldn't have been more wrong.

George asked, *What do you read for leadership? What do you read for culture? What do you read for news?*

I furiously took notes while George expanded my To Do list considerably.

I took all of his advice seriously, but the list was overwhelming. My boys were 3 and 7. I commuted between 2 and 3 hours a day depending on traffic. I tried to maintain both a meditation practice and regular exercise. I worked a ton. Where would I fit in all this reading?

Nevertheless, at George's recommendation, I subscribed to *Vanity Fair* and *The Economist*. Although that was only a tiny fraction of my new recommended reading list, it was all I could handle. They were good suggestions, however and I maintain those subscriptions to this day.

Over the years, George has been an exacting mentor, rivaled only in his expectations of me by Scott Moore, who expected equal but different achievements. Even though I was reticent to show emotions on the job, I soon came to trust George completely, able to share with him my greatest challenges at work. It was years before I was able to share my emotional challenges; it wasn't that kind of relationship. George was a hard-driving, exacting mentor who provided the kind of tough advice that I needed and wanted to hear.

One bit in particular came in handy every day.

CEO Mentor

I referred to George as my *CEO Mentor* because of this story. As I was relaying one of my challenges, George listened patiently before sitting up, leaning forward, and relaying this bit of wisdom. George was formal by nature, and this was the only time I heard him cuss.

Tisha, when you are a CEO, every day you are going to come into the office and there are going to be five buckets on your desk. Every day. Every day those buckets are going to be full of shit. The only question is what shit you're going to have to deal with. So stop wondering when things are going to be easier. Just come in, expect the buckets, and deal with them.

The imagery was so graphic and my response was so visceral. I could smell these buckets of shit, and I knew them well. For me, every day I had a full schedule with no room for error, a pile of work and correspondence that needed to be dealt with after hours, and invariably there would be some combination of a hostile media call, an angry member letter, an incensed legislator, and a personnel conflict.

Buckets of shit.

It was strangely comforting to stop looking for the break. There was no eye in this storm and there never would be. In fact, it was critical that I rearrange my schedule to allow time to get work done and to handle the daily, unplanned crises. George's buckets of shit changed the way I planned my days and perceived my challenges. It also removed the glamour I'd anticipated with finally being the big boss.

Being a CEO is not glamorous; it's where the bucket stops.

25

National Precedents

Five national precedent-setting rule makings in five years is not a good way to make yourself popular with your membership. To some, it proved I was a mole with a liberal agenda inside the tent. In fact, I didn't think we had any other options.

As the controversies around oil and gas drilling got hotter and hotter, I was determined to navigate a "responsible development" path that would allow reasonable people of any political persuasion to support oil and gas. When the National Petroleum Council released its *Prudent Development* guidance, which identified the potential role of natural gas to lower emissions, and cited national objectives for the economy, environment and security, I was delighted.[50]

> Although these days the word *prudent* always makes me think of poop. I don't know why.

The more hard looks I took at studies and data, and the more time I spent in basins around Colorado, the more I became convinced that oil and gas development was both essential and could be done safely. The key was to craft appropriate, meaningful regulations. On the flip side, I also came to believe, very strongly, that to have responsible development, you need good, reasonable opposition that will come to the table with industry to find consequential compromise, and ultimately be willing to celebrate shared successes.

That became increasingly difficult.

In my first legislative session, the Clean Air-Clean Jobs bill was passed. I don't get any credit for the substance or success of that bill, because I just rode the coattails of others' work. The bill represented a very substantive move from coal-fired electricity generation to natural gas-fired generation, and could have heralded a new age of climate peace between environmentalists and the oil and gas industry. It did not. Although the bill was a success in Colorado, it did not become a national model. In just a couple of years' time, the low price of natural gas would shift market forces such that coal-fired generation dropped dramatically across the country without further such regulations.

Naïve Success

The effort that I will take 100 percent credit for was creating the first baseline groundwater sampling program in the country. This is a perfect example of both my naiveté and my success, and from it you can draw many conclusions about the efficacy of my time at COGA.

I started off with a modest proposal, which took months of one-on-one and group meetings with individuals and companies to gain traction: COGA would host a voluntary baseline groundwater-sampling program. At the time, the dominant public concern about fracking was groundwater contamination. In the San Juan basin located in southwestern Colorado, there had been a mandatory baseline groundwater-sampling program in place for 10 years due to the shallow nature of the groundwater and the natural intermingling of natural gas and water. I'd had great success presenting the data from that sampling program to public groups to demonstrate that, even where groundwater was very shallow, drilling, fracking, and development could be compatible with protecting groundwater.

So why not take that show on the road?

In the COGA voluntary program, whenever a company drilled a new well, they would take a groundwater sample from a nearby groundwater source before drilling and then another sample one year later.[51] It took months of work, but I ultimately got Board approval, and then worked the phones for many more months, until we had over 98% of oil and gas operators in the state participating in the program.

This was a game changer, but not in the ways that I had anticipated.

Environmental groups were not impressed. This was perhaps my most devastating disappointment. While they routinely said both publicly and privately, "Companies should innovate. They should exceed regulatory requirements. They should go above and beyond," now, these same groups were publicly dubious, saying that nothing other than a mandatory regulation would be acceptable.

I cringed. My Board had said that's exactly what would happen.

In real terms, the voluntary baseline water sampling program was a massive success. It demonstrated that operators were willing to be proactive to assuage the concerns of the public. Another year later, the program would become a state regulation with official COGA support. Years later, tens of thousands of water sampling data points were publicly available for assessment and analysis. And, fundamentally, it took the question off the table of whether oil and gas development was systematically contaminating groundwater. It was not.

In reducing tensions in the oil and gas wars, however, this program did nothing but escalate conflicts. Environmental groups, including important, reasonable partners like the Environmental Defense Fund, lambasted the rule as inadequate. My membership crossed their collective arms and silently glared "We told you so" to me. And the topic of public concern about oil and gas development quickly morphed into new issues.

There was not one minute of peace in the valley.

Reader, it's really worth reflecting on this for a few moments. In Colorado, one of the most environmentally progressive states in the country, the oil and gas industry created a voluntary baseline water sampling program and then supported it becoming a mandatory regulation. There was not one shred of evidence that oil and gas drilling was systematically contaminating groundwater; in fact, there was plenty of proof that it was not. So the industry proposed, supported, and implemented an entire new program 100 percent to assuage public concern. And what did they get for it? Nothing. In fact, less than nothing…public critiques of the rule said that it did not go far enough.

Now, you tell me, where was I supposed to go from there?

I kept going. Because I was naïve and optimistic and hopeful.

Onward

I was fortunate to have an amazing partner in Governor Hickenlooper and his personnel. Although they were excoriated any time we all accomplished anything meaningful, I felt empowered by their pragmatism, desire to make progress, and willingness to piss off critics. They provided exactly what I needed to have the courage to persevere. I dare say over the same five-and-a-half years, they became as exhausted as I did at the difficulty in making any substantive progress.

At the time, the heating-up opposition didn't leave a lot of alternatives but to keep trying.

Before the baseline water sample became a rule, fracking disclosure was the first national precedent-setting rule that I presided over. And although the head of the state regulatory agency at the time went over my head and negotiated directly with companies after I had said *No*, he was successful. Although I never trusted him again, I did appreciate the progress he made.

After the baseline water rule, we then negotiated mandatory setbacks from buildings, in particular, sensitive structures like schools. Although a good and important rule, there was no reward for the effort.

The rule-making to create a better process for stakeholders and public notification was a similarly reasonable and responsible one, but months of negotiations did not result in any kind of public recognition for the effort involved.

And did I mention that every single one of those rule-makings occurred over Christmas?

What I didn't realize then that I know now is that these weren't even the big battles. It was an important regulatory progress, and I'd pursue those rules if I had to do it all over again. But in a do over, I wouldn't imagine that they would create any peace. They won't.

Creating peace is up to the rest of us.

26

Breakthrough or Breakdown?

Navigating the middle ground is not a clear proposition. Pulled between the external environmental forces acting on the industry and pushed by the traditional positions of oil and gas operators, I spent the better part of each day trying to navigate to a middle ground. What are the goals and objectives of the middle ground? Those were unclear, even uncharted. I needed to figure this out.

I was spending the better part of each day in conflict...either with my own members trying to devise the best path forward, or with our critics, who were suddenly everywhere. Never mind my personal life where nearly everyone I encountered, it seemed, was hostile to my job and demanded an explanation. I needed a structured philosophy to guide my decision-making and give me confidence among so much disagreement.

A best path?

There were both personal and philosophical elements to the question of identifying a best path forward. Best for whom? According to what values, what goals, and what objectives? I had already learned that no one person could identify the best solution to a given problem... there is value in a collective process and engaged, iterative decision making. However, I was leading an organization in a treacherous time and I needed a philosophy to fall back on, to use to guide my leadership. The problem was, neither the traditional environmental movement nor the conservative political environment I found myself in seemed to offer that philosophy. I did not see a framework for decision-making that seemed functional, responsible, rational, and pragmatic.

Take the role of science in political discourse, for example. It seemed to me that the oil and gas industry was irrational, anti-science, and downright obstinate when it came to any discussion of climate change. On the other hand, liberals brought those same characteristics to any discussion of fracking. I was baffled and confused that smart people with good intentions on both sides could not see this dichotomy.

It would be many years until I understood
what was happening there.

So I charted a new course, one that acknowledged the risks of climate change while valuing the important role of fossil fuels. I scrutinized contradictory studies on climate, fracking, renewables, energy use, and oil and gas development seeking to understand for myself the real issues, risks, threats, and opportunities. It was and continues to this day to be a slog. It takes real effort to discern credible studies from questionable ones. And then to make sense of partial or contradictory results. I understand why most people aren't willing to make this effort.

How *does* one craft a pragmatic, environmentally friendly solution? I looked at the challenge from three vantage points—globally, nationally, and from Colorado. Each of those looked more or less like this.

Globally:

- ◇ Worldwide energy demand was (and is) expected to double by 2040 as 1.3 billion people strive to leave energy poverty.[52]
- ◇ At that time (and still today) more than 80% of the world's energy is provided by fossil fuels.
- ◇ Countries that need to raise people out of poverty are going to focus on access to affordable energy rather than environmentally friendly energy.
- ◇ A pragmatic solution must acknowledge this reality rather than prioritizing concerns about global warming over energy access.

Nationally:

- ◇ At that time, half of the country's electricity was provided by coal. Ninety-five percent of transportation fuels was provided by petroleum products. Adding in heat and petroleum as feedstocks to everything from plastics to fertilizers, there is a massive demand for fossil fuels.
- ◇ Even should energy demand flatten, which indeed it has, fossil fuel infrastructure is massive and would be very expensive and energy intensive to replace.
- ◇ To me it seemed that transformations of our energy system would be most efficiently addressed through improvements to the fossil fuel mix rather than wholesale replacement by wind, solar, biofuels, or some unknown future solution.
- ◇ I didn't then nor do I now see a new, wholesale solution that is energy-, resource-, and footprint-efficient.
- ◇ Nuclear power, however, does make sense. But we won't open that can of worms just yet.

Colorado:

- ◇ As the representative of 40,000 direct employees in the oil and gas industry, I was painfully aware of the very direct economic benefits of this industry. Every threat to oil and gas livelihood to me felt like a personal assault on the industry I was representing.

✧ Colorado's electricity generation was fueled by about 50% coal, like the nation's, during my tenure. The transition of electricity generation to natural gas has since had the single largest effect on reducing greenhouse gas emissions.

✧ Wind and solar has its place in Colorado. But to me it was a resource- and space-intensive endeavor with mixed results. The concept of energy being good or bad by definition made no sense.

This assessment resulted in a personal worldview. With much reading and soul searching, the path I charted about two years into my tenure at COGA looked something like this:

✧ Climate change is a real threat worthy of consideration and planning.

✧ World energy demand is going to double, and we need an affordable, realistic set of fuel sources to meet that demand.

✧ Natural gas is an important part of addressing climate change.

✧ Renewables are an important part of an all-of-the-above strategy, but they aren't energy dense enough to address the world's current or future energy needs.

✧ Natural gas is also an important part of reducing other pollutants, too.

✧ No one is proposing a realistic replacement for transportation fuels; we need a solution there too.

Pragmatic Perspective

Part of my responsibilities at COGA were to oversee the annual conference, the Rocky Mountain Energy Summit, an event that had first introduced me to COGA. Planning the conference was a year-long effort akin to the scale of planning my wedding every year. We had a steering committee to identify speakers, but the vast majority of the legwork in identifying speakers by this time was done by me.

By habit, I still jot down great potential speakers or interesting personalities I read about in the press. Filling a three-day program with great speakers is no easy task, and so I was (and by habit still am) on the lookout for captivating potential speakers. Which is why in April 2012 I was struck by an article in E&E Daily news, about Peter Kareiva, the then-Chief Scientist at The Nature Conservancy.[53]

I read the article through my own lens of frustration and helplessness. Here was a person in a critical leadership position at perhaps the most famous environmental organization in the world, talking about the importance of integrating humans, humanity, and human culture into our view of environmentalism. He wanted to be both reasonable and realistic. For the first time, I could envision breaking down the camps of being pro-nature OR pro-humanity, instead creating a worldview that would include both. The article was a long one, and I devoured it.

And that article linked to other articles.

I sat at my computer transfixed. Reading about people who, like me, were striving to navigate a new kind of environmentalism that acknowledges the realities of human aspiration around the world. At length, this journey led me to the Breakthrough Institute. I spent most of the weekend reading *Love Your Monsters*,[54] which was a collection of essays by environmental thinkers. The key premise felt brought to me by the heavens: They argued that environmentalism was stuck in an old paradigm and that, if it did not evolve, it would itself become an obstacle to addressing the environmental challenges about which its proponents most cared. I couldn't agree more! And what's more, it wasn't a negative, apocalyptic vision of people, the future, technology, energy, or nature. It was positive and optimistic!

At last, I had found my people.

I remember the time like one remembers falling in love. For weeks I was floating about in gratitude that there were people like me out there. People who considered themselves environmentalists, but were not aligned with what had become the mainstream environmental movement.

That very weekend I left phone messages for both Michael Shellenberger and Ted Nordhaus, founders of the Breakthrough Institute. I didn't know how we could work together, but I knew we had to. Ted and Michael had written the excellent and exceedingly controversial book, *The Death of Environmentalism*. In their own way, they'd come to the same conclusion that I had: the mainstream environmental movement generally is not promoting positions and policies that will meaningfully allow for world improvement.

They were more rigorous and more thoughtful than I had ever even aspired to be.

One of their first causes was nuclear energy. As an energy dense, no-carbon electricity generation source, there is no better alternative. And yet traditionally and to this day, world environmental organizations oppose nuclear energy. The Breakthrough Institute has taken this on in many ways, from scientific studies to policy papers to the movie *Pandora's Promise*.

When I had my first conversation with Michael, he directed me to a just-published report reframing the North American natural gas revolution as a success story of federal research dollars combined with U.S. company ingenuity. They also made a compelling case for the role of natural gas in a transition to a more sustainable energy mix at a time that this position was becoming increasingly unpopular thanks to the fracking wars.

Over the following years I stalked Peter, Ted, and Michael and had them speak multiple times at COGA events. I continue to follow their work closely and, as a result, my thinking continues to evolve through thoughtful analysis of their detailed science and policy work.

In 2012, exposure to the Breakthrough Institute offered me two important cornerstones for my future thinking. First, I now understood that I was not alone. Words on this page cannot express how heartening it was to realize that there was a community of people interested in true environmental progress. The second cornerstone was a new lens through which to view energy-environmental issues. All credit goes to the Breakthrough Institute to raising my awareness about the critical importance of lifting people out of poverty around the world.

And that has changed the rest of my life's work.

Their most important influence has been to allow, even require, that I develop a flexible approach to energy and environmental issues, letting my opinions be reshaped by new studies, information, and the thinking of others.

I've also met remarkable people through the Breakthrough Institute. People who, in their own way, embody contradictions like I do. For example, Rich Tafel, a Republican thought leader, who founded the Log Cabin Republicans and has become a lifelong friend. The Breakthrough Institute also connected me to Paul Robbins, a self-proclaimed socialist who is skeptical about capitalism but recruited me to the Board of Visitors of The Nelson Institute at the University of Wisconsin so I can create connections to the business community for his programs and students.

I opted for breakthrough, rather than breakdown, for now.

27

Community Engagement Budget

It soon became inevitable that COGA would have to expand beyond state-level regulatory and legislative work and expand down into the city and county levels of government. In hindsight, I could and should have made that more of a deliberate decision. In real time, our responsibilities slowly bled into that area as one community after another started passing limits on oil and gas development.

Our staff was up to six, but that wasn't nearly enough to keep up with our full state regulatory and legislative workload, and now we were adding city council and county commissioner meetings, sometimes an hour's drive away. Then Doug's wife became gravely ill, and pretty much all of that responsibility fell on my shoulders.

I could not anticipate the tsunami of work, opposition, and controversy that was coming our way… instead I just saw these slowly building tensions as I prepared for my second COGA Board strategy retreat in the early fall of 2011. During the retreat, the COGA staff prepared an update on our work and proposed projects for 2012.

I had a few modest proposals to put in front of the Board.

I had thought the *Niobrara Outreach Strategy* was a no-brainer. West Slope COGA had successfully been running a program for years called

Community Counts. This effort was staffed by one employee, and essentially served as a combination *Neighborhood Watch* for issues related to oil and gas operations and monthly meetings for group accountability. They had a staffed hotline to channel complaints from residents about truck traffic or noise to the correct operators. Monthly they gathered to make sure these were all getting addressed and try to prevent repeat offenses. Quarterly a diverse group of affected stakeholders, from the local regulators to the residents, gathered for dinner to build rapport.

It was a very effective program and I wanted to repeat it in northeast Colorado where new oil development was expected to expand dramatically. Weld County is a politically conservative county with a long history of oil and gas development. It was overwhelmingly a friendly place to develop this kind of program. My proposed budget was $40,000 from the COGA budget with a plan to raise additional funds from local operators and contractors.

The Board was both unimpressed and uninterested. There was virtually no discussion and the general sentiment was overwhelmingly summarized in this narrow thought: *Why would we place signs to call a 1-800 number? We are just asking for trouble where we don't have any.* In discussion, Board members were dismissive of the idea, and I had the good sense not to call for a vote.

> I like to think that that program would have
> prevented a lot of later heartache.

Over the next several years, COGA had to engage in community engagement whole-heartedly, and it cost a lot more than $40,000. At one point we had three dedicated staff and two teams of contractors, and we ran political campaigns in four cities opposing fracking bans. We also eventually sued three cities to overturn their bans. Millions of dollars.

28

The Shift: Move Over, Climate Change

Not long after I discovered the Breakthrough Institute and devoured *Love Your Monsters,* I met with a long-time friend of mine for coffee. We had moved to Boulder the same year, she, just a few months before me. When I had first moved to Boulder, I tried out for all three women's Ultimate Frisbee teams, not sure which one I would make. She was a dominant force on the team that I made, the best one, where I would spend all my free time for the next several years.

People in industry often bandy about the term *professional environmental activist* to represent those who work in the environmental movement full time. It is generally used derisively. But my friend Rachel has worked in the environmental movement as both her career and her life's purpose. Until I went to COGA, we had more in common than we did not. Once I took the COGA CEO position, our relationship became strained, but we both wanted to stay close.

Earlier in our friendship, before I'd had kids, we met weekly for breakfast. It was a lovely ritual, but one I could not figure out how to sustain with the pressures of being a working mother. Up until I took the COGA role, we tried to get together at least monthly. Once at COGA it was nearly impossible to get together. I had an hour-plus commute each way, I worked all kinds of crazy hours, and I needed to spend any free moment I had with my boys.

But my heart ached to find common ground that would keep our friendship intact.

Making the Case

This was early in my thinking on energy poverty, and I wanted to make the case to her that we (meaning all of us do-gooders who want to save the world) should consider fossil fuels as an important part of addressing energy poverty world-wide. At that time, I still thought of us—my friend and I—as "we," meaning we were on the same side, with the same intentions and the same long-term objectives.

We met at this cute, kind of fancy café on The Hill in Boulder. It wasn't one of our traditional haunts, but I'd wanted to have a fresh start. Before our drinks had even arrived, I was off. I spoke with the breathless passion of the newly converted. I was certain, absolutely certain, that I had happened upon a solution that could, that *would*, put our paths back in synch. The wine arrived.

I made my case; she listened patiently.

I laid out the conditions of world poverty, much as I described them in Chapter 21. I talked about the importance of energy access as a cornerstone of raising people out of poverty, providing examples of all the known benefits of getting basic electricity to poor people around the world. I sipped my wine. She sipped hers. I framed the realities of fossil fuel consumption, cultural interconnection with fossil fuels, and the very real projected demand for more and more fossil fuels around the world.

I laid out the good old hierarchy of needs and the reality that as people get out of poverty, fertility rates decline and communities have more interest in pollution, energy mixes, and things like climate change. As I built my case to a mildly buzzed crescendo, I concluded triumphantly: *Don't you think it's more important that we rally the environmental movement around raising people out of poverty than climate change? By raising people out of poverty, we will be able to mobilize people and address the factors contributing to climate change!*

I smiled, held my breath, and waited for the much anticipated on-the-spot conversion. I was high with the thrill of my carefully crafted case and paradigm-shifting conclusion. I was still operating under the thrill of falling in love with my new life philosophy and I expected everyone else to do the same.

She did not hesitate; her patience was exhausted from my enduring narrative. She responded, *Poor people are screwed with climate change.*

Wait... what?!

Perhaps I didn't articulate a good case. I tried again. With no luck. We both left, angry and frustrated, but putting on a conciliatory face. We truly loved each other, but we were not finding common ground.

Making a Better Case

I've had several years to refine my thinking, learn more about the issues, and wrestle with important questions. However, this line of thinking has been repeated to me: *The planet cannot tolerate raising*

1.3 billion people in the developing world to the developed world's level of consumption and quality of life. Period.

The follow-on arguments vary, and are truthfully somewhat compelling. Climate change will make another 1 billion people poor. The poor will be the most dramatically affected by climate change. What's the point of raising a billion people out of poverty if we simply fry the planet?

I have heard these arguments so often from well-meaning environmental leaders and members that I have been forced to deeply reckon with them. More recently, intelligent members of the public, who have embraced climate change as an important cause, even if not *their* cause, have also made these arguments to me after my public talks.

The more good-natured, subtle audience members phrase the question more sensitively, but equally irresponsibly. Their line of query goes something like this, *If we get everyone on the planet access to energy, we are going to increase carbon in the atmosphere, and ultimately exceed the two degree threshold.*

Won't the poorest people be the most affected?

That was a few years ago. My early reckoning back then lacked sophistication and grounding in the real world. I have since had the opportunity to meet with and work with people from the developing world, from India, West Africa, and East Africa, to discuss these issues and learn from their perspectives. The most compelling case is made by putting yourself into the shoes of someone living in the developing world. If you were living in a lean-to in a city located in an area prone to extreme weather... would you rather have access to lighting, cleaning cooking fuel, motorized transportation, mechanized water pumps that will (literally) empower you to make the most out of your life, or would you rather have bureaucrats around the world lowering their carbon emissions?

The world's energy development provides your answer.

My colleagues from developing nations were unequivocal. While willing to acknowledge the importance of reducing carbon emissions, getting energy to real people whose lives it will transform is the priority. Period. My colleagues visibly bristle when citizens of developed nations such as the U.S. preach about the importance of limiting carbon emissions. From their perspective, the developed nations have *already* used up more than their fair share of the world's carbon budget while developing their economies. One of my colleague put it most starkly: "Telling other nations that they cannot develop using carbon after you have is best summed up as 'climate imperialism.'"

I have to agree.

There is a fiction perpetuated in this developed-world narrative that the developing nations *don't need carbon.* In this storyline, developing nations will *leapfrog* industrialized development, powering their service-driven economy with renewable energy. Although this sounds great, there's absolutely no evidence that any economy can develop without manufacturing the goods and services required for a population moving from subsistence living to a thriving middle class. Even cell phones, that great transformer of lives, have to be manufactured somewhere. And manufacturing requires abundant, consistent, affordable energy.

The Market Case

The other important take-away from that conversation with my friend was the second line of argument she made, also repeated to me often since. *We cannot accept that current energy is provided 84% by fossil fuels and world-wide demand for fossil fuels is expected to double. We have to drive markets to change.*

It's a fair point.

The idea that you can't accept the status quo and must drive change inspires me daily. Before and since that conversation with my friend, the environmental movement had been and is very successfully driving change through a combination of public actions (such as preventing construction of the Keystone Pipeline) and regulatory changes (such as authorizing the Clean Power Plan).

I would now argue that the idea that the world will be powered through an unidentified, unrealistic combination of unknown clean energy sources, only articulated as wind, solar, and electric cars (and generally not including nuclear or hydro) is downright nonsense. Producing energy and moving it to people who need it is an enormously technical, complex task requiring the participation of nearly every element of society.

With what plan? With what policies? With what realistic scenario?

In their defense, it is not and has never been the job of the environmental movement to innovate energy solutions. It is, however, emblematic of several of the key problems with the mainstream environmental approach to energy, environment, and climate.

The overarching thinking is so committed to the idea that fossil fuels are evil, no one is interested in paradigm-shifting approaches to addressing climate change. Unless, of course, that paradigm shift is a world powered by wind and solar, which at this point is not particularly innovative nor radical.

Magical Thinking

To be fair, I have devoted my adult life to these questions and pursuit of their answers. My friend and many, many devoted environmentalists have focused on the cause and its fight. From their perspective, they are on holy ground and engaged in a righteous war. From my perspective, this righteous narrative is short-sighted, counterproductive, and possibly destructive to our shared objectives of achieving sustainable energy-environmental goals.

But these conversations have further informed my understanding of the mainstream environmental movement: magical thinking is the order of the day. If you *believe* you can do it and if you adequately *vilify* fossil fuels and *obstruct* projects related to their development, you will drive innovation and markets to your solutions. And your solutions will magically become more economic and efficient and ultimately save the world.

I get it, but I don't buy it.

Prioritizing Energy Poverty

I wish that I thought of it myself. Memory is a tricky thing, and I wrestled with many concepts during my five years at COGA. You would think I had some brilliant insights. But this one I have to hand to the guys at Breakthrough.

For my first couple of years at COGA, I stayed committed to the concept that I was working for the oil and gas industry because I believed that the oil and gas industry was most likely to contribute to meaningful solutions to address climate change. I later became enthralled with the realities of our total interdependence on petroleum as well. My approach was to address these two competing realities: climate change is underway, and we are a nation fundamentally reliant on fossil fuels. My intent was to navigate through the controversies to propose and participate in the best solutions.

Then the enormity of world energy poverty moved to the center of my frame of reference.

The Breakthrough Institute offered a new, shared lens through which to look at energy-environment issues: reducing poverty around the world. As described in Chapter 21, energy poverty is a reality on a massive scale. And the most important thing you can do to raise someone out of all forms of poverty is to give them access to energy.

Here's the beauty of a new, shared vision. Right now, discussion of climate change makes most people break out in hives. If you are for prioritizing climate change, you may feel emotions ranging from guilt to panic when the topic comes up. Just a few weeks ago, I was walking with a friend and she said, "*Sometimes I just don't know what to do. It's so scary! It's so big…*

And then I don't end up doing anything at all."

The other option is to be dubious or even downright angry about all the climate change hype. In that case, you get called names like *denier* and feel you must defend everything from our quality of life to our dependence on fossil fuels.

The words "climate change" divide any room into two groups.

And this isn't just in the U.S. If you are in a room with people from the developed and the developing world, discussions of climate change immediately split participants into camps of energy haves and have nots. You will be hard pressed to find a person from the developing world who will prioritize climate action over the immediate well-being of their citizens. It gets tense pretty fast.

The shared vision offered by the Breakthrough Institute allows people of all walks of life, political backgrounds, and experiences of quality of life to imagine a world where people are lifted out of poverty. As communities gain access to energy, their citizens move up the hierarchy of needs (I added more about this in Chapter 35). As families improve their shelter, gain access to work opportunities, and are able to educate their children, their concerns become more civic in nature. Concern for environmental issues grows as prosperity grows.

But it is even more concrete than that. As communities become more prosperous, birth rates fall. So you have stabilizing populations combined with citizens more able to contribute meaningfully to shared policy goals, like addressing climate change.

It is inevitable that carbon emissions will rise.

If my dream comes true, citizens all over the world will gain access to electricity, clean cooking fuels, transportation, and increased goods and services. The consumption of fossil fuels and the resulting carbon emissions will happen. I, for one, am willing to focus my environmental muscle on planning for a more than 2-degree-Celsius world where more than a billion people are raised out of poverty.

I think you could argue that people will gain access to energy with or without the well wishes of climate activists everywhere. Abstract concerns of a changing climate are not motivating in the face of the kind of poverty that countries are working to address.

Although I failed once before, I will try again.

I would like to make the case to environmentalists and climate change activists everywhere: if you want to address climate change, talk about something else. Let's create a positive, proactive, productive goal that people of every political stripe can get behind: addressing energy poverty. By mapping out pathways to energy access first and sustainable energy access second, we can transform the conversation.

There are three major advantages to moving "reducing energy poverty" to the top of the priority list, even if climate change is your life's work.

First. You just doubled your audience. In a polarized political landscape, half the people you want to mobilize just changed from being actively hostile to your cause, to at least neutral, and possibly supportive.

Second. You'll conserve your energy. Rather than spending all your time fighting over science, swimming upstream in difficult political currents, and making a case for action, you can invest that energy into policy action. Although the path to energy access is difficult, and the devil is always in the details, it has broad public appeal.

Third. Combining forces for good. You aren't pitting the developed world against the developing world. U.S. emissions are falling and energy demand forecasts are flat. The rest of the developed world is in a similar situation. At the same time, billions of people around the world see access to energy as their ticket to a better life. Framing the top worldwide issue in a way that obstructs that momentous goal unnecessarily divides the world into those who do and do not have access to energy.

Environmentalists in the developed world cloak themselves in concern for those most vulnerable to climate change around the world. But communities in the developing world require meaningful access to energy to begin to realize their potential. Abstracting the people of the developing world using a carbon budget is the height of a painful hypocrisy that we are all guilty of participating in.

I find it more engaging to set goals related to empowering people and communities to raise themselves up through the hierarchy of needs. If energy is what they need to get started; let's get them energy. As for the resulting climate change, we made our part of the mess. We will need to be critical participants in the world's preparation and adaption for whatever is to come. A big part of that is empowering the countries of the world. More in Chapter 40.

And as for my friend and I, we are still striving to find common ground.

29

Trail Running

During my fourth year at COGA, a new trail opened near my house—and changed my life. About half way down the mountain, a new single-track trail was created that connected to two loops. One of my neighbors and I checked it out one Saturday morning, when it wasn't open to bicyclists. That figure 8 track became one of my greatest bridges to mental and physical health.

I have always done my best to exercise regularly. But having two kids and a long commute will really take a toll on you. I was more disciplined than most about hitting the gym at 6 am, but once the gym became another place that people wanted to talk to me about fracking, even *that* became just another exercise in endurance.

This was different.

Before the opening of this trail, which those of us living up here just refer to as The Trail, running had always been a chore. I ran because it was an efficient way to get in exercise. I'd run three miles usually, four on a good day, and five for a huge workout. I'd analyzed the map of The Trail and worked out that I could run a four-mile loop, a seven-mile loop, or cover the entire thing for nine miles.

My neighbor and I started with the first four-mile loop—it seemed like a solid but feasible amount of exercise. We alternated walking and running, keeping an easy pace and catching up on our kids. It went so well, we decided to keep it up until we could make the nine miles. That was three years ago.

We now run the nine miles every
Saturday that it's not covered in snow.

There is something amazing about a single track in the woods. Running isn't scary, like mountain biking where you can easily break your elbow, and eventually it became as straightforward and mechanical as walking. I promise you I cannot run five miles in a city. Running in the woods is different. It's magical.

At the time, the pressure of the COGA responsibilities was compressing my body and my spirit. I had developed sciatica that tortured my back most days. Right before the trail opened, I had also developed carpal tunnel, which I knew was stress and not repetitive-use induced. I was in constant pain, but I kept most of it to myself most of the time.

These Saturday runs left all that stress behind, and allowed me to start each new week fresh. Michelle, my running partner, wasn't particularly interested in my job. She had always known me as a mountain mom, another mother of two boys, and we kept our conversation focused on our families and our 30,000-foot discussions of what was happening in the world.

On some level, those runs saved my life. I would accumulate all my troubles during the week, and scatter them behind me like a popcorn trail, dribbled out over two hours. I loved the smell, the feel, and the relief of that time in the woods.

Occasionally, when Michelle wasn't available, I'd run by myself. I struggle to motivate to do any workout alone, but once I get started I'm always fine. On this summer afternoon, I was about four miles in and was just starting to decompress. My heart was still tight and my breathing shallow... I wondered to myself when I might start to feel better. Sometimes I had to run faster, really wear myself out, to start getting out of my head and feeling some relief in my body.

Suddenly I heard screeching and a giggle, like teenage girls ahead. It was an odd noise, and I cocked my head to make sure there wasn't someone in trouble. Nope. Not trouble, just your average screeching teens. I kept going. The trail twisted and turned a lot, so sometimes you could hear people a mile before you saw them.

I came down a little drop into a ravine, crossed the metal bridge, and started up the other side. This part is one of my favorites because the path looks like the packed clay of the redwoods in California. It feels like you've turned the corner into another world. The little ravine often has water in it and makes the drop feel cool and refreshing.

I looked up and saw the bear.

The smart thing would have been to turn back, but I had a full loop ahead and I really needed this run. The juvenile bear wasn't very big, but he blocked the entire trail. *So this is what the screeching and giggling had been about.* He must have encountered some other hikers coming toward me, and they'd turned around and gone the other way. I looked up and down the steep hillside; there was no way to get around him.

I already had my pepper spray in my hand. I walked slowly toward him. "Hey little guy, why don't you beat it?"

He looked at me and didn't budge. I stopped. There was about 20 yards between us and one of us was going to have to move. I knew from an accidental spray in the house that winter that pepper spray sucks, and the person who sprays it is as likely to get hit as your intended target, so I really didn't want to spray him. The spray was also as likely to land me heaving on my hands and knees as it was to get this bear out of my way.

I took one step forward. "Hey, little buddy—time to go home."

This little buddy stood up on his back legs, now about six feet tall. Small for a bear, but bigger than me, and then he came down on all fours and started loping toward me. *Oh, shit!* He didn't seem threatening, but he did seem intent on finishing his adventure in my direction. I didn't want to turn my back, so I grabbed a tree with my left arm, and swung off the path to the right, dangling over the steep side. I looked down… if I had to, I'd just have to roll down the hill, which would suck, but wouldn't be fatal.

He got to the 8-inch diameter tree I stood behind and stopped, staying in a crouch, looking in my eyes, the same height as me in his crouch. I could touch him, in theory. I was precariously teetering off the edge, holding onto the tree with my left hand, pointing my pepper spray with my right. "Hey, little guy, I *really* don't want to spray you with this pepper spray. It sucks, I know. What do you say we move along?" I shuffled to the left trying to get off the path, he leaned in toward me, so I shuffled to the right. He tipped his head around the tree and looked at me.

He's so cute, I thought. *And, he could accidentally maim me with one swipe of that paw, which is bigger than my head. I better figure out how to get out of here.* I shuffled back to the left, intending to roll down the hill, and the bear just loped up the trail in the direction I had come.

Whoa! Mission accomplished!

"Bye, little dude!" I called, and looked around. When something like that happens, you really want to tell someone. I'd felt a strange bond with that little bear.

I brushed myself off, took a deep breath, looked back over my shoulder and saw no sign of the bear returning. I continued with that run, thankful for all my blessings.

30

A Girl Who Changes Her Mind

It's pretty clear, when you're working in a political environment, that evolving one's thinking, a.k.a. "changing your mind," is not an acceptable practice. "Flip flopping" has become as gruesome a verb as "compromise." Learning to acknowledge and even embrace change, including gathering new information and changing my mind as a result, has all been part of my development.

My thinking on climate change is still in a perpetual sequence of adaptions. In college I'd attended an early Earth Day rally in San Francisco, bought a Mother Earth t-shirt, and proudly wore it until it fell apart. Climate change wasn't on the agenda in the early 90s. After college, with my degree in Earth Systems with an emphasis in Geology, I worked at the U.S. Geological Survey (USGS) on a team studying ocean sediments to unlock information about historic temperatures.

My scientific interest in climate change was born.

That work had begun with a spring break internship my junior year. Instead of another western road trip (how I'd spent my first two spring breaks), I had the opportunity to join a research vessel for two weeks. The boat seemed intimidatingly large as I boarded it with my fellow student, Remy. The smell of diesel and saltwater permeated my senses (and today always reminds me of that moment) as I took the stairs below deck to drop my bag in the bunk we shared.

Once I finally threw up in the metal toilet three days later, I got over the sea sickness. A horrible, mind-numbing sickness that immediately evaporated upon that purge. (On my second cruise the following summer, I knew to throw up right away—get it over with.) We worked 12 hours on and 12 hours off and I was assigned to the night shift. As interns, Remy and I were on alternating crews working in the Geotech lab below deck. The USGS team was hardworking and gruff, but ultimately kind and considerate and, over those two weeks, let us have a look at all their myriad operations.

Science on a boat is cool.

The boat cruised west from the Bay area, and then proceeded down the coast. We would stop periodically and the crew on deck would throw a long tube over the side, which cored ocean bottom sediments by the weight of its fall. They would haul the core back up and divide it into manageable lengths, which would then be sent below deck. A different team would split the core lengthwise and wrap up half to send back to the big core-housing warehouse at the USGS in Palo Alto. The working half would be divvied up for the various teams. In Geotech, we twisted, prodded, dried, and weighed, writing down mysterious measurements that were hard to contemplate in the grand scheme of things.

I had the good fortune of working for the USGS for two years, and got to see those obscure measurements turned into a report, which even listed my name as one of the authors. The gist of our effort was measuring marine sediments for evidence of climate history on the planet. So I got an early education on the research efforts contributing to later discussions of climate change. There was no drama or politics then.

If anything, climate science was geeky, dry, and very, very detailed.

When Al Gore put out the movie *An Inconvenient Truth* in 2006, I was spellbound, and excited to jump on the climate change bandwagon. I knew about climate science! The narrative of this movie fit comfortably into my worldview. I didn't feel the need to dive deeply into the Intergovernmental Panel on Climate Change (IPCC) reports, even though I have the background and temperament to be a sophisticated connoisseur of climate change science.

I was a believer.

My Comeuppance

During my first few years at COGA, I had crusaded to convert the oil and gas industry's best and brightest to climate change activism, or at least interest. I failed miserably. I beat my head against this wall for some time until George of *The Museum*, my very important mentor and friend, told me his story.

George was a long-time conservative who was becoming more moderate; he had decided that climate change was in fact human-caused and that engaging conservatives in the conversation was critical. He shared that after a similar frustrating process of trying to convert his colleagues, he had decided to skip the "believe in climate change" phase, and just focus on the "what are we going to do about it?" process.

I took his advice.

George and I started at opposite ends of the political perspective and both moved, slowly and systematically, to the same place in the middle. George got there on his own, but I was in the process of moving toward the middle, and having someone like George as a mentor was a critical component. In addition to being someone I could bounce ideas off of and ask for advice, George modeled for me how a mature, thoughtful leader can develop his or her thinking. George was proud that his perspectives were evolving, and that gave me permission to grow and change my mind too.

I often thought of those buckets of shit.

Climate change was an important topic to have such a valuable mentor because nearly everyone has a strong opinion, and yet most people's justification for their opinion is quite shallow. Thanks to George's pinpointed advice, I no longer spend any of my public speaking or consulting time trying to convince people that climate change is real. I don't even talk about my personal opinions, unless asked.

So, since you asked...

I've discovered several obstacles to having an intelligent conversation about climate science, which are best navigated with a light touch.

First. Exaggeration sucks. Some climate change advocates exaggerate scientific data, the media amplifies it, and the result makes a mockery of the things that are true. Take for example, the oft quoted "97% percent of scientists agree." I just read it in an article today. It's not correct,[55] [56] but furthermore, it ridicules the idea of science by misusing scientific data to talk about scientists.

Second. Data rocks. The exaggeration of science with regards to climate doesn't mean that there isn't good data. There is. We humans are adding a shitload of carbon into the atmosphere.[57] We have, in fact, permanently altered the planet.[58] Our emissions are a measurable part of the geologic record.

Third. Zombies, anyone? Those things don't mean the apocalypse is on the horizon. The unrelenting portrayal of climate change as the end of the world[59] (rather than the end of the world as we know it) is demoralizing and alienating. We just don't know what's going to happen.

Fourth. Outcomes unknown. I'm interested in a range of possible scenarios. We can't forecast oil prices, or markets, or even snow storms; why are we talking about the most complicated systems on planet Earth as if we have any idea what is going to happen? The results of more human-caused carbon in the atmosphere will have consequences. Some, like severe weather, will undoubtedly be terrible. Some, like higher productivity of crops,[60] , will be good.

Fifth. Curious cat. This all leaves me curious. Curious about what we will learn. Curious about what we can do now to prevent additional carbon going into the atmosphere. Curious about what will motivate humanity to act. I read through a bunch of articles about climate change science and policy with a big shovel to move all the polarizing shit out of the way to try and find out what can inform my thinking.

Sixth. Focus now. As a result, I AM concerned about what additional carbon in the atmosphere may do to the climate. I DO worry about if, when, and how the climate will change and what the consequences will be. I FOCUS on what part I can play in addressing climate change (you're reading it). I DECIDED that the status quo isn't it.

Even writing these words fills my stomach with anxious butterflies, because we just don't know what's going to happen. Even so, I am dedicating my life to creating shared goals and finding common values that will ultimately help us live together as long as possible. And none of this alarms me as much as compassion moves me to want to create a world where people do not have to live in poverty.

Period.

In My Backyard

I have found that this framing is extremely compelling to moderates of all stripes. It is not, however, convincing to people who face and oppose oil and gas development in their backyard, nor should it. In other chapters, I will discuss how I have wrestled with the concerns of citizens about nearby development.

The vast majority of U.S. environmental activism at this moment is driven by climate change. Although most people have no idea what 2 degrees Celsius really means in terms of the practical considerations of naming a world-wide energy temperature, just about any good liberal will cite news quotes and factoids about climate change when justifying their energy-environmental positions.

Through the climate change lens, nearly every environmental organization supports "getting off fossil fuels" and a "transition to a clean energy economy." It sounds nice, and, interestingly, the position doesn't require YOU to get off fossil fuels, so it is a free stance to take. A position without consequence. This rationale then drives all kinds of specific movements, such as:

- ✧ Opposing every type of fossil fuel-related development, from oil and gas drilling, to fracking, to pipelines.
- ✧ Supporting divestiture from fossil fuel-related companies and projects.

✧ Creating policies and regulations that support the above, regardless of economic and environmental aftermath.

Some organizations have very effectively translated this anti-fossil fuel message into localized campaigns to prevent all sorts of community projects. This approach obfuscates issues and demonizes companies and employees working to deliver energy to a public who demands it. Take, for example, natural gas pipelines in the eastern United States. For years, communities there have paid a premium for natural gas due to pipeline constraints, or worse, have been limited to the less environmentally friendly fuel oil to heat their homes. Yet natural gas pipeline projects that have been requested, even demanded, for years are now under ubiquitous assault.

The tactic is effective, I'll admit.

It also takes hypocrisy to a new level, where people have access to energy, but want it produced, transported, and delivered somewhere they can't see it. It also takes advantage of community members' legitimate concerns about development projects, turning citizens into soldiers in the anti-fossil fuel war. Those communities would be better served focusing on their actual interests and concerns and negotiating directly with local companies and engaging on their real issues with area regulators.

31

Feeling the Loss

In hindsight, the most important tests are the ones that tug at your heart. The lost friendships and numerous perceived betrayals. The most interesting are probably the most superficial. So I'll cover some of both.

Let's start with the night I knew the shit was hitting the fan.

I showed up in Longmont to give 10 minutes of "Oil and Gas 101" to the city council, at their request. I had mildly prepared, having given the talk dozens of times to various civic groups, and showed up half an hour early, as I am always inclined to do.

The staff met me in a preparation room to make sure my PowerPoint worked and to go over the evening's plan. The agenda started with public comments, then a few business items. After that, I was up for "Oil and Gas 101." The city council then had some other agenda items they would cover but I was free to leave. The meeting started at 7 pm and they expected, if there were significant questions, I'd be out of there by 8. I hadn't eaten dinner.

I should have eaten dinner.

At a quarter to 7, we moved into the meeting room, which was unexpectedly packed. The room buzzed with a tense excitement I would later come to know well, but at the time it was just confusing to me. *Longmont citizens sure are engaged!* I thought. I took my seat in the first row, off to the side so I would be out of the way during public comment. I unwrapped a granola bar.

The first order of business is always public comment, and the city council called the meeting to order and got to work. In my experience, a city council meeting usually has three to five people who want to say something during public comment. Often, the city council members know them and welcome them to the podium on the floor by name.

As I sat in the front row, off to the side, I familiarized myself with the proceedings and the audience. I believe it was the mayor pro-tem who presided over the meeting; he was brisk and efficient, informing the audience that public comment would be limited to three minutes each. He explained the ground rules including "no exclaiming" from the audience; I was curious what all the fuss was about. I had attended dozens of city and county meetings and I had never heard any "exclaiming."

Three-minutes at a time, members of the public got up to speak about the dangers of fracking and oil and gas development. I took stock of the packed room and several things began to dawn on me at once. These people were here for my talk. These were interested, engaged, and ANGRY citizens. Apparently, I should have brought some trail mix.

And maybe reinforcements.

The misinformation, fear, and hyperbole were shocking to me, and I took furious notes, wondering how I could possibly dispel all of these myths in my ten minutes of remarks. The personalities and their comments would later become so familiar to me that I could give their remarks myself, but at that moment I was shocked. Shocked by the anger. Appalled by the misinformation. I waited my turn, taking more notes.

I was certain that I could bring comfort to these dozens of enraged people.

At three minutes each, 20 people can speak per hour. As the hours wore on, I was shocked that the city council would invite a speaker (me!) and let that speaker sit by, in numb, hungry silence, as public comment went on and on and on. I wasn't sure what proper protocol was. Should I go get dinner and come back? Should I leave? What kind of reception could I possibly face after this onslaught? I sat alone. Quiet, scared, numb.

Every single comment was hostile, except one.

I moaned inwardly when my counterpart from another oil and gas trade association got up to speak in public comment. What was he doing here, speaking during public comment, when I was on the agenda? He got up and delivered a pat, three-minute, standard oil and gas oratory on the importance and safety of oil and gas development. It went over like a slow, silent, deadly fart. When he finished, he looked at me and smiled, and nodded, as if to say, *See! You aren't alone! I'm here.* At which I slid down in my seat hoping no one noticed that he had looked at me.

Who needs enemies when these are your friends?

At ten minutes past midnight, that's right, MIDNIGHT, I was called up to give my 10-minute oil and gas 101. It was doomed before I began. Although I acknowledged the tension in the room, and said

I'd be happy to come back and address all the concerns raised by the public, the tired, cranky, hungry city council members looked down on me with narrowed eyes and crossed arms. The audience hissed and scoffed at every one of my remarks. If the city council members asked any questions, I don't remember.

At nearly 1 a.m., I started the hour plus drive home, thinking, "We are fucked."

And the Shit Hits the Fan

Within months, our tiny COGA staff was overwhelmed with local governments going through their own version of Longmont's public controversy and process. The COGA Board was constrained in its response, and I took my Chairman to a Longmont public meeting to experience the fuss first hand. He sat in the room in shocked silence, much as I had done the first time, and by the end of several hours, understood that we were in uncharted waters. He is the only one of 30-plus Board members who made the trek, despite his encouragement to all of them to attend. It was not an experience one could understand through press clippings alone.

I think they thought, *That's what we pay COGA for, right?*

My right hand man was going through a health crisis within his family and couldn't share the burden of these community meetings like he normally would have. As a result, I practically killed myself going from meeting to meeting, town to town. Many nights I arrived home after midnight, driving hours per day up and down the Front Range. I'd wake up at 5 and do it all again.

I squared my shoulders and articulated a zero-tolerance approach for failure to my staff. I felt that we at COGA represented 40,000 plus oil and gas jobs and every attempt to prevent oil and gas development was a risk to the entire state. My whole career, I had achieved my personal and professional objectives through force of will.

My will would meet its match in Colorado's anti-fracking movement.

As the number of communities with anti-oil and gas efforts mounted to a crescendo, over 30 communities had public processes underway to ban or make difficult oil and gas development. With the belated support of the COGA board, the COGA staff grew to 13 and our approach became more refined. We built a community outreach team of three talented, energetic young professionals, who spent all their time going from town hall to city council and back again. We hired consultants to fight local ban-fracking ballot initiatives. We tried just about everything.

And we lost. A lot.

Throughout the fracking wars, I faced personal and professional challenges. The industry was not of one mind on how to face the fracking wars. Some wanted to engage in the softer side of building rapport and winning over hearts; others wanted to fight to win and take no prisoners. Every new battle required an approach, a plan, buy-in from the Board, and then fundraising to execute the plan. While it felt like Colorado was burning in these battles, I spent a great deal of my time trying to raise money from my members to fight battles they didn't understand, take seriously, or necessarily care about.

And during it all, I worked myself and my staff to exhaustion.

Battles raged in my own county, with anti-fracking "education" messages going out in mountain resident community emails, discussing the threat of fracking and encouraging residents to *Ban fracking before it's too late!* Although oil and gas development in our mountain community was so unlikely as to be absurd, I shuddered at the all-encompassing battle that raged.

Going anywhere in public became a nightmare. My 6 am workouts, my last haven of Me Time, was not even sacred. Before the sun was up, people I'd swum with for years were asking me *How do you live with yourself?* Adding, *You're a mother, how do you justify what you're doing?* Friends stopped inviting our family to dinner and on trips. And it was just as well, because I was running out of energy for anything but the barest survival of the fight.

There were personal, professional, and scientific lessons of this long, arduous period of the fracking wars.

Personally

There's no way to avoid sounding melodramatic. The times *were* dramatic. Five towns banned fracking by a vote of the people. My family was ostracized by most of our friends and much of our community. We rarely could go out in public without some kind of difficult conversation about my job and fracking.

The challenges came from within the organization as well. The politics of running a trade association under siege are brutal, and on more than one occasion, the members were more divided internally than they were united to face the public challenges. Individuals and companies had strong opinions about each of the many challenges we faced, and they would lobby each other and me for the outcome they desired. It felt like incessant fighting on every front.

I took all this personally.

At the end of the day, the buck stopped with me, and my will to lead COGA to success was strong. I fought mightily to overcome the conflicts within the industry and to present a cohesive, positive, proactive face to the public. Our team had developed a series of processes to get as close as possible to consensus on regulatory and legislative decisions, and I spent countless hours in committee meetings working to facilitate agreement. I worked myself into several health crises, all of which I hid from my colleagues while I silently persevered. I kept myself aligned with that three-question test, and I returned day after day, working harder to face every new onslaught.

By the end of my time at COGA, I felt that nearly every single person I worked with had betrayed me in some way. The stakes were high, opinions were diverse and emotions ran high. COGA was often under siege externally and I was under siege internally. I later developed a clearer understanding of the situation, and have since come to believe that *betrayal* is too strong of a word.

I now understand that most people are living in a world where they are the sun and everything happening is revolving around them. In my own world, I was the sun and all the other people were actors in my main stage production. However, in their world, I just had a two-bit part. And actions that felt like monumental betrayals to me were, for those people, straightforward actions in their own best interest. I may have not even entered their stage, or their thoughts.

This understanding really puts relationships and work-related drama into a realistic perspective. From there, the only action that really matters to you is the action that you choose to take. And once all the relationships and dramas associated with work take on the character bit-parts that they are, you understand that you have to set your own guiding principles, and you have to stay true to yourself.

Learning to self-calibrate to my own standards was a wonderful result of surviving these trials.

Professionally

You can't win them all. *Maybe YOU can't win them all!* I hear my old self saying. That fact, now clear, was heresy to my all-in, take-no-prisoners, straight-A's-in-life, overachieving self in my early COGA years. It took working myself to the bone and several lost ban-fracking votes for me to change my expectations for the COGA team and for myself. I did everything within my power, sacrificed sleep, practically abandoned my family, cajoled, threatened, strategized, engaged, fundraised, and still we lost. Again and again.

Losing was a novel experience for me.

It transformed me. Later we, COGA and Colorado's oil and gas industry navigated our way to success in community engagement and winning hearts and minds. But I learned humility and, eventually, grace in defeat…and how to keep going.

I hope as a result of this experience that I now have more of the quiet, patient gravitas that I so value in my mentors. I used to think you set a goal and then moved heaven and earth until you achieved it. Now I think you set a goal, expect the best, do everything in your power, and then accept the range of possible outcomes. And then you take stock and take another run at it.

Less sexy, more healthy.

I made mistakes. It took a lot of meetings with my corporate psychologist to set aside the idea of working toward professional perfection. It looks silly on paper: professional perfection. At the time I understood that to be my only option. Now I recognize those scars I have from mistakes I made are, in fact, the battle wounds that make me more interesting as a person.

Sounds like something an old woman, wearing purple, would talk about, so let's move on.

I also learned that the higher the professional stakes, the less likely professional loyalty is to exist. I know that I'm a leader that builds a loyal team of people who will follow me from job to job. And yet, whenever the shit truly hit the fan and the stakes were extremely high, I learned that every man, woman, and colleague will fend for their own interests. I used to take this personally; now I understand it's just the way it is. Interestingly, most of these folks have since come back and we look for opportunities to work together.

Unfailing loyalty is no longer a condition I hold my colleagues to.

It does not exist.

Lastly, one of the benefits of moving away from a culture of batting 1000 and perfection is empowering the team to articulate their doubts. I now understand that a loyal team of overachievers is essentially worthless on the battlefield. Yes, *worthless*! However, an empowered team of people willing to question authority, articulate their concerns, and contribute to the best possible outcome is the team I want for my future adventures.

Non-lemmings, please take note.

Socially

As is true with most jobs, there were many different communities within which I worked. Each community requires a unique approach and relationship. One was the oil and gas industry, of which COGA only represented a microcosm. A diverse, complex microcosm, but still only part of the broad industry we were working to represent. A key component of COGA's ultimate success in Colorado was our coming to appreciate the different social groups that we needed to understand and, ultimately, it was imperative that we earned their respect.

First, there is a Colorado political community. These insiders understand politics, the media, the legislature, and the rule-making process. This relatively small group of people knows how to get things done politically, legislatively, and through regulation. Getting to know them, respecting their talents, and engaging their support was extremely important.

Then there are the actual communities with drilling conflicts. Each one has its own culture, dynamic, players, and influencers. In any town, there are only a small number of people who engage with and influence local elections and government proceedings. This group is unique, dynamic, and key to its community. Each community had to be treated as if it was the only one that exists.

Then there were the other interest groups, like COGA. I learned that everyone from hospitals to auto dealers has an association. There is the Farm Bureau and the state Cattlemen's Association. Each city has its own chamber of commerce and often an additional economic development group. Fortunately for us, no matter what the group, they each had a connection to oil and gas and an interest in our ultimate success. This allowed us to engage them in our work. Our job was to understand their worldview, and make connections between our mission and theirs.

I learned to respect the diversity and unique interests of these dozens of social groups within which we had to navigate to accomplish our work. Most importantly, I came to understand that, whatever microcosm you are working within, it is all-important to those involved.

On any one day I might run from the Colorado capitol for a legislative hearing to a town one hour away for a meeting negotiating regulations, conducting a press interview along the way. Each of these required a totally different paradigm, focus, and hat. And I had to learn how to show up completely and seek to understand each context from the perspective of those working in it.

Scientifically

In community conflicts, here are the things that matter.

- ✧ Each community's concerns will be unique.
- ✧ It is crucial to understand who is influencing decisions, what is motivating them, and where they gather their information.
- ✧ It is also critical to appreciate who will make decisions and how; in many cases, the decision makers and decision-making process are not tethered to the on-the-ground issues.
- ✧ Much of the community concern will be emotional, which will not be addressed by providing scientific information or technical explanations.
- ✧ Understanding and empathizing with the emotional content is critical.
- ✧ Building relationships…showing up again and again and again…is the only way to make progress.

Science wasn't on that list. After developing dozens of fact sheets to address citizen concerns, I learned that there is a very limited role for facts and science in the challenges we faced along the way. I have details in Chapter 36.

The things people are scared of often are not the things that will bother them when drilling is underway. Helping a community navigate their fears, the real-world realities of drilling, and finding a reasonable process require building, earning, and maintaining trust.

More on that coming right up.

32

Urban Is not Necessarily Urbane

The area of work most personally challenging for me was the conflict in communities that were affected by drilling first-hand. No one wants any kind of construction activity happening near their home. Think how annoying a barking dog is at 2 in the morning! Oil and gas development is a 24-7 activity during drilling operations happening at an industrial scale.

Twenty-four hours a day.

I empathized deeply with the people who lived in a community and suddenly found their world turned upside down. The impact of drilling is similar to a strip mall being constructed in your neighborhood: earth moving, traffic, and noise. Except drilling has to be conducted around the clock; so add lights and disturbed sleep. The drilling of a well generally doesn't last too long, but while it does, it is happening all the time and can be very disruptive to nearby neighbors.

Although there are many advantages to centralizing wells onto one pad, one downside is that the nearby neighbors have to contend with a much bigger well pad and much longer total drilling time for the many wells on that pad. Although fewer people are affected, those that are affected endure more intense disruptions for a longer period of time.

Personally Acknowledging the Effects

I wanted to stay connected to the citizens that COGA interacted with. So each morning I would drive to work and imagine a well pad and a rig on my neighbor's property. How would I feel? Not great.

Interestingly, a big factor affecting a household's receptiveness to drilling activity is their support of the industry in the first place. I was often baffled by how one set of neighbors would welcome drilling and describe how benign the experience was. Meanwhile, another set of neighbors would report illnesses, disturbed sleep, and a feeling that their lives were truly ruined by the experience. Each experience was valid. Their values affected their perceptions. Their perceptions affected their actions.

And all of that became my reality.

I spent a lot of time in these communities. As we traveled the state each year, I took Brian and the kids to countless barbeques, rodeos, awards dinners, and potlucks. I attended hundreds of hours of public meetings, listening to the public comments, trying to put myself in their shoes. Community supporters of oil and gas were amazing, and I will always be grateful for their words of encouragement to me. For them, drilling was a critical part of our state's history, its livelihood, and our society. Mineral owners and oil and gas supporters also felt under siege, and they were generous with COGA staff and me. They would often hug me and tell me how important my work was. They would inquire after Brian and the boys, and tell me to never give up.

Community opponents were often shrill and always angry. They would stand inches from my face and yell, often with spittle flying. Yet I must admit that I felt more natural kinship with opponents than with supporters. I could imagine how I would have responded if I lived in a parallel universe and received the knock on my door from a neighbor telling me to, "Come to the community meeting! They are going to poison our children!" I would probably have come to the meeting.

And I might be carrying the sign myself.

A critical lesson from my time among opponents is that *concerned community members are not professional environmental activists*. They often look the same. Concerned citizens are often spurred on and informed by professional activists; they may carry the signs and shout the same slogans, but their motivations are fundamentally different. They want to protect their families and their homes.

I can relate.

And so I plodded along. Empathy and compassion is a tough road to hoe. The sound bites and dismissive stance of much of the industry is something I understand, but it's not the way I wanted to engage. Conflicts over development are not limited to energy, and they are never easy.

After much soul searching and many interactions, I ultimately came to the following conclusions:

Treat everyone as a concerned citizen. Although you may find yourself in a room full of hostile, angry people who look like professional activists, you will always have better luck if you assume they are all concerned citizens. This softens your approach, and allows you to learn what their issues are. Although concerned citizens may be misused by activists, that doesn't change the fact that their issues and concerns are valid.

Who is directly impacted? Of concerned citizens, there are those that dislike the *idea* of drilling and those that are or will be *directly* affected. Both create pressure, very tangible pressure on local government officials, like members of the City Council. All must be addressed uniquely, with a curiosity about their motivations and a willingness to seek solutions that help them.

The unfortunate reality. Although it is extraordinarily difficult to admit, some individuals and families will be inconvenienced by drilling just as construction or other types of projects in their communities will inconvenience others. For them, the drilling activity is just going to suck. You can focus on ways to minimize these effects, but strong understanding and empathy are in order. Their best bet is to negotiate directly with companies and regulators, understanding exactly what is going to happen and requesting remedial actions that will help, such as traffic diversions or noise controls.

Compassion. Understanding that people feel helpless when drilling comes to town is a key component of engaging with concerned citizens. Building trust is crucial. Ultimately, a lot of the interactions about oil and gas are emotional in nature. I go into this more in Chapter 36. For now, let's just say that all of this fundamentally comes down to relationships between people. Whichever side of the debate you are on, things will go better if you show up and participate *as a person*, and listen to the other participants *as people*. It's too easy to vilify the other team. Making progress requires conversations among humans.

There are limits. All in all, I focused on working with and addressing community concerns as best I could, understanding that some concerns were valid and simply could not be adequately assuaged.

You simply cannot make everyone happy.

33

Floods

I was sitting in a large Denver auditorium in a row very close to the front next to Roxane White when my phone started buzzing. I had noticed that Roxane had been looking at her phone a lot, but she was the Governor's Chief of Staff, so that really wasn't unusual. I, however, try to make a habit of not looking at my phone during a talk, but the buzzing was so insistent that I took a peek. I had never seen a message like this before: "Emergency Message: Flash Flooding Underway, Seek Higher Ground Immediately."

I looked around. Everyone seemed really calm. I looked sideways at Rox. She seemed agitated, but not "seek higher ground immediately" agitated. I showed my phone to Rox and she nodded, leaned over and whispered, "Flooding in Boulder County."

Oh, okay, so this was my "Reverse 911" message for where I lived, more than an hour away. My body flooded with adrenaline. Natural disasters, of which I have now had more than my fair share of experience, bring on the same response in my body that you get when you narrowly avoid a car accident. When you are cruising down the highway at 70 miles per hours, and you suddenly see the cars stopped, and you brake hard, but hopefully not too hard, and glance in the rear-view mirror hoping the car behind you isn't going to hit you. Then you glance forward and think, *Oh God, I'm not going to make it!*

But then you see there's room on the shoulder and you brake harder and place your car there. You have to take a deep breath because you were sure you were about to be crushed, and your body fills with adrenaline.

A natural disaster feels like that.

I completely tuned out the talk in front of me and took stock. Ever since the fire, our canyon flooded pretty regularly. One time, I couldn't get home because a critical road junction washed out and I ended up sleeping on my sister-in-law Wendy's couch for the night. Usually I raced home at the first sign of significant rain to make sure I wouldn't get separated from my family.

It had been three years since the fire, and we had received abundant warnings of the likelihood of a flood event. As a result, we had a huge overnight backpack full of food, socks, and rain gear always ready to go by the back door. We had tied a rope from a tree to help us ascend the steep slope behind the house in the event of flash flooding. We kept one set of shoes for each of us and a leash for Sasha by the back door at all times in the case of a quick evacuation.

We were also ready to be stranded for about two weeks, should the roads wash out like they did in the 60's. We had heard from our neighbors about how from Wall Street to Sunset, five miles away, they had shared whiskey and food rations until the county could clear a road up to them.

It sounded rather glamorous.

I hadn't planned to return home that night, so roads washing out wasn't going to be an issue for me. I was headed down to the Broadmoor in Colorado Springs for our annual Board retreat. Yes, once again a natural disaster was underway in my home and I was heading to COGA's Board retreat in the opposite direction. I never considered missing it—I took my leadership responsibilities very seriously.

So I didn't need to worry about getting home. I knew Brian had access to fire department updates and he had a radio. The boys, now 6 and 10, were well prepared to either evacuate or shelter in place. I was concerned, but not frantic.

That would come later.

I took deep breaths in through my nose and out through my mouth and endured the rest of the programming. Ever since the fire, I had suffered from some vague but pressing anxiety where I felt I smelled smoke at the oddest times when there was none. This situation was definitely triggering that anxiety. But I'm nothing if not good in a crisis, so I sat and breathed and endured. My heart beat slightly too fast and my hands were sweaty.

When the talk finally ended, I followed Roxane out and she immediately disappeared. We had made plans to meet at the follow-on networking event, and I decided to go ahead and make that appearance, but first I went to my car and called Brian.

He was frantic.

He was home with both boys and his dad, Papa Norm, who was visiting. I could hear the radio blaring emergency responder updates and I only had about 25% of Brian's attention. I knew the worst part for him would be that he couldn't respond because he was home with the family. I asked him if I should head home (I figured I could leave super early in the morning to get back down to Colorado Springs for my 9 am start).

He was exasperated: "Tisha, you would never make it. If the junction hasn't washed out, it will within hours. No, you absolutely should not try to make it. It may be weeks before you make it back up here."

Weeks? I sighed inwardly, not because I thought it would be weeks before I made it home, but because Brian was almost incoherent in his stress, and I was annoyed. In fact, he was right. It would be weeks before I made it home.

> To get there I would have to drive an hour
> and hike an hour to see my home again.

Fortunately, I didn't know any of that, and I was normal-spouse annoyed and upset that there was nothing I could do to help. I felt I was letting my whole family down, but I didn't know *how* I could help. I asked Brian to call me if anything changed.

I went to the networking event, and awkwardly let Roxane introduce me to important people who I should already know but didn't. My heart wasn't in it, and I slipped out as soon as I could. I made my way down to the Broadmoor, checked in with Brian at home, and went to bed.

I called home in the morning to get an update on conditions, and Carter told me that Dad was on a call, short hand for a fired department call. He seemed fine, said they were watching Netflix. On the morning news, I watched people get rescued from cars. By now I had given up on the boys joining me. They had planned to drive down after school and spend the weekend with me at the Broadmoor. I had a huge, gorgeous room that felt cavernous and lonely now that I knew they wouldn't be coming.

By the time I arrived at the meeting room, the widespread state of the flooding was becoming apparent. Huge swaths of northeast

Colorado were experiencing emergency conditions. In addition to my canyon, most of Boulder County and nearly all of Weld County, where one-third of Colorado's oil and gas production took place, were experiencing severe flooding.

As I learned during the fire, I have a different gear for crises.

So I, along with the COGA team, executed the Board Strategy meeting flawlessly. In addition to our regular agenda, we gave hourly updates on the flood crisis, and used the opportunity to gain the Board's support in rallying oil and gas resources to help with flood response. This would go on for weeks. Oil and gas companies ended up donating an amazing amount to relief efforts and mobilizing hundreds of people with heavy equipment to help with delivering supplies, moving debris, and conducting cleanup.

I knew that at home, Brian was leaving the boys with his Dad and responding to urgent flood-related calls. Later, I learned that in the middle of the night, Brian had also responded to a medical call. One of our neighbors who lived at the most dangerous intersection of floodwaters had a chronic medical condition and needed oxygen. Then in the early morning hours, he had returned to participate in her evacuation, which took the better part of the day.

They had had to load her onto a stretcher, and then with teams on either side of the now washed out road, transfer her in a Tyrolean crossing, a rope contraption that pulled her across the washed out road, in the air above it, to an ambulance waiting on the other side. When that effort was complete, he had a crew from the fire department that was surveying damage in Salina to pick up in our truck.

Over the radio, they received word that a particularly brutal burst of rain was coming. He loaded the crew into the truck and onto the back. In the pouring rain, the road began to calve off into the creek. The crew chief on top of the truck yelled in to Brian, "Drive! Just keep driving!" He drove through blinding rain, past the house crushed by a mudslide the night before, through water obscuring what was left of the road. Mud was coming down the hill on the right and the road was disappearing into the creek on the left.

"Just keep driving!" the crew chief yelled to Brian.

The only other alternative was going down the creek with the mud. He kept driving. When they reached the Wall Street fire station, adrenaline was super high. The crew jumped out, and Brian took the truck up the Melvina Hill road to get another group. There would not be time to rest for days.

Fortunately, I didn't know about any of this for weeks. To me, things at home seemed scary but stable.

I was on edge, but high functioning.

Meanwhile at the Broadmoor, we transitioned from our successful, concluded meeting to our late afternoon cocktail and hors d'oeuvres gathering of the Board. Spouses were invited and a few came. We organized the meeting on a Thursday so the COGA team could do follow-up meetings on Friday and anyone who wanted to could stay and enjoy the weekend.

Once everyone seemed happy with cocktail in hand, and I'd made one round of visits, I decided to step away and call home. It felt like half of my heart was left behind up in the canyon, and I needed an update now that my COGA responsibilities were over. Carter picked up the phone immediately, which was unusual.

"Mom! The bridge just washed away! Dad's on the other side!"

"Carter, where are you?" The noise was horrific—I couldn't tell what it was. Turns out it was a combination of rain and the sound of our once docile creek eating our canyon alive. Carter was also exceeding the distance of what our little cordless phone could handle, so the static was incredible. We were both shouting. I was shouting loudly enough that one of my staff came to me with big eyes and stood next to me, as if to say, *Is everything okay?*

"I'm outside looking at the bridge. Dad's on the other side. Oh my God, Mom, what do I do?"

"Carter, get in the house."

"But Mom, Dad's on the other side."

"Carter, get in the house. I'm not talking to you until you're in the house."

My mom-panic was intense. Carter was a very athletic, impulsive kid, and I was imagining him somehow trying to get to his dad, or help in some way, and I was terrified. I also needed to understand the situation. Was a wall of water moving toward them? Were the waters rising? Where was Alec, where was Papa Norm? Were they in immediate danger and needed to run up the hill? If they did, could they do it without Brian?

"Okay, Mom. I'm in the house. Why did I have to come in the house?"

"I was scared. And I couldn't hear you."

"Mom, I wouldn't go near the creek. It's crazy."

"How high is the water?"

"It's still down below."

"Is it covering the patio?"

"No."

"Is it rising?"

"I don't think so."

"Okay, I want you to keep an eye on the water. If it starts rising, I want you guys to think about going up the hill."

"Okay, Mom."

"Where's Alec?"

"He's right here playing cards with Papa Norm…Oh, Dad's here!"

"Put him on."

Brian had returned from his harrowing adventure and had been about to cross the bridge when he saw that it was going to wash out. He'd immediately driven a quarter mile up, parked the truck on the right side, and backed in, on what he hoped was higher ground. At least he'd have a vehicle on that side later, the roadside, of the creek--if he could get to it.

That turned out to be good thinking.

He had hustled with his fire pack across another bridge, which was still intact (although not for long), and bushwhacked with the 40-plus pounds on his back to the house. Thank heavens.

He said, "We're fine. I can't talk now." And hung up.

For heaven's sake.

And then I reached my breaking point. Or, more accurately, what I thought was my breaking point, but this crisis was just getting started. It's good I had no idea what the next 12 hours and then the next week would bring.

Flooding in Earnest

I called over two of my staff, explained the situation, and said, "I can't do this. Can you keep everyone happy?" They agreed—we were wrapping up anyway. I returned to my lonely, cavernous room to decompress.

I tried to figure out how to best monitor the situation from afar, without wasting needless energy when there was nothing I could do. I figured out the Twitter hashtag for the flood, turned on the news, and had a glass of wine. I knew from my fire experience that people, including me, tend to waste a lot of frantic energy trying to get news and updates, but natural disasters unfold slowly, and take weeks to recover from. I knew I had to conserve my energy. But I was also desperately lonely and scared.

Again, I felt I was letting my family down,
but there was nothing I could do.

Sometime around midnight, I figured I might as well go to sleep. I turned the TV off and made one last Twitter check. What I read instantly froze my blood: Four Mile Creek debris dam burst, 30 foot high wall of water making its way down from Emerson Gulch.

Oh my God. Emerson Gulch was one mile above my house.

I sat straight up and I called the house. Ring… ring… ring… voicemail. I called again. Ring… ring… ring… voicemail.

Oh my God.

I turned the TV back on. Nothing. Argh! I got back on Twitter asking, *Can anyone verify?* The poster of the tweet sent a link to the U.S. Geological Survey Four Mile creek water level measurements, which, in fact, showed a huge surge of water.

Oh my God. They could all be gone. The house, our things, the cars. My Brian. My boys. They could all be gone.

I drew my legs under me crisscrossed on the bed and sat up straight. *You can't think like that, Tisha. You have no idea what's going on. It's time to get some support… who can you call? It's midnight. I'll call Brian's sister, Wendy. No, then she will be as panicked as I am. If something has happened, might as well let her have a good night's sleep. If it's nothing, no sense freaking her out. I'll call one of my COGA team, and they can come keep a vigil with me.* I knew that I was living in a first-hand nightmare, and I ultimately decided that there was no sense dragging anyone else in. It would be hours, if not days before I knew what had happened, and it was best if I paced myself, and spared anyone else this horror.

This is when I discovered that I have another emergency mode.

I looked at the clock. 1 am. *I will sleep for 5 hours, until 6 am, then I will wake up and figure out what to do next.* I made sure my phone was on in case anyone called. I turned out the light, put my head on the pillow, and pulled up the covers. I closed my eyes.

Through some inexplicable miracle, when I opened them, the clock said 6 am. I sat straight up. I checked my phone—no calls. I checked Twitter…nothing…nothing…nothing…relevant to me. I queried: *Anyone heard anything about Four Mile?* I turned on the TV. Horrible scenes of people being rescued from flooded cars.

At 6:05, the phone rang. It said, "Home."

"We're fine. We got a call from Kristen's boyfriend, who saw something on Twitter, and we ran up to Cheralyn's and slept on the floor there. The house is still here. I've gotta go."

"Okay, please call me as soon as you can."

And, of course, I burst into tears.

Big, long, dragged out, hiccupping sobs. They were alive.

That was the last time I would hear from Brian for several days.

We don't know why Brian was able to make that call, because the phone was out the next time he picked it back up. I'm fully willing to accept that call as a miracle.

Fundraising

I had two more nights at the Broadmoor. Nights that were going to be a trip with my family. There was no point leaving because I had nowhere to go. All of Boulder was flooding, and the state patrol advised staying out of Boulder. Even Wendy's basement was full of water and so her tiny condo was now packed with her belongings that once sat in the basement. I thought about sitting down and getting some work done, but my head was too scrambled for that.

So I called Gino Greco, the CEO of the Red Cross and told him my situation. I said, *Let's raise some money.* I told him, *I think I can raise you a million dollars*, and he laughed and said, *If you do, I'll buy you a really nice bottle of whiskey.* I didn't have anything else to do, so I sat down and started making a plan.

The fundraising lasted about 10 days, and exceeded all of our wildest expectations. Noble Energy came in early with a $500,000 gift that they were willing to characterize as a matching gift, so we were able to use that to raise another $500,000. And so we got started. I worked my relationships and the phones, and when it was said and done, the oil and gas industry donated $2.3M to the Red Cross.[61] They donated probably as much to other causes as well.

Their generosity was staggering.

But writing checks wasn't enough for any of us, so we also organized teams. I had to end up dedicating one staff to managing the effort full time, because we were overwhelmed by the response. We queried local responders and governments for their needs, and paired up trucks, heavy equipment, and people with gloves and shovels to families that needed help digging out of flood debris. The work was never glamorous, but nearly always appreciated.

In one instance in the city of Boulder, the residents turned a crew away once they learned they came to help from an oil and gas company. Fine. We reassigned them.

The situation got more complicated for me, personally, but the response I saw firsthand from industry at every level, was my point of greatest pride in the industry I represented.

The Evacuation

After I had spoken to Brian at 6 am, I had tried the phone an hour later and it went directly to voicemail. I figured that's the last I would hear from the boys, and by Brian's own explanation, it might be a week or more before I heard anything again. I knew they had plenty of food, fuel for the generator, and although they might be uncomfortable, they would be fine. As long as the storm didn't get any worse, which at that point, was anyone's guess.

Was there anything else I could do? I asked myself. Well, I could check in with my contacts at the state. I texted Mike King, the Executive Director of the Department of Natural Resources. Usually when there was any kind of crisis in the state, the entire cabinet would be mobilized into a leadership response. I let him know Brian and the boys were at home, they were cut off from communication, and if he heard anything about Four Mile and Wall Street, could he let me know? I was super self-conscious about further taxing people I figured were completely maxed. But.. *if they heard something on the radio, could they just let me know?*

Of course, Mike replied. *Rox is about to get in a helicopter, let her know.*

I would never have dared. As far as I could tell, Rox ran the show when any crisis could hit the state. The Governor was excellent on the front lines, and Rox would run all the behind the scenes logistics with the skill of five generals in one compact frame.

Hi. I'm sure you're swamped. Brian and boys cut off in Wall Street, in Four Mile. If you hear anything, can you let me know?

I'm in the helicopter now. Whoa! Apparently flying low enough to get cell service! Despite my personal crisis, I was so impressed with Rox's role and influence. *I'll let you know if I hear anything.*

That's when I got to making my calls. I worked the phones until I ran out of calls to make. At some point, too exhausted to make more fundraising calls, I opened a bottle of wine and started a chick flick marathon.

Rox texted me, *Rescues in Four Mile are underway. Let me know when you hear from your boys.*

Wow! I called Wendy to see what was happening in Boulder and her house. She was personally maxed. Her tiny condo's basement had flooded and they'd moved everything to the first floor, which meant their family of three was down to about 500 square feet on the second level. Roads into Boulder were still flooding, and I let her know I might need some help if the boys got out, and I couldn't get into Boulder to get them.

Then nothing. Eventually I fell asleep in front of the movie, my cell phone on my chest. Sometime after midnight, the phone rang and I sat straight upright. It was Wendy, the boys and Papa Norm had been airlifted out and Papa Norm had called here. They were now at her house. Everyone was crowded in. It didn't seem wise to show up there in the middle of the night with everyone exhausted. I told her I'd be there first thing in the morning.

I was quietly knocking on her door at 7 am.

A Long Hike for a Roller Bag

Things had not eased up for Brian. After the long brutal night with the wave of water, he got word the next morning that evacuations would begin within a few hours. The world had been divided into people on the north side and the south side of the creek, because all of the bridges had been lost and miles' long stretches of the former road were gone.

He had one inexperienced volunteer firefighter on his side of the creek, and he hustled him down their side to find a place they could land a helicopter. We live in a tight canyon and most of the houses on the south side of the canyon are built on the old railroad grade. About 1 ½ miles down from our house, he found a place they could make a clearing, and he put the other guy to work chain sawing down trees. He took out an old fire shelter, which looks like a big shiny piece of tinfoil.

He secured it down to mark a landing spot.

Brian is a good firefighter and he did all of this with his pack on. That's at least 40 pounds of equipment. In a flooding situation you can easily get stranded by a mudslide, and so you have to wear your gear. He then started hustling up and down his side of the creek, telling people that planes were coming. Of course, these are mountain people, and nearly all of them said, *No thanks.*

One exception was our neighbor, Kristin, with her three kids. Her middle son had broken his arm right before the flood, and had it in a temporary cast, waiting to get it set. The flood had trapped them and his arm was still temporarily set. Their house is really close to the creek, and they had spent the previous night on the hillside under a tarp, terrified. I cannot imagine how hideous that must have felt.

They grabbed their belongings and made the two-mile trek to the landing site.

Brian stopped by our house and told his dad and the boys to each pack one backpack of gear. At this point, everyone was exhausted and no one was thinking clearly. Brian continued his hustle from house to house. One couple with their 90-year-old aunt agreed to line up for evacuations. Meanwhile, on the other side of the creek, firefighters prepared people as well. Brian warned people that this might be their only shot. After that, he couldn't guarantee emergency response support or another chance to leave.

He got word that the first Black Hawk was on its way. He hustled back to the house where his dad was waiting with his roller-bag suitcase. Both of the boys had their school backpack as instructed. Brian took one look at his dad and the bag, and told Carter to run and get another backpack. He flung the bag open and said, "Grab as much as you can put in that backpack."

The roller board was left behind for several months.

Papa Norm, our neighbor, Cheralyn, and my boys were on the first Black Hawk that landed. Brian had to get them out so he could focus on everyone else. Carter, was 10 at the time, and he could appreciate the cool experience of a military evacuation in a Black Hawk. Alec, age 7, on the other hand, was open mouthed and terrified as his Dad said good-bye, sending him off to, where, he did not know.

It was months before we learned what was going on in Alec's head. He had been quietly compliant with everything happening, watching and observing, wondering where his mom was, but afraid to ask. He then overheard on a radio news report that seven people had died, and he had assumed I was one of them. Now he was being put on a helicopter by his dad. He assumed he would never see either of us again.

The resulting trauma would be intense for more than a year.

Thankfully, Wendy is the best surrogate I could pick to love my boys in a crisis, and she quickly took the situation in hand, filling everyone with love until I arrived a few hours later.

It was also months later that I was telling this story to Mike, who'd been my first text the morning of the evacuations. He said, "I'm sure Rox got your boys out." I had the opportunity to ask Rox about that shortly thereafter, and she was dismissive. "I pointed out where people were, and command set the priorities."

I love you, Rox.

We were blessed six months later to honor the 4th Combat Aviation Brigade from Fort Carson with an award at the Red Cross 100-year Ball. Brian and I did not nominate this group, which had executed the largest airlift rescue in history, but we did have the opportunity to give them their award. We did so as a family.

That evening was magical, and as we introduced ourselves to the men representing the unit, it turns out that we happened to meet the two men who flew the helicopter who picked up our boys. Brian said, "I was the one on the radio who landed you."

The Captain said, "With that little piece of tinfoil on the ground? That was some crazy shit! That was crazier that anything I ever had to fly in my tours of duty." Then he took a look at our boys, "Were you the two boys? You were our first pickup!"

They had flown rescue flights for days.

That night we all stood on stage together, celebrating our military, emergency service workers, and, most importantly to me, this big extended family that it took to get us all out of that alive.

Brian's Long Hike

Getting his dad and the boys out on a helicopter had taken a huge weight off of Brian's mind that night of the flood. But he would not get any physical rest. He spent the next two days escorting people and their pets to the landing site, radioing in the helicopters, and getting them out. A handful of the hard core stayed behind, and Brian checked in on them. He also set our house up for what might be a long wait until we could return.

We had minor damage where water had run down the hillside and flooded a back corner. The water level had dropped about four feet and our well was now dry. The bridge, of course, was gone. But compared to many of our neighbors, we were in great shape.

Once everyone who was going to leave was gone, Brian was ready to leave himself. It had been days since he'd had any real sleep and he was ready for a shower, electricity, and a clean bed. But the weather had different ideas.

It was still raining.

So Brian arranged with a crew on the other side of Logan Mill to pick him up on their all-terrain vehicle, and started the long hike out. He had periodically run the generator and been able to keep his phone charged. When he reached a high point, he gave me a call. I had been glued to my phone, and answered immediately.

It was pouring and the ground was saturated and difficult to cover, but he was making his way out with his fire pack and our dog, Sasha. There was still the possibility that he could get caught in a mudslide or isolated by one, but at least he was on his way.

The hike was about 45 minutes to where the guys picked him up in their UTV, then drove him to a fire station, and he caught a ride down in a truck to the Boulder airport, where he called me. I was so relieved to finally see him that, after we made it to the house of friend who was putting us up, I stood in the bathroom while he took a shower.

I was afraid to let him out of my sight.

The Generosity of Friends

During the fire, our friend Jennifer Moore had offered to have us come stay. We hadn't known her very well then, so we had of course declined. She had then proceeded to wow us with her energy for helping organize clothes and bikes for displaced families in our community.

This time I would not turn her down.

I was embarrassed to impose, but I knew we needed the help and Jen had a beautiful house with plenty of room. I said, *3 days only!* She poo pooed me.

Stay as long as you need!

We were there seven weeks, and I stayed off and on throughout the next six months.

As if a family of four wasn't enough, we also had Sasha. But Jen made us feel not only welcome, but as if her life was improved by our presence—and the dog's. It was a remarkable lesson for me in both generosity and patience.

It feels like we are now all connected forever.

What Really Happened

Dealing with the flood kept us busy for the next several weeks, but we did slowly have the opportunity to compare notes and figure out what had happened. The flood surge was the greatest mystery to me, and here's what we pieced together.

There had in fact been a debris dam break in Emerson Gulch, which is about one mile above our house. Brian had both heard the traffic on the fire radio and, rethinking it later, had heard the rush of boulders and trees and peoples' bridges in terrifying crashes.

Separately, there had been a surge in a different part of Four Mile Creek, in north Boulder County, where the USGS had a water meter. The events were unrelated, but strangely correlated. By the time I had seen the surge and Brian had received the phone call, both events were over.

Damn strange coincidence.

34

The Longest Day Ever

Once Brian was out and we were all settled at Jen's house, I was ready for a break that I would not get. As soon as floodwaters had risen over much of Weld County, activist groups started reporting that tens of thousands of Colorado oil and gas wells were leaking. One group rented a helicopter and took reporters on flyovers, showing them so-called "proof" of leaking wells… floating tanks and discoloration on the water that looked like oil slicks. The Denver Post ran a front page headline claiming, "Oil Spilling Into Mix"[62] and, as is often the case, the much smaller, second page correction[63] barely warranted a glance. These reports would shape my longest day ever.

Fortunately, COGA and I were prepared.

We had mobilized the COGA staff the moment flooding had started, in the event that there were any real emergencies at oil and gas sites. We had companies reporting in their shut-in operations, the status of their facilities, and making crews available to help with bringing crews and supplies to stranded communities.

Oil and gas companies prepare and drill for natural and human-caused disasters all the time and are adept at it. In Colorado, before the first floodwaters began to rise, the larger companies had set up remote emergency operations centers and started shutting in their wells from a distance. Smaller companies had sent out crews to manually turn taps that shut off wells, drain tanks into trucks, and remove any hazardous materials from well pads. This meant that even if everything on the surface of a well pad was swept away, there would not be any spillage from the site.

COGA staff mapped floodwaters and systematically contacted every operator to confirm the status of shut ins, surface facilities, and assess the potential for spills. Floodwaters rose for days and it was more than a week before they receded enough that every site could be visited. COGA also coordinated with state, county, and city resources in flood-impacted areas, to stay informed of issues and also to keep them apprised of field crews available to help if needed.

While my family was being flooded, evacuated, and resettled, we were coordinating all of this at COGA. To the best of my knowledge at the time, we had no major issues, but I wouldn't know for sure until the flood waters receded, and every site could be visited and confirmed.

In the meantime, news reports were going insane.

By Monday, I had to hit the news sites. National and international news outlets were reporting that tens of thousands of Colorado wells were flooded and leaking. The scale and scope of the unconfirmed misinformation was staggering, and we figured that the only way to counter it was to put me on the news. So Doug, my loyal lieutenant, scheduled interviews starting at 6 am.

I made several critical logistical errors that day. I was emotionally and intellectually exhausted to begin with, and I had no idea what the day would hold for me. I should have had one of the COGA team drive me and keep the schedule; however, everyone was busy on flood-tracking duty, and I hadn't wanted to impose. I was out and conducting back-to-back interviews for over 14 hours, so I should have brought abundant food and water. I had two granola bars and one water bottle.

I would complete one interview, check in with Doug, and then head out to the next. I did local TV news, CNN, radio, international news, and on and on without a break. I would close my eyes in the car; breathe deeply for a few moments, and head in to the next one. About the middle of the day, I got a pounding headache. I took two Advil and kept going.

The questions were all the same. My answers were all the same.

"What are you going to do about the tens of thousands of leaking wells?"

"It's important to note that there has not been one confirmed leaking well. Oil and gas companies activated their shut-in procedures, and we are working to confirm that all wells in the flood area have been shut in."

The questions became increasingly hostile and I stayed calm and stuck to my messages. I have to say, I was really good under this kind of pressure and I never caved.

The final interview of the day was in a hotel in Boulder, and I was so exhausted that two of my team came to support me. I think they were worried I'd just collapse! It was for a national news show and would be an extended interview. We went over the questions with them before I sat down in front of the hot lights. It was 7 pm.

The interview was so brutal, so hostile, that finally I said, "You've already asked that question. I think we are done here." I took off the microphone and walked out, not in anger, just at the limits of my endurance.

Interestingly, less than half of those interviews aired. Without a smoking gun story, or a hostile interview with a defensive representative of industry, there really wasn't a story to tell.

Although that day was a kind of living hell, I learned that I have reservoirs of strength that I didn't know I had. I also knew that I could stand up to nearly any kind of pressure.

Physically exhausted, I went to my new, temporary home, asked my kids to lie on either side of me, curled up in the borrowed bed, and fell into a deep sleep. The alarm was set for 5:20.

I had another radio interview at 6 am.

Don't Tell Me *New Normal*

We live about 10 miles from Boulder, and I learned that about 2/3 of the two roads that connect us to the town lost at least one lane. For a few weeks, the only way we could get to our house was to take our truck about an hour up into Gold Hill and leave it, and then hike down an old mining road for another hour to the house. We would grab the things we needed and hike out.

One irony was that the creek was just a trickle that we could easily jump over.

Just three years earlier, the Four Mile fire had devastated our canyon, and I can't really describe how painful it was to see the steely trauma in the eyes of my neighbors and our local firefighters. We knew how to do this, we had done it before, but it was taking a serious toll on everyone. We'd lost another dozen houses and everyone was displaced… again.

I took some comfort in the fact that even if we wanted to sell our house, we couldn't. Property values plummeted and so we had no choice but to keep on keeping on. This time the boys' school was not affected, so as soon as they could move home, Brian and the boys moved home. That was about seven weeks after the flood. The formerly 15-minute drive up to the school was now a serious four-wheeling 45-minutes… but that was still shorter than a commute from Boulder. I stayed for a few more weeks living at Jen's house in town, which made my commute about 40 minutes instead of the 1.5 hours it would be once I moved back home.

Everything felt traumatic.

You couldn't drive to work or home without seeing the destroyed houses of friends and neighbors. None of them moved back. The logistics of getting to and from home were so difficult that the absence of water at our house was just another inconvenience. When the water table dropped four feet, it dropped below the level of our 150-year-old hand-dug, brick lined well, and then we had no water. We hauled water in buckets from the creek to wash hands and flush toilets. The boys showered once a week at Aunt Wendy's. Brian and I showered every few days at the gym.

When it got cold, you had to break the ice on the top of the creek with the bottom of the bucket before you could fill it up. I stopped sending the boys down to do it, afraid that they would slip on the steep banks and fall in. We kept this up through February, when we were finally able to get our well fixed.

There became an unspoken agreement between everyone in the canyon that you would never, ever say *New Normal*. Anyone offering services and support would strive to comfort us with that phrase. It was over two years before things did, in fact, start to feel normal in our canyon again. Several years later, if you get any critical mass of four-mile residents together, someone is bound to choke up. It had been a painful few years.

On the family front, we all had work to do. The experience traumatized each of us in different ways, with Alec taking it the hardest. Right before the flood, he had begun the normal separation of a 7 year-old—asserting himself as one of the big boys, wanting to be with Brian and Carter instead of me. I had been in silent mourning, watching my baby grow up before I was quite ready.

The flood changed all that.

While I had been far away in Colorado Springs, and Brian had been conducting flood rescues, the radio had been playing constantly at the house. Alec, silent and stoic, had been watching and listening, but not saying a word. He had heard that seven people had died, and he was certain that I was one of them. Why else wouldn't I have come up? I always came home. If Brian or my kids ever needed me, I always dropped everything and rushed home. In fact, since the fire, any time it even threatened rain, I rushed back to the house.

When asked later why he hadn't said anything, or ask, he said, *Everybody was so busy.* So while panic slowly gripped his 7-year old heart, everyone went about their business. When I finally came to Boulder to pick him up, he clung to me the same as I clung to him, and I didn't think anything of it. But as you can imagine, the experience triggered a need that took more than three years to soothe. Frankly, it has been fine with me because I have the same scar.

I can cling to him while he clings to me.

35

The Thorniest Question

And life went on, school resumed, work continued, I breathed easier and once again, immersed myself in COGA. I love to take questions at my talks, and I often ask for "Question, critiques, or comments?" to encourage the audience to contradict me or challenge my presentation. On this day, I stood before a senior-level environmental studies class with the reluctant attention of students who hated me upon first sight. After four years of running COGA and putting myself in such challenging situations, I am habituated to this feeling, but it always hurts, and I have to resist the impulse to win them over at any price.

I was about 25 minutes into our 75 minutes together when, finally, one brave student sitting in the second row put up his hand and asked the question that I used to dread, "Won't more people be hurt by climate change than helped by new energy?"

Often talk of climate change comes in a self-righteous tone of voice and I find myself easily able to dismiss the imperatives. Much of climate change direction comes from people sitting in rich, developed communities who are enjoying a standard of living unimaginable to billions of poor people around the world.

This question was motivated by compassion.

Won't more people be hurt by climate change than helped by new energy?
I could have hugged that young man. Exactly!

Dear reader, it is my hope that my response to him will help explain
to you why I've changed everything about my approach to energy and
the environment based on my own journey. Here goes.

Let's work under the common assumption that climate change is
happening right now, and it is affecting poor people around the world.
(I know this will be controversial to some, but it's worth using this
as a starting point, so stay with me.) Climate change is happening.
Poor citizens living in lean-tos are being affected by rising sea levels,
increased flooding, and longer droughts, and these challenges are
exacerbating their already difficult living conditions.

> What is the best way to develop a common
> cause with these citizens of the world?

Is it to show them that we care, and we want to help? Is it by working
to slow, stop, and reverse "climate change," which will take decades
and massive worldwide resources? I don't think it is either of these
tactics.

The best way to share goals with the world's poor and work to alleviate
their suffering and prevent future suffering is not an environmental
solution. It is to work with them to raise their standard of living. As
mentioned in Chapter 21, creating meaningful access to energy is a
start. Are you best prepared to deal with climate change if you are
relatively rich or relatively poor? Which would you prefer?

> I think the answer is obvious.

That day, I expressed this dilemma to the environmental studies seniors who had been sitting arms crossed and heads tilted in frustrated disinterest. Now hands shot up around the room. I had their attention! Emboldened by his classmate, another student raised the even thornier question that everyone was thinking but no one else was willing to ask: *But if we raise 1.3 billion people out of poverty by giving them access to energy, won't that really accelerate climate change?*

And herein lies the real challenge.

Making climate change a priority is not free. It comes at the expense of other priorities and programs. International banking and policy programs have, for example, limited funding for fossil fuel-related energy access programs in the developing world, seriously hampering those efforts. For example, the Overseas Private Investment Corporation (OPIC) is not allowed to invest in natural gas projects. Yet allowing OPIC to invest in natural gas in developing African countries would provide electricity to millions more people and alleviate one of the biggest impediments to the growth of Africa's private sector.[64]

The truth is, YES, if we prioritize raising people out of poverty, we will need to use fossil fuels in more places around the world, and YES we will increase emissions and YES, that may exacerbate climate change in ways no one fully understands.

And I think it's worth it.

If you and your family were facing rising sea levels, would you rather have a bank account and a mobile phone, or promises from the rich world that they will reduce emissions?

A New Approach with Hierarchy at Its Core

Even if I still thought addressing climate change should be our highest worldwide priority, there are very real political obstacles. Climate change has become so polarized, but addressing worldwide poverty has not.

Maslow's hierarchy of needs is not a sexy name for such an important topic. The concept behind the hierarchy is that people can only address the issues most pressing to them (Figure 35-1).

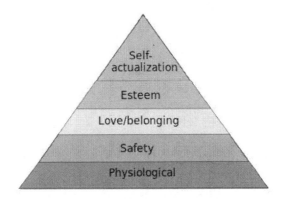

Figure 35-1. Maslow's hierarchy of needs pyramid[65]

When my family was evacuated from our home during the wildfire, even though I had many hours of down time a day, I was so preoccupied with the basics of survival that I couldn't work or even read a novel.

The hierarchy can be applied here.

It also applies to our thinking about climate change. Throughout history, as cultures go from poverty to prosperity (or in reverse), their priorities understandably change. A society can focus on arts, culture, and even the environment only after the basics are taken care of. And the data proves that out.[66]

This has significant implications for addressing climate change. It is truly a blessing to have the means and lifestyle to worry about a problem as abstract and unpredictable as climate change. For countries around the world striving to bring energy to their millions or billions, climate change is certainly a tertiary concern. Although air pollution in developing countries, for example, is gathering significant attention and positively affecting energy decisions, that can be viewed as a direct health effect, and therefore much more relevant to the population than something one can't put their fingers on, such as climate change.

It is the height of hypocrisy to propose addressing climate change by preventing other people's climb to prosperity. So, let's imagine a different approach. Around the world countries large and small, rich and emerging, commit to goals focused on raising people out of poverty. These countries acknowledge the importance of doing so with as little impact on the environment as possible, including consideration of water, air, wildlife, indigenous peoples, and potential effects on climate. In the U.S., right and left can rally around energy access goals, particularly when they are framed in the context of creating prosperity and self-reliance. By focusing on energy access with a mind to tradeoffs, countries expand the opportunities for prosperity within their borders. As we discussed in Chapter 21, energy access increases life expectancy, education rates, and health outcomes.

It also does two very important things that people who currently prioritize climate change care about. First, it reduces birth rates. Even under current scenarios, worldwide population is expected to peak in the next century at 11.2 billion.[67] Second, it moves people up the hierarchy of needs. Ultimately, this will create more prosperous societies that can prioritize environmental outcomes if they so choose.

A Passionate Middle

At the heart of a lot of polarization is the reality that most people don't care about these issues all that much, and most of us do not want to invite conflict into our lives. The result is that for hot topics like energy and the environment, passionate people with strong opinions dominate the conversation. And that doesn't generally include a lot of moderate people interested in compromise.

Instead of ceding the field, we all must participate. We don't have to have strong opinions or have all the answers; we just need to care enough to not give up. I've met people along the way who have strong opinions and even extreme views who have also decided to join the passionate middle.

Politics are fiery, passionate, and sexy—but policy is where things get done. Although engaging in policy is complicated, it's worth the effort because that is where you'll find intelligent and informed participants charged with creating the best outcome for the most people. To do this well, policy makers have to anticipate unintended consequences and thoughtfully balance perspectives.

In Colorado, this comes up repeatedly with the setback of oil and gas wells from structures. It sounds simple, "Keep oil and gas wells pick-your-number-of-feet from a structure." But, in reality, there are dozens of stakeholders in this equation: mineral owners, land owners, home developers, and local governments, and a myriad of considerations, such as surface and subsurface trespassing, distance from property lines, and technical feasibility. Policy affecting complicated decisions requires thoughtful participation and considered compromise.

In other words, it's no place for loud, divisive, uninformed politics.

I'm passionate about the rejuvenation of compromise as a lost art. It's a quality I admire in civic leaders of all types. We live in a diverse society, and we cannot be led by people only willing to have everyone succumb to their viewpoint! That would be a dictatorship. Finding common ground and compromise is an important way that we can live together.

The gridlock created by bitter, divisive politics inhibits progress in all its forms. Moving forward toward difficult solutions crafted by thoughtful, intelligent people is preferable to a morass of angry stagnation, wouldn't you say?

And how does a passionate moderate declare himself or herself within the reasonable limits of human patience and endurance? A few starter suggestions that I might have said to that astute student that day.

Stay attuned to the conversation. Whether controversy is taking place in your neighborhood or on the editorial page, we all have a desire to tune it out. Keeping a dispassionate eye on what's happening is important.

Become a student of all sides of the debate, even if you are locked into one side. Why do they think what they do? What do they want out of this? What would they consider a win?

Assume good intentions. Generally, everyone thinks they are on the righteous side. Why do they think that? You don't have to agree, but you will have a more intelligent assessment if you seek to understand them.

Hold off on having an opinion until you actually need to have one. Most people who haven't avoided a controversy will rush head long into having an opinion. There are actually very few situations where you are required to have an opinion. Try it; it really broadens one's perspective.

When necessary or appropriate, participate modestly and with humility. Vote. Support thoughtful candidates. Write letters. Submit comments.

Prioritize. Most importantly, engage in conversations as someone passionate about civility, intelligent process, and compromise.

We could use you in this conversation.

36

So You Think You're Rational?

Nearing my five-year anniversary at COGA I realized I was going about the energy debates all wrong. Although I had now made peace with the idea that I would routinely change my mind, I didn't know that my entire decision-making paradigm was about to be upended.

I was assuming that each of us behaves rationally. I spend a lot of time evaluating my position on things with facts and figures, and I work to draw the best conclusion. I think that I'm doing this rationally... analyzing the data for what it is.

Turns out, that is almost impossible.

COGA had built dozens of fact sheets. I had spent countless hours building solid scientific cases about what could be done safely in the oil and gas industry. And yet, time and time again, beyond the cold hard facts, I found myself in impossibly emotional situations with people who didn't trust me and didn't want to hear what I had to say.

I didn't come to these conclusions quickly. I came to them slowly and painfully. I am pretty sure I made every communication error in the book before I found an appreciation for the social sciences, particularly behavioral economics. After years and years of arguing with the best facts, I concluded that I could not make any headway in a discussion or a debate until I could establish trust and rapport with my audience.

> Newsflash: facts and figures aren't the key to
> successful energy engagement.

This is so painful to acknowledge! Both because I love facts, data, and a well-constructed argument, and also because I invested so many years, and industry dollars, into carefully analyzing and communicating facts and figures. Even among conspiracy theorists, arguably the least rational among us, their conspiracies are built carefully upon the facts and figures that describe the motives and plans of the agents of conspiracy.

Although I think that I am behaving rationally, science tells me that I am not. And neither are you.

> Definitively.[68]

It turns out that science also tells us it is nearly impossible for a human to digest the fact that we are not behaving rationally. So don't bother! I will assume that I am behaving rationally. You may assume that you are behaving rationally. But to effectively communicate amid the energy wars, it is critical that you have a basic understanding of the irrational decision-making framework of others.

In both my consulting job and then as head of COGA, I have essentially spent my career collecting, analyzing, packaging, and repackaging facts for the consumption of my audiences. Assuming that facts and figures will wins hearts and minds is fundamentally flawed.

I'm not a psychologist or social scientist. I'm just an environmental scientist who engages in a lot of heated debate, and as a result I have made an informal study of understanding how to navigate this minefield of data and emotions. This understanding dawned on me fully the *second* time I tried to read, *Thinking Fast and Slow*. Every 18-year-old should have to read this book before they attempt to make their way in the world!

To my kids: you have been warned.

We have two ways of engaging our mind in a given situation: Kahneman describes these as system 1 and system 2. System 1 makes quick, intuitive decisions about the material before us. System 2 engages in discerning analysis.

The important thing I learned about this is that most of us are operating in intuitive mode (system 1) most of the time. And in that intuitive mode, we bring all kinds of biases to the table to help us make sense of our world. An example of a bias is something called the *affect heuristic*.[69] In the affect heuristic, people make decisions based on how they feel—*Do I like it?*—and then assign rationalizations to support their emotional preference. Think about your last car purchase and you'll get an idea of how the affect heuristic affects your thinking. I, for one, decide what I want.

And then come up with some great rationalizations for why I should get it.

So, years too late, I figure out that that most people I'm engaging with about oil and gas development think they are making rational, discerning assessments of what is safe and what is not. But really, they are quickly processing the available information and making intuitive decisions. As a result, most people are making these intuitive judgments based on their identity... such as, "I'm a Democrat, and Democrats don't support fracking." People may look like they are gathering scientific information about energy and environmental problems but, really, the vast majority are making very cursory, intuitive judgments.

Disguised as deliberative decisions.

This is further exacerbated by confirmation bias. Confirmation bias will really break your heart. This is where people accept or dismiss news stories, or even scientific data, based on their pre-existing beliefs. When you hear a story, pay attention to the moment where you say, "This reporter is so biased!" or "That study was funded by industry!" While some of these judgments may be true, they often point to the early trigger of confirmation bias.[70]

Oh, reader, I'm sorry to break your heart!

The result of our subconscious biases is the effortless divisions we have created into camps on hot-button energy issues like climate change and fracking. We know what "our people" think, we digest news and science that supports our opinion, and we further dig in to our own side.

How does this inform how you engage with others on energy and environmental issues if you want to have an intelligent, informed conversation? You may be motivated because you are implementing outreach for a project or because you simply want to have intelligent, informed conversations.

The good news is you can use the miracle of the social sciences to deescalate tough conversations in any hot topic. Here's what I've learned can really help in these situations.

Acknowledge the emotional, irrational nature of the playing field.
It is actually empowering when you give up on the idea that the best facts will win. They won't.

Understand that relationship building is primary; science and data-based discussions are secondary. Your obligation here is to be an interesting, engaging human being, not a data-driven robot. Get to know the people with whom you are engaging, and be curious about what informs their point of view. The more you engage the person and build rapport, the more likely that you will be able to introduce facts and figures to the discussion later.

Cease imagining that you will ever change anyone's mind. Yes, even me! Even you. *Even engineers!* Despite what many of us have imagined over the course of our lifetimes, we do not engage in conversations to change people's minds. We engage in conversation to build relationships. Do you like someone trying to change your mind?

Plan on multiple conversations and multiple iterations on your engagement approach. The best process of engagement starts, stops, and continues; it goes backward, forward and then forward some more. If you are charged with informing a public group in an outreach project, plan multiple meetings so that participants can digest what you have to say without having to get dug in to their own opinion. A series of engagements allows for the more subtle process of building rapport and trust.

Listen and understand, to inform your next conversation. Iteration is only helpful if you are seeking to learn from your audience. You will grow your perspective along the way, and this will help you build more interesting and subtle perspectives on the issues. Beware! You will learn something too.

Allow for breaks. Once you understand the emotional and intuitive nature of decision making, you can recognize the importance of letting people go away and reset to some extent. You also need time, because inevitably your positions will change as well.

I struggle to admit that I do not behave rationally most of the time. But I have probably influenced more constructive conversations and participated thoughtfully in more difficult conversations about energy and the environment since I put away my facts.

And opened my heart.

37

Daily Threats

The threats against myself were so painful that I still fold my body forward, rounding my shoulders in, whenever I think about them. By the time they peaked, I had become so raw internally, so worn out in spirit, and so hardened to the external world that most people in my life didn't even know about them.

I'm grateful to one of my staff, who during a Board meeting, passed her phone around to Board members, showing them an example of the type of threat I faced daily. I never would have done so, it seemed self-indulgent and weak, and on top of that, I honestly didn't think that they would care. That's what they paid me for, right?

But I was wrong; they were horrified.

That particularly Twitter antagonist was new, and, I assume it was a "he" described various forms of ways that I should die amid sexual violence. I had shown my team that morning because I had them monitoring and tracking my various harassers in case I ever needed to make a legal case against them. I tried to delete them quickly and move on. I could have gotten off social media, as my corporate psychologist suggested, but again that struck me as self-indulgent and weak.

One of my Board members interrupted my update and said, "You guys need to know about this!" He described the tweets and, interestingly said, "Tisha, have you called the police?!" His concern shocked me, but his naivety struck me more.

For more than a year, my family had regular check-ins from the Boulder County Sheriff. We had removed all identifying names and numbers from our house and mailbox. Our neighbors and the Four Mile Fire Department had pictures of people who had threatened us.

And we had a mountain-style neighborhood watch underway.

The boys often had a sheriff at their school, ever since one group of activists had posted their pictures, school, and school address with descriptions like "Disgusting". Prior to that, a significant part of our team had been targeted on a website flagging each of us, our spouses, our home addresses, and various tidbits of personal information encouraging site readers to "make us pay for our crimes against humanity."

This had been going on so long that it had become normal.

The COGA team had been followed, threatened, and harassed. They'd had their cars keyed and creepy "I'm watching you" notes left for them at home. At various times we were protested, delivered mean "declarations" on live video, and had events disrupted by incognito protestors.

In some ways, these threats brought all of us closer together. The COGA team instituted travel-by-pair policies. We often hired off-duty police to support our efforts and events. We supported each other, because, frankly, it often felt that we were up against the world.

There were, of course, blessings. The love I feel for my neighbors and my community is overwhelming. One of my neighbors, who for years put *NY Times* anti-fracking articles in my mailbox (just in case I didn't get that he thought it was unsafe, I suppose), ended up putting a "Coloradans love fracking" bumper sticker on his snow plow truck. This truck was always parked conspicuously in front of his house. He explained to me, "I don't love fracking, but I do love the Schullers, and if any of those Anti people come here, I want them to know that they are in the wrong neighborhood."

Life in Boulder became unbearable. Earlier in my time at COGA, I relished the opportunities to engage in conversations, passionately committed to winning hearts and minds. Now I was tired, and I wasn't sure that Boulderites were interested in being engaged. As a family, we stopped going out to eat or play in town. I was too easily recognized, and people were too aggressive with their opinions. I even moved most of my workouts to Denver, or snuck in and out of the gym as fast as I could, avoiding eye contact and the potential resulting conversations.

I was tired. And scared.

There were painful personal consequences for me. After making excuses for the isolated behavior of deranged individuals, I lost all of my patience for the mainstream left and the mainstream environmental movement. *I thought that we were about peace? About love? About higher consciousness?* Although these nasty people were not representative of everyone, environmental and liberal groups never spoke out or condemned their tactics. I realized that these groups were about winning... winning a battle that wasn't about the highest and best outcomes, just about winning. And there was a kind of implied judgment... that I, my family, and the COGA team deserved this treatment.

With a little space behind me, I no longer consider that kind of behavior *normal*.

In the end, we were fortunate. I got local, state, and FBI investigative support. That scared away the amateurs. Thankfully, we were never seriously targeted by people who wanted to do us harm. I like to think we handled the threats gracefully, taking the higher ground.

38

Meditation or Meds?

Somewhere around 25 years old I really started taking my spiritual practice seriously. But it's hard to balance all the expectations on a liberal, healthy, spiritual perfectionist. Should I do yoga or meditate? Bake bread or go for a run? I landed on 10 minutes of meditation per day, with pretty low expectations of that 10.

By the time I was at COGA, my daily routine was pretty well set. I would wake up at 4:30, make coffee, and then while it was brewing, read a page or two of whatever spiritual book I was making my way through. I would then close my eyes and sit for 10 minutes with no particular agenda. I set a timer on my phone so I didn't look at the time incessantly and just in case I fell asleep, which did happen. If I was particularly time-pressed, I skipped the reading. On weekends, I tried to sit for 20 or 30 minutes.

A tremendous challenge of work at COGA was that I already was doing everything one could humanly do to manage stress. I exercised 4 or 5 days a week. I meditated nearly daily. I went to a yoga class whenever I could, and practiced on my own for a few minutes each day. I had a family who I adored and, who cherished me. But the stress kept piling up. About 6 months in to the new job, I developed sciatica, which didn't clear until a year after I left. At its peak, the pain dominated my life. I couldn't sit for more than few minutes and so stood or grimaced through most meetings. I got where I couldn't drive anywhere for more than an hour without having to stop and stretch.

Back pain was my constant companion during the COGA years.

To manage the sciatica, I got regular therapeutic massages, which helped keep the pain in control, but just barely. A couple of years in, I also developed carpal tunnel, which came and went. My arms would go numb and sometimes I couldn't move my fingers, and I had to text with my pinkies. I knew it was stress, but I didn't know what else I could do to manage it.

After the Four Mile fire, I also started experiencing a new kind of anxiety. Sometimes it was triggered by things that made sense, like strong winds, or the smell of a campfire. But other times, it was completely nonsensical. I'd be in my 6 am swim class, swimming laps like everyone else, and I'd feel a kind of claustrophobic panic. Starting in my chest, I would get a feeling like nervousness, but more consuming, and it would move into my face, then out into my extremities. I almost couldn't move my arms or legs. Sometimes I would feign a leg cramp so I could catch my breath and try to calm my heart without attracting the attention of my lane mates. At those times, I would often smell smoke, even though there wasn't any.

I kept all of this to myself. It took me years to understand that keeping the daily stressors of my work out of my marital conversation was going to be a recipe for disaster. I was trying to protect Brian, and definitely the boys, from what I experienced to be daily crushing difficulties.

I don't think I could do all of that again.

I was trying to protect everyone from everything. I strove to be an intermediary between my difficult members and the staff, frequently asking them to critique me rather than my team. *Their* job was hard enough. I tried to keep the daily pressures from my family, and walk in the door each night with a calm face and a big smile. Meanwhile, I knew that, inside of me, things were beginning to break down and that there was a limit.

> I assumed it would be horrific: a car accident,
> a nervous breakdown, a fatal cancer.

I looked around and saw people with more stress than me functioning better, and I told myself to suck it up. I was a mom, the family breadwinner, the head of an organization, the face of an industry, and this was no time to be a wimp. I knew I was weaker than most, had a tendency to get sick, and could not for the life of me get that sciatica managed. I was not prepared to accept that weakness.

> I am now.

It's funny that what finally made me cry uncle wasn't people posting pictures of my children on the Internet, or some horrible member screaming at me for failing at an impossible task. It was what felt like a final act of betrayal from someone I loved very much.

Sue probably didn't even have me in her mind when she organized the letters from local governments to the governor to oppose oil and gas development. She and I had played ultimate Frisbee together back in the day, and we had been very close. Although she didn't approve of my position, we strove to remain friends. I described the scenario to my corporate psychologist, Julie, who by this point was my one lifeline to reality. I told her everything. She was a no-nonsense gal who I had known a long time and I knew that she had the smarts not to let me get away with anything. She often cocked her head at me and said, "You know this isn't normal, right? You know there *are* jobs where these kinds of things don't happen?"

So I expected Julie to be as outraged at my story as I was.

"Sue didn't have to get involved at all," I told her. "She made an issue and then rallied people, and got involved, got involved in oil and gas, just to get back at me?" I was nearly in tears and my sense of self-righteous indignation was washing over me in waves that made it hard to breathe.

Julie looked at me and cocked her head as she often did, but she didn't say what I expected. I expected her to say that I had been terribly wronged and this was not normal, and that I needed to find a job where people behave sensibly and my long-term friends did not betray me and break my heart.

Instead she took a deep breath and said, "This doesn't seem like that big a deal. I want you to consider something. I think things are getting to you. Would you ever consider going and talking to your doctor about anti-depressants?"

My mind jerked forward in parallel streams, two waves of thoughts competing for my attention. One was a wave of pure relief. I had finally reached the breaking point and I could get some help. The waves of panic in the early morning hours and in the pool raced across my mind, the smell of smoke when it wasn't there, and my fluttering, panicked heart. This thought stream's fraternal twin was the stoic, upstanding part of my psyche, which said, *Never!* I could do this without medication. I would meditate more, exercise more, sleep more, whatever it took. These two waves crashed together and I just looked at Julie with my mouth pinched, brows furrowed, and breath coming in shallow bursts.

"I'll think about it."

Something in me must have broken then as the battle between my will and my exhaustion flourished. The next day I called in sick and made an appointment at my doctor's office. By the time I got there I couldn't stop crying, and when I saw the nurse practitioner, who I had never met before, I simply said, "Ever since the fire I have a lot of anxiety. I'd like to try Lexapro." She wrote me a prescription, gave me some appropriate warnings, and made me commit to coming in and seeing my primary care doc within 3 weeks.

I drove straight to the pharmacy and filled it, now buzzing at a level of anxiety that I didn't know was humanly possible. When the prescription came, I practically ran to my car, ripped the bag open, and skipped reading all the warnings, which I am usually very good about, and popped the prescribed dose of 5 milligrams. I had been warned that I would feel worse before I felt better, and it would likely be 3 to 4 weeks before my sense of wellbeing improved.

Within 30 minutes, I felt notably better.

The walls of panic that had been closing in around me dropped down. I could think. I could breathe. I hadn't realized the level of stress that I was sustaining all the time. It was making it difficult for me to complete mundane tasks, such as laying out my clothes the night before I went to bed. A soothing calm kicked in immediately and never completely left.

I am neither proud nor ashamed that I stayed on Lexapro through my remaining time at COGA. I didn't tell anyone but my closest family and Julie. I experimented with lighter and heavier doses and found a very modest dose worked perfectly for me.

By the time the flood hit, I was so grateful that I had Lexapro as one of the resources in my survival toolbox. During the intense flood response period, I also called my doc and requested a prescription for Ambien to help me sleep. This former yogurt-making, organic hippie mom was now representing the oil and gas industry and taking pills to both function and to sleep. I didn't feel ashamed, just adaptable and resilient.

And most of all humble.

I used to expect the impossible out of everyone in my life. I would push myself and push them too. But there are limits, and I'd met mine. Meeting my limits has made me a gentler person.

Although I no longer take Lexapro, I will again, should the circumstances merit it. I've dropped the expectation that I can get through anything through the force of my will. COGA certainly taught me that I can get through challenges beyond my wildest expectation, personally, professionally, emotionally, and even physically. But being tough for the sake of getting shit done just made me miserable and kind of mean. I am glad to know that I have reservoirs of endurance.

But I am a better person for understanding that I can adapt, be resilient, and be gentle.

39

Culmination in Disaster, Again

When I started at COGA, I planned to stay for three years. That seemed like a respectable amount of time to take on a big challenge and a two-plus hour daily commute and still return to my reasonably normal life. My previous company told me I was welcome back anytime, and that's what I planned to do.

Somewhere around two years at COGA, my now-beloved chairman, Scott (then he was just a task master! See Chapter 22) realized that my departure was nearly imminent and decided that we should negotiate a retention agreement. We picked a time that seemed extraordinarily far away, May 31, 2015. It allowed for continuity, a well-planned search for my successor, and a transition after the legislature ended in a non-election year. This was smart, because when the time came, the communication about my departure and transition to the new CEO was really well done. When my time was up, I would have been on the job a total of 5.5 years.

At the time, I really loved my job and could imagine staying in it forever. But a challenging job like that requires a fresh face periodically with fresh perspectives. I and my approach to the job were not universally beloved.

I didn't want to overstay my welcome.

And, how long can you be the environmentalist in oil and gas before you just become the oil and gas gal?

I did have an agenda for my tenure. It developed over time, but became my daily mantra:

> Externally, put the best foot forward on behalf of
> Colorado's oil and gas industry.

> Internally, bring out the best in the industry.

These guideposts, combined with the Three Questions, gave me the direction I needed to handle the daily challenges and dramas of leading the industry during such a contentious time.

These guideposts were not always appreciated.

There's an interesting phenomenon that occurs in the oil and gas industry; I don't know if it occurs in other business arenas, but I think it's a cultural phenomenon fueled by long years of embattlement. There are those in industry that would simply like to duke it out with the opponents of oil and gas. This isn't a mild inclination for conflict over compassion, this is a deeply held preference for full-scale battle against environmental activists.

I really have a great deal of empathy for their perspective. After five long years of compromise in the form of five nationally precedent-setting rules that did not seem to meaningfully transform the conversation, I came to be reasonably embattled and bitter myself. But the state of mind is a choice, and the choice that these participants make is to fight every step of opposition and regulation, fearing that "if you give an inch, they will take a mile." They have a point, and there was plenty to be said about this in Chapter 25.

A key, culminating conflict happened in the last year of my tenure. Ultimately it led to a Board "vote of confidence" in me. Which was a goofy, humiliating way of deciding whether or not they were going to fire me. Fortunately for my motivation and the herculean efforts that were about to be required of me, I never could have anticipated the vote, or its outcome.

Which brings us back to that boardroom where our story began.

Exhausted from a series of regulatory compromises, dozens of community-level battles, and several lawsuits underway, the industry was besieged by anti-oil and gas ballot initiatives supported and funded by my very own Congressman. The industry was exhausted, and so was I, but there was no time to rest, or even think, as we made our way through a contentious legislative session.

There were a handful of oil and gas leaders who were keen to find a legislative compromise that would result in the removal of funding from the ballot initiatives. Although civic and business leaders of diverse political persuasions opposed the statewide ballot initiatives, they were polling well and represented a serious threat to the industry and the state's economy.

I devoted myself to diplomacy on every level of the conflict: externally with people who could influence a compromise and internally with oil and gas leadership. I lit candles on my altar at home, seeking help wherever I could find it.

I was tireless in my pursuit of compromise.

As the legislative session led to a close, many people feverishly worked to draft, edit, and build support for a legislative compromise. I was not one of them. Our organization's members were bitterly divided. The largest operators with the most to lose in the state if one of the measures was to pass generally favored a reasonable compromise, if one could be found. Most others preferred to "kick their ass" at the ballot box, cherry picking data to support their vision of a win, which was uncertain at best. I continued to focus my efforts on diplomacy that would support reasonable assessment of a compromise, if one could be reached, so that my members could vote to support or not support something, fully informed.

I was neutral on the particulars but passionate about the necessity of the compromise. I felt that a fighting, belligerent industry played right into the stereotypes portrayed by our opponents. We had business, civic, and political leadership from across the state and both parties with us; it was critical that we not blow that support by behaving like the "cave men" our opponents caricatured.

It was in this boardroom that I facilitated the first meeting, representing over 20 companies, many of them hardliners. Over the course of two tense hours, the executives, often CEOs, weighed in on the elements of a potential compromise. My optimism was high but my expectations were low. I didn't allow myself to show any emotion at all, not fear, not elation, as we seemed to build toward a crescendo of a reasonable compromise.

The details were mind numbing. Lines of legislative language dissected out what cities and counties could and could not regulate. Lawyers argued over specific words and the placement of commas. My job was to keep the conversation moving forward. When we had accomplished as much as we reasonably could, one of the CEOs, who it was well known had never liked me much said, "Good job, Susan. You'll circulate to all of us to review, right?"

Susan?

I could only guess that he had confused me with the only other woman who had participated in the negotiations, an accomplished lawyer from one of the member companies. "Tisha," I said, "and of course."

"Great, thanks Susan."

I had just navigated my most challenging, successful meeting that I had ever had to lead. The stakes were high, tempers were piqued, and we not only got through the meeting, but left with a draft that exceeded my wildest expectations for reasonable compromise. I was inwardly elated, outwardly stoic.

And, really, that fucker didn't even know my name?

I ended up facilitating a series of such meetings on the legislation until we were ready to present our draft to the other side. Even that meeting had to be carefully crafted diplomacy… held on neutral ground, limited to three people "per side" and with all participants sworn to secrecy. There were so many people who wanted a compromise to fail—and one leak to the press, or hostile forces on either side would have killed it.

Our mistake was showing up with a reasonable deal.

There would be no returning to the industry side. They had given away as much of the farm as they were going to, and this was a take-it-or-leave-it offer. It was generous beyond everyone's wildest expectations.

But the other side rejected it.

Why? I'll never know. On some level, I think the opponents weren't yet ready to compromise. I think they were also shocked to get what they wanted, and therefore felt they had to ask for more. Whatever the reason, we had several tense meetings where they countered this and countered that until finally they gave me their "best and final" to take back to industry. As I expected, they were disgusted.

We told you, Tisha.

After that the industry really threw up its hands and prepared for battle.

As a result of this experience, one company CEO became intoxicated with the idea of replacing me, and he set his executive who sat on the COGA Board to the task. He did figure out my name was not Susan. Impressive.

I became aware of the effort at first through rumors. Then my chairman at the time informed me that "some of the guys want to hold a vote, it's no big deal really, just to see if the Board likes the direction you're taking things."

"You mean to fire me?"

"Well, I'm sure it won't come to that."

I was well aware of the effort happening to build votes, but, honestly by this point I was so completely exhausted from the work underway, the work that still had to be done (we were busy on very many fronts,) and enduring the ire of the opposition personally and professionally, that I decided not to fight.

If they wanted to fire me, let them.

I had many allies who kept me informed of the progress of the effort to remove me from my position. I kept my staff in the dark because everyone on the COGA team was working to the point of physical and emotional exhaustion, and I did not want them to think a referendum on me was a referendum on *their* work. I mentally and emotionally prepared to be removed, and firmly refused to consider the ramifications it would have on my life and career.

It was the culmination of my newfound humility and exhaustion that I continued to be resolved not to fight. Several of my allies thought they had the votes to remove me (it would only require a simple majority of our 40-person Board). I knew that I would probably be devastated, but there was no way I could both consider that and get through my day-to-day. I was also tired of representing people who didn't appreciate the effort I was enduring at every level.

The week of the Board meeting I prepared exhaustively, as usual. The COGA Board met monthly for two hours, and the preparation of a Board packet a week in advance, timely updates, and a strongly facilitated meeting was one of my most important responsibilities. The morning before the meeting I gathered my executive team, and told them the Board would be going into executive session at the end, and we would all leave.

Then I told them why.

I looked around my office and prepared to pack my boxes. I told my team if I was voted out, we would behave with our now habitual stoic grace. They were open mouthed with horror, but held their tongues. My tone did not open the door to our usual open debate.

I still remember the step-by-step walk over to the Board meeting four blocks away. I was strangely calm and seemingly prepared for my fate. I ran a good Board meeting and my staff later marveled that I betrayed no inner conflict or fear. Strangely, I didn't feel any.

Once we were excused for the executive session, my staff and I left and I went to lunch with my counterpart from the western slope. Everything was normal, but all of life was moving as if it were underwater, strangely suspended.

My current Board chairman called, and I answered, feeling the first flex of a nervous stomach.

"Hello, this is Tisha."

"Everything is fine," he said, "We'll talk later."

"Ok" I pronounced, my voice sounding strange to myself. "Wait!" I interrupted his goodbye, "Do I still have my job?"

"Yes," he said. "Of course you do."

40

A New Environmentalism

It turns out that there was only one vote to get me fired. My informants were terrible, and my antagonist clearly didn't have much of a plan, or know how to count votes, or wasn't particularly committed to the task. I'll never know which.

Now how to proceed?

I had a defined departure date about a year away. If I was completely honest with myself, I wanted to stay on the job for a couple more years. The job was challenging and relevant, the COGA team was now comprised 100% of people who had been hired during my tenure, and they were fabulous. Many of my supporters on the Board asked me to stay. But I just felt in my heart of hearts that it was time to go. I had accomplished what I could; it was time for someone else to take the reins.

I sat down with my compensation committee and completed the negotiations for my departure. And that was that. It took less than 20 minutes.

A few months later, we rolled it out to the Board, and six months later, announced my departure and the ensuing search for my replacement publicly.

In that intervening six months, between decision and announcement, I was then left contemplating what my legacy would be. There had been a time when my community outreach program was the shining jewel in my personal crown of accomplishment. I loved the comprehensive, engaging, non-partisan approach we'd built in over a dozen communities around Colorado. Unfortunately, that effort was largely co-opted by another, competing, organization that was better funded and more aggressive, so that would not be my legacy.

I was excessively proud of the staff and the programs that we had built. We had an always-sold-out Industry Ambassadors series, and we had created a yearlong EnGen program for emerging industry leaders. The alumni from this program were vibrant and engaged. I figured that a COGA successor would probably change out staff and programs, so it was unlikely that any of that would be my legacy.

And that led me to where we are today, contemplating a new kind of environmentalism. My legacy, it turns out, would be internal, the development of a philosophy, which informs all the work I do today. This internal legacy now drives my work, including this book, written for you:

- ✧ Acknowledging that most people want the same thing, a reasonable quality of life, the opportunity to improve their circumstances, and access to beautiful, healthy, natural environments.
- ✧ Understanding that although we nearly all share these objectives, people have wildly different ways of going about pursuing those dreams.
- ✧ A discerning environmentalism requires letting go of some traditional positions that don't stand up under scrutiny.
- ✧ This new, true environmentalism is available to people of every political, socioeconomic, and cultural persuasion.

✧ There is no such thing as good and bad fuels; all energy sources have tradeoffs.

✧ A commitment to honestly assessing tradeoffs and seeking the best energy solutions with a mind toward energy density, footprint, transportability, affordability, and environmental effects.

✧ Prioritizing addressing world energy poverty can create a unifying vision for addressing global human and environmental challenges.

It could be that it's too late to use the word "environmental". It has so much baggage for both people who ascribe to the working identity and those who are alienated by it. I, though, take comfort in my environmental philosophy. I take solace and rejuvenate myself in natural places, as often as I can. This is a core of who I am and what I want to contribute to. That's not where the fights are now, though, for the most part, and we need a shared philosophy that can include a broader tent working toward shared goals.

My kids say, shaking their heads, "Yup, mom's still a hippie."

41

Now, What Do You Really Think?

The summer after I left COGA, I was finishing up a leisurely 7 am workout when I ran into one of my gym acquaintances. "9 am!" she remarked, "Aren't you the woman of leisure now?"

I smiled because indeed I was. She continued, "Is it too soon for me to ask... 'What do you really think'?"

Confused, I queried, "What do you mean?" Barb had never discussed my job with me, and so I assumed she either didn't know what I did or didn't care. She elaborated: "All those times I heard you on the radio or read about you in the paper...you were doing your job. And doing it well. But now I want to know what you really think about oil and gas."

I was immediately defensive.

If I had learned nothing else at COGA, I definitely knew how to combine a poker face with a Mona Lisa smile. That morning, I had been off my guard, but my guard was back up. It took me a moment to understand why I was so taken aback... the query assumed that I had been lying in some way, "for the job." I decided to respond as straightforwardly as possible, minus the defensiveness.

"I think exactly what I said in all those interviews."

She looked surprised, and then recovered quickly. This was not the answer she expected. And the innocent look on her face made it clear to me at once that she wasn't trying to corner or badger me, she just assumed I had another, different opinion than the one I presented to the public in the course of my COGA responsibilities, and she was honestly curious about what it is.

I let my guard down a tad.

"I took that job, Barb, because I wanted to help people understand that oil and gas is important, and it can be developed safely. The more I learned, the more I became confident in the industry. If anything, I'm more of a supporter now than when I started."

Surprised again, eyebrows wide, she simply said, "Oh! Good! I'm going to give that some thought."

Maybe my work on behalf of the industry would never be done.

I spent years and years giving talks debunking the most common oil and gas myths, to the point that I practically have a narcoleptic fit anytime someone wants me to explain fracking to them. But I will make one, last heroic attempt here to debunk those myths. Even though I want you all to know I could be surfing, or running, or really doing anything thing else in the world.

After this... someone else will have to carry this baton to the next leg of the race.

Fracking

Yes, it's a horrible word. Yes, I just spelled it with a "k." Hard core oil and gas folks still want to write frac'ing or fraccing, or stick to hydraulic fracturing or hydraulic stimulations. We debated this robustly for years at COGA and finally decided we needed to go where our audience was, and our audience was using fracking.

No number of c's is going to get the public to start loving fracking.

Fracking is one little part of the oil and gas drilling process, formally called hydraulic fracturing. But several years ago, various groups started using the word as a synonym for oil and gas drilling. We argued about that for years, but it was a waste of breath... So while it's important to understand what fracking actually is... people will often use the word "Fracking" when what they mean is "any oil and gas drilling".

And that's that.

So after you drill a well, you need to create tiny fractures in the rock to allow the oil or gas to flow out. This oil and gas is often a mile or more below the surface of the earth, and it's very dense. You inject water with sand and a small amount of additives under pressure to create microfractures in this rock... they are so small that the sand grains are used to prop them open. (The sand grains are called "proppant" – get it?!)

This action has been done millions of times all over the U.S. and it can be done safely. As I mentioned in Chapter 25, in Colorado we have thousands of data samples showing groundwater before and after drilling and fracking, and there is so much solid ground between the oil and gas layer and the shallow groundwater layers that impacts are extremely rare.

Water Contamination

For years there has been widespread concern that fracking and water contamination go hand in hand. This simply isn't true. But there are important things that must happen to protect groundwater during oil and gas drilling.

And I'll tell you about those.

In a lot of the country, including Colorado, oil and gas development has been happening for over 100 years. Old wells can create problems, and addressing those are important. Most people aren't worried about these, but fortunately state agencies are. In Colorado, there's a significant fund of money in place to address old oil and gas wells when they are found.

Then there are the "in between" wells, those that are maybe 30 or 40 years old and still operating. Companies can run tests, such as cement bond logs, to make sure that those wells are operating correctly and not allowing oil or gas resources to leak out on their way to the surface.

The most important thing that must happen when oil and gas wells are installed is being cemented correctly. Ground water resources are relatively shallow, and the oil and gas is brought up from very deep, often over a mile. The well creates a straw that allows the oil and gas resources to be extracted at the surface and collected on the well pad. At the surface, water is removed, and it's held for transportation in either a truck or a pipeline to market.

Still with me?

These days, the drilling and follow-up tests for new wells are so sophisticated that companies can assess the quality of the well and address potential issues before the well goes into operation.

You will read about oil and gas operations contaminating groundwater or soil. The vast majority of these cases are old wells that have not been properly maintained. If you read these stories carefully, you can discern what went wrong, and use this to inform your understanding of the millions of wells that are operating correctly. It's imperative and is expected that companies follow regulations and, especially, that old wells are maintained.

Lighting Water on Fire

The images of people lighting tap water on fire have probably created more unnecessary fear than any other anti-oil and gas campaign. It's effective, but upsetting. I know firsthand because I faced many mothers, often with infants in their arms, crying in genuine fear about what oil and gas will do to the health of their family. As we discussed in Chapter 32, oil and gas development does affect its neighbors, but the hyperbole and exaggerations about the dangers were very distressing to me.

Have you ever lit water on fire?

In fact, people in Colorado and Pennsylvania have been lighting water on fire for more than 100 years. There are layers of rock that can be described as coal or coal bed methane that often are very porous and hold both water and natural gas in them. Sometimes these layers are deep below ground. In some places in Colorado and Pennsylvania, they are quite shallow and even appear as a rock outcrop at the surface.

Where they outcrop at the surface, there is generally flowing water, and people have been able to light these places on fire for over a century.

This activity is well documented in both states.

Where those layers are held below ground surface, homeowners have often created a groundwater well in those layers because they are very porous and the water flows well. It's an interesting phenomenon that when you take the water out of the coal layers, it creates methane, or natural gas. So, in the simple act of pumping water for your house or your livestock, you create a byproduct of natural gas. As a result, people can light their tap on fire.

Methane in water came to public attention in both Colorado and Pennsylvania because these states are also great places to produce natural gas. When water tables rise and fall, either due to seasons, drought, or water pumping activities, more methane is produced. In fact, in two basins of Colorado, the process of dewatering coal seams is used as a way to produce natural gas. This natural gas is called coal bed methane.

Earthquakes

Earthquakes are scary because they seem much an act of God. In my second month at Stanford, I was there for the 1989 Loma Prieta earthquake, which closed a significant portion of the Stanford campus for my four years there.

So I share the healthy fear.

The discussion of earthquakes is nuanced, but important. So bear with me.

Fracking itself does not cause earthquakes that you can feel at the surface. The pressure required to break the rock is the equivalent seismic event to dropping a gallon of milk off of a kitchen counter. Because this is happening far below ground, it does not shake the ground service. Because the vast majority of new development is regular oil and gas wells, communities do not need to fear that each well will cause earthquakes.

There have been instances where water disposal wells have caused earthquakes. In a handful of areas, many now famously in Oklahoma, where there are faults, these can be triggered through the disposal of large volumes of water deep underground. The careful management of this handful of wells is important, and states such as Oklahoma and Colorado have put processes in place to prevent earthquakes and respond when they do happen.

> There is not, however, any widespread danger of earthquakes from oil and gas development.

42

A Guide to Engaging

The man chased me down the open-aired corridor. "Tisha!"

I still bristled and expected the worst, although generally by this point most of my audiences were friendly. It still takes an act of will to stay and attend to the line of people who want to talk to me after I've given a speech. I try to keep my guard down, but after I've given an hour keynote, I am so spent and vulnerable that this effort always costs me something. Once I've politely taken cards, answered questions, and accepted suggestions, I generally flee for solitude to recover. Often, I have a splitting headache and have to close my eyes. Adrenaline races through my veins for a couple of hours and I try to find some balance.

So, the chaser was not a welcome intrusion.

Was I far enough away to keep going? Perhaps, but two people walking toward me in the hot but breezy hallway said, "Tisha, he's trying to get your attention."

"Thank you!" I said, big smile on my face. I consider keynote talks a performance, and my job is to be gracious and engaging until I fall over. I turned it back on and turned around to meet the chaser.

"Oh, whew! You had a line and I wanted to let them talk to you. Want to grab a cup of coffee?"

"I'm so sorry, I have some work I have to get to, but I'm happy to talk here for a few moments." The other two who had flagged my attention joined us.

He jumped in. "Tisha, I loved your talk. You were amazing. So smart. I just don't understand; how can you vote for Hillary?"

This is what he wanted to talk to me about?!

It was actually funny, and I let my guard fall about three-quarters of the way. I was familiar with this line of exchange. The life-long Republican who found me smart and therefore couldn't understand why I openly declared myself a Democrat. This was one of the many ways I saw political identity override common sense and common cause.

It was the summer before the presidential election and the two nominees, Trump and Clinton, had more or less just been sorted out. One of the standard points in my speech was, "It doesn't matter who is going to be President, the expectations of communities for more proactive, transparent engagement is not going away." Throughout my talk, I articulated my personal political philosophy, generally to try to demonstrate that one doesn't have to let their political identity dominate all of their views.

Point not well made, apparently.

We exchanged a few light-heartened opinions, punctuated by the two companions encouraging the chaser to "leave her alone, she doesn't have to support Trump." When it became clear that the good-natured chaser absolutely intended to convert me, I begged off.

Ironically, I used the skills that I had covered in my *Deescalating the Energy Wars* keynote, which turn out to be applicable to just about any contentious conversation you might find yourself in. They key is to emphasize engaging thoughtfully, civilly, and persuasively.

You are not in it to win it.

Since I've done a lot of thinking about this, I've come up with some pointers that might help you out, reader, should you be chased down a corridor by someone who wants to change you.

The First Rule

The rules of engagement are simple—on the surface. In practice, the rules require self-awareness and more of a commitment to having a conversation than to being right. I probably don't need to mention that this can be very challenging. But, you're banging your head against a concrete wall unless you try something new, so you might as well give these rules a try.

Rule No. 1: Treat everyone like a concerned citizen, even if they look and act like an activist.

Take that chaser, for example. It would be too easy, and frankly lazy, to dismiss him as a right-wing nut. Similarly, people who oppose oil and gas may look or sound like activists. People on both sides dismiss their opponents as extremists routinely, and it is not helpful. It alienates an awful lot of people who can, should, and ultimately will join the pragmatic conversation about energy development.

Many, many community members get worked up and scared over what they have heard about oil and gas development in general or fracking in particular. Similarly, people in the industry are exhausted by regulation and genuinely fear it is affecting or will affect their livelihood.

A lot of people hear things but have no idea what's fact, what's fiction, and what's relevant to their life. So, step one is to respect their fear, and seek to understand it.

Upon encountering that first challenge, whether during a family gathering or over a keg of beer, take a deep breath. Engage your curiosity and ask yourself, *What is driving their perspective?* Here are some example questions that you might ask your protagonist, to get this conversation started on the right foot:

"That's an interesting perspective; can you tell me a little more about it?"

"I have never heard that before, but I have some understanding of the topic. Can you tell me more about where you got your information?"

"It sounds like you are really focused on that issue. What is most concerning to you?"

"I have access to some information; would you like to gain another perspective?"

"I have some experience with this topic, would you like to hear about what I've learned?"

You'll notice that these are questions, not statements. Which brings us to the second rule.

This Is About to Get Interesting

Rule No. 2: You are a student of the conflict.

It's easy to find ourselves defensive in discussions about energy and the environment because others will often take what they believe to be the higher ground. It's quite fashionable in liberal circles to be opposed to fracking, for example. And on the right, opposition to all forms of government intervention are taken for granted. Then, without much thought, people become accustomed to being in the right.

Whether they are right or not.

Too often, we play right into the villain role by becoming angry, condescending, or spouting facts. It's important to let go of the good-guy bad-guy paradigm and make a calm study of the conflict.

By putting our attention on the conflict, rather than being right, we allow our curiosity to drive the conversation to the next level. Make yourself a relentless student of understanding people who feel like opponents. *What makes them tick? What motivates their thinking, behavior, and actions? What will they consider a win?*

You will be a much more effective advocate for your positions, and, incidentally, a much better conversationalist, if you understand who you are talking to. And there is a distant chance you just might enjoy the exchange.

Getting to the Point

Rule No. 3: Let the conflict lie. You cannot win.

The biggest mistake we all make when we advocate for our position, is we lord the facts we have over others. In fact, *this is not the point.* The engaging conversation is the point. Learning about what people fear, why they are motivated, and how we can engage more effectively is the point. Humanizing yourself and the perspective you represent is the point.

Building trust is the point.

In a discussion about oil and gas, for example, who is the most influential person to your average citizen? Someone they know who works in the industry. It's not because that person will know everything, or have all the facts, it's because ultimately this is a person they know and trust. You can't win trust by spouting facts and dominating an interaction. You build trust by conversing, and listening, conversing, and listening.

Be the Change, Even Though It's Cliché

Rule No. 4: You're representing your perspectives. Be trustworthy.

Whether you're an employee, a supporter, or a consumer, it's important that the conversation about energy and the environment become about people, not faceless opponents. We can be labeled big oil or crazy hippies. These labels are the cop-outs we all use to blame faceless others for conflicts that we don't want to take responsibility for or take part in.

Enough already.

There is not any "they." Every group is made up of people. If we aren't going to cede the most important conversations happening about energy to all the nutty extremists, it comes down to each of us sucking it up and participating in a meaningful way.

Yes, I know you want to run and hide in the bathroom when that awkward conversation begins, but you can't. When you think about it, each of us is part of the conversation about energy and the environment because, when you think about it, our lives are entirely interdependent on these resources.

So engage with grace, patience, and compassion.

43

Is There a My Life's Work?

It was an absolutely surreal day. My boys had stayed with me at a downtown hotel, and they kissed me goodbye and headed to school. I took my time getting ready and heading into the office because I literally had nothing to do except put some boxes in my car. May 31, 2015 was my last day at COGA.

Originally my plan was to take the summer off and look for a job in the fall. But I had the opportunity to work for COGA part time on the summer conference and Stanford University part time on their new Natural Gas Initiative, so I decided to make it six months part time and look for a job in the New Year.

Jim Davis, a good friend had spent most of his career in the FBI before a stint heading up safety for Colorado, a position that involved sitting in the Governor's cabinet. He had then moved on to his consulting career, and gave me some pointed warnings about my upcoming break. Having worked nearly around the clock for five years, working in my subconscious even when I wasn't working, he let me know that my body was addicted to stress and the hormones associated with stress. He did not sugar coat his prediction.

"It's gonna feel like hell."

I didn't believe him. I was ready for a break!

Jim was right.

I woke up every day with a pit in my stomach and a pressing sense that there were a lot of really urgent things that I needed to get done. But there weren't. It's particularly challenging to suffer from the withdrawals of stress, anxiety, and debilitating workaholism when everyone you see thinks you're on vacation. "Congratulations! Living the dream, eh?!"

"Woman of leisure now... nice!"

The friends and colleagues I encountered assumed I was loving my new life, and I let them. Yet, I woke up every morning with a strange anxiety... *What was I supposed to do?* I knew there were things that needed to done. I had been sure I would clean out every closet in my house (that never happened). Working ½ time was like not working at all. The absence of a brutal headwind was disorienting! Luckily, Jim had warned me and I now processed his warning seriously.

I treated that summer like I was going through detox, and in many ways I was.

The most painful questions that plagued me were those of identity. I had been an environmentalist, then the face of the oil and gas industry, and now, *Who was I?*

Was I a success or a failure?

By whose measure?

How did I want to spend my summer?

How did I want to spend the rest of my life?

I vacillated wildly between being motivated and productive… waking up early, getting in my workout, knocking out my work. And other days I would drift around the house wondering when I was going to clean out all of those closets I'd promised myself I'd clean out in the summer. *Should I be reading? Working? Sleeping?*

What matters, who matters, what's the point? I slept a lot more than I had for five years. I still am sleeping a lot more and I hope I do forever! I trained for and ran a half marathon. I decided I could meditate more, but I needed to think less.

I wrote this book.

And here's what I've found is important.

- ✧ There are times in your life where it's critical to work hard. Really, really hard. But making a habit of ambition without an intelligent purpose is silly.
- ✧ If you can swing daily meditation, daily exercise, and eight hours of sleep, you should.
- ✧ Create time and space in your life for perspective. You can't know who you are, what you are doing, what you want to do without regular time for reflection.
- ✧ Creative pursuits require some space. You can't crush productivity into every minute and expect to be able to create. Whether its art, music, writing, thinking, or speaking… making some space is its own discipline.
- ✧ I love speaking to groups who are interested in the topic of energy and the environment. I love offering a path forward that isn't combative.
- ✧ Contributing to politics, policy, and thought leadership that can move people out of poverty— now that makes my heart sing.

Epilogue

Being the face of an industry had its advantages. I had an enormous platform, including a staff, financial resources, and lots of access to the media. Now, I am no longer hamstrung by representing the industry, but there is a different kind of pressure, an internal pressure to participate meaningfully, but by what right? For what purpose? To what end? So many questions I have been asking myself.

It's more complicated to be a free agent and an honest broker. *With what authority do I speak and who will listen?*

I want to participate in transforming the world as we know it.

As I make my way striving to figure out how to contribute to the dialogue meaningfully, I have decided that the most important trait for me to nurture in myself and seek in others is this: *One must be more interested in working toward solutions than committed to the ideological warfare of the energy-environment debates.* On paper this seems quite straightforward, in practice, we are emotional, tribal beings. The war has become a habit.

And so I have developed my "energy-environmental ideology."

Ideology, not theology!

The first step is to remain flexible. The world is changing, scientific understanding evolves, and we—you and me—can change our minds. Scientists, industry, think tanks, and policy makers are perpetually creating new bodies of knowledge. I love having the opportunity to contemplate energy sources, environmental problems, and the ever-changing menu of solutions. I enjoy that light-headed feeling I get when some piece of knowledge I took for granted was wrong. But I have to remember that learning from new information along the way is key. It's easy to get stuck in one's current thinking!

Here's where I propose we start.

Pro-humanity

There will be environmental leaders who view humans as a plague on the natural environment, but it's not a position that holds up to very much scrutiny. I propose a worldview that puts humans first, to a point.

There are very few people living a subsistence living who view the wonders of the natural world as superior to the needs of humanity. It is a position that can only be espoused by the fabulously fortunate. Pretty much all of us reading this book are astonishingly rich by historic and worldwide standards of quality of life.

I admit that the idea that *nature without human interference is superior to our current experience* does resonate somewhere deep in my selfish consciousness. The idea that there is this beautiful planet full of amazing natural wonders that humans are screwing up is thought-provoking and provocative. But it doesn't hold up to an honest inquiry. Have you seen *The Revenant?* Do you want to be left to your own devices in the wilderness for very long?

This worldview fails in two fundamental ways.

The first failure of the *precious, fragile nature* worldview is that even it is anthropocentric. A human who views this amazing planet in its wonder, glory, history, and diversity needs only to think for a few minutes in geologic timescales to know that the planet was just fine when it was a fiery soup and perfectly content when it was covered in ice. Mother Earth was at peace with massive rainforests and battling dinosaurs, and Mother Earth will be just fine if humanity makes a disastrous mess of things and pollutes us to extinction.

It requires a profound hubris to imagine that we humans with our massive gifts and extraordinary failings are more than a blip on the history of this planet. We are just a blip. and I haven't even gotten started on how irrelevant we are in the context of the galaxy.

Or the universe.

The second failure of the *precious, fragile nature* worldview is that it ignores that life without modern quality of life is pretty awful for humans. Hunger, cold, disease, and despair are the currency of life in the natural elements pretty much everywhere on this planet when living directly with nature. Ever watch *Naked and Afraid?* I didn't need to watch more than one episode to be convinced that I want to wear underwear if I'm going to sleep in a swamp full of mosquitos.

To truly value nature and natural systems, one has to enjoy a minimum of a middle-class quality of life. Otherwise every rainstorm is an exercise in endurance, and a summer heat wave becomes a fight against dehydration. To make sacrifices for nature and natural systems, a family has to have all of their other hierarchy of needs met.

Because I live a middle-class life in the developed world, I take refuge, solace, and refreshment in the natural world. My reverence for nature is deeply rooted in my spiritual values. My entire life is set up so that

I spend the majority of my time in the woods. I wrote this book at my desk overlooking a creek and forest.

I am privileged beyond measure.

For others to join the quest to value and uphold the best natural world sustainable for the longest time, we need to increase the number of people who have the quality of life to enjoy this worldview. And we need to understand that good people will not necessarily prioritize environmental values over other economic development priorities. However, we stand a fundamentally better chance of increasing the number of citizens of the world who prioritize environmental protection by first envisioning a world where all people have the basic dignity and quality of life that allows such a choice.

Therefore, I propose that we prioritize humanity by reducing world poverty through creating energy access. This can be done explicitly with the goal of creating a world citizenry who enjoys the basic quality of life that allows them to care for the planet as a whole.

Will there be a cost in increased energy use and the associated environmental effects such as increased emissions and, particularly increase carbon emissions? Yes.

But here's why it's worth it.

The current framing of developed world vs. developing world and economic development vs. environmental protection has the majority of energy and attention going into the battle rather than into the solutions. If that collective interest and attention could instead go to reducing energy poverty and building support for sustainable systems and solutions, how much more could be accomplished?

I propose a humanity-first approach to environmentalism that seeks to care for the most vulnerable among us in both the developed and developing world with the explicit goal of creating a world where people can choose to love and value the environment.

It hasn't really worked to try to coerce them anyway.

Let Go of Your Fuel Antagonism, Support R&D

Fossil fuels are not capable of being evil. They are carbon atoms put together in chains of varying lengths. Using them to keep people warm, light up cities, and move goods and services around the planet is useful, not malignant. Other ways to get these things done are not inherently angelic either; energy sources are stuff being used to accomplish stuff.

Coal is a rock. It does not have a personality.

There are, and will forever be, better ways to accomplish the tasks that we conduct today with smaller footprints and different tradeoffs. It makes sense to align ourselves toward increasingly efficient, effective, accessible, affordable energy sources. Looking at sources of energy without cultural baggage allows us to weigh the tradeoffs and thoughtfully make informed decisions.

Fuel antagonism is a silly worldview that frankly makes no sense. It is not only polarizing important energy policy discussions, it is leading us to make energy decisions that hurt the planet and its people. Take, for example, the closing of a nuclear plant. In 2016 alone, these are unlikely to undermine the massive carbon emissions reductions credited to the growth of wind power.

Sound dumb? It is.

I am confident, however, that an energy agnostic approach to energy policy and development will ensure that we don't make senseless choices based on irrelevant value judgments. Efficiency, prudent development, access, and affordability should be our guides moving forward.

We don't know where the next energy breakthroughs will come from. Investing in perceived angelic technologies is one approach. A better one is to make massive commitments to energy R&D across the spectrum of fuel sources.

> Let's discover the best energy solutions,
> not project values on inanimate objects.

How the Divest Movement Misses the Point

I understand the feeling behind the Divest-from-Fossil-Fuels movement, and I've talked with a good many well-meaning individuals who want to be a part of moving to a cleaner, greener world. The idea of using the stock market against capitalist enterprises, like oil and gas companies, sounds smart. In some ways it's a nod to the importance of free market forces and a desire to put one's money where one's mouth is.

> The problem is, it is misguided at best,
> and counterproductive at worst.

Generally, when an organization encourages divestment, they want the target entity to stop investing their money in companies that do business in the area of fossil fuels. So, if I'm a university, and I have an endowment that I invest to create annual income for university activities or scholarships, the divest ask is that the university limit its investments to companies that don't produce, transport, or burn energy from coal, oil, and natural gas.

Sounds easy enough, and that's part of the problem.

It is, in fact, incredibly hypocritical to ask SOMEONE ELSE to divest. It makes people and organizations feel good about themselves, without thinking about all the key issues raised in this book.

- ✧ It ignores the important role that fossil fuels play in powering the world.
- ✧ It ignores the need to have diverse, abundant, affordable, transportable, practical energy solutions.
- ✧ It provides no reasonable or functional alternative.

The second important reason why divestment is a bad idea: It does absolutely nothing to change demand. If you really want to put market forces to work for a cause, you must disrupt demand. Not only do we continue to demand fossil fuels and their related goods and services, we are extremely sensitive to changes in gasoline for our cars and heat for our homes.

Divestment does not disrupt this fundamental demand driver.

There are very practical, real reasons why an organization shouldn't divest. Investors are tasked with providing returns on investment. Although external forces may feel that divestment is free (to them) and that someone else should prioritize "people over profits" and the like, the reality is that organizations that invest for, say, school teachers' retirement, need to provide returns on that investment.

Now, imagine for a moment that all the data is wrong, and that investment decisions do not have to account for their returns, let's just play out what successful fossil fuel divestment could mean in the world. Let's say oil and gas exploration companies, pipeline companies, and power generation companies all took massive hits on their stock price because no one would buy their shares…what would be the outcome?

Public opinion further vilifies fossil fuels, making it more difficult to build and execute projects. Companies' bottom lines are hurt, reducing their ability to invest in infrastructure, growth, and R&D. This does not do anything for demand, or energy alternatives, so one of two things will happen:

✧ Prices go up, and infrastructure investment goes down
✧ Other country-owned fossil fuel companies, such as oil and gas interests Russia, Venezuela, and Saudi Arabia source fossil fuel resources, unconstrained by divestment

If you want to meaningfully transform the world, you have to look at demand, and either transform that, or seek practical solutions. Divestment simply cannibalizes our energy ecosystem, if it does anything useful at all.

Fracking, Nuclear, GMOs and other Boogie Men You Can Support

There are some key themes to this worldview.

✧ There are no easy answers
✧ Think for yourself
✧ Technology can be humanity's and the planet's friend
✧ Solutions keep evolving

It's perfectly appropriate to ask questions about technology solutions, to be aware of unintended consequences, and to be skeptical about new, radical solutions. In traditional environmentalism, many environmental positions have become stuck and unwavering. It is critical that humanity evolve its understanding, scientific base of knowledge, policy solutions, and technological advancements.

Environmental positions must evolve along the way as well.

In my early environmental days, I was opposed to all kinds of things I now think it's important to support: natural gas development (aka fracking), nuclear power generation, genetically modified foods to feed the world. In their own ways, each of these is a technological advancement that addresses a growing humanity's need for increased efficiency in energy and food production.

What I hope I've laid out for you in this book is that being opposed to something, such as fossil fuels, doesn't make you a good environmentalist. It makes you a good, mindless foot soldier in a battle that isn't serving anyone.

In fact, it makes you part of the problem.

An evolved energy-environmental ideology requires intelligent, caring, compassionate, and thinking participants. There will not be one policy position. There will be intelligent debate of data, ranges of solutions, potential unintended consequences, and tradeoffs.

A Case for Compromise

Which brings us to the final, most important tenet of an evolving worldview: compromise is required. I don't know where along the way compromise became a sign of weakness, but it's foolish and we must grow past the notion.

Compromise is fundamental and required.

Addressing world poverty, energizing humanity, feeding the world, protecting and sustaining important places... these are complex challenges that will not be solved by shouting politicians thumping their fists on podiums. To even envision making meaningful progress, we need engaged, diverse teams of innovators, inventers, policy makers, entrepreneurs, established multinational corporations, and even accomplished bureaucrats. We must have difficult, long, creative conversations about priorities, paths forward, tradeoffs, and costs. No two people will think about these things the same, nor should they.

And so, the paths forward will be, by their very nature, winding. They will have false starts, involve mistakes, require circling back, and ultimately create advancement through the best combinations of ideas and execution. The undercurrent of this stream is engaging, thoughtful compromise.

I say, let's get to work.

Acknowledgements

My reason-for-everything is my family: thank you Brian, Carter, and Alec for being you.

Several kind people read and commented on drafts in formative ways. Thank you, Todd Hartman, Resa Furey, Max Potter, Barb Munson, and Paula Gant. Rest in peace Fred Julander, and thank you for the confidence in me that made these experiences happen. Much love to the Four Mile Fire Department and Boulder County Sheriff for so much care and concern for the Schullers.

Without Lindsey Gage, this book would still be sitting in a sad, lonely corner of my hard drive. Thank you for bringing Accidentally Adamant into the daylight, Lindsey!

Endnotes

1. Data converted from USDA National Nutrient Database. https://ndb.nal.usda.gov/ndb

2. Google calorie information. https://www.google.com/webhp?sourceid=chrome-instant&ion=1&espv=2&ie=UTF-8#q=strawberry

3. Google calorie conversion. https://www.google.com/webhp?sourceid=chrome-instant&ion=1&espv=2&ie=UTF-8#q=convert+kilocalories+to+megajoules

4. Y. Chisti, "Biodiesel from microalgae," *Biotechnol. Adv.*, vol. 25, no. 3, pp. 294–306, May-Jun. 2007.

5. Murphy, S. Wootton, AA. Jackson, "Variability of fecal energy content measured in healthy women" Department of Human Nutrition, University of South Hampton, UK. *American Journal of Clinical Nutrition*, Issue 58 (2) pp. 137-140

6. Energy Content of Some Combustibles. Adapted from C. Ronneau (2004), Energie, pollution de l'air et developpement durable, Louvain-la-Neuve: Presses Universitaires de Louvain https://people.hofstra.edu/geotrans/eng/ch8en/conc8en/energycontent.html

7. Smil, Vaclav. "Power Density Primer: Understanding the Spatial Dimension of the Unfolding Transition to Renewable Electricity Generation". May 14, 2010.

8. Denver Post, 2011 Oil bash turns into political brouhaha. http://www.denverpost.com/ci_14290542

9. Science Daily. 2011. Methane levels 17 times higher in water wells near hydrofracking sites, study finds. https://www.sciencedaily.com/releases/2011/05/110509151234.htm
https://www.sciencedaily.com/releases/2011/05/110509151234.htm

10. Sheppard, Kate. 2011. Natural Gas: Worse than Coal? Mother Jones http://www.motherjones.com/politics/2011/04/natural-gas-worse-coal/ April 12.

11. Robert W. Howarth · Renee Santoro · Anthony Ingraffea. 2011. Methane and the greenhouse-gas footprint of natural gas from shale formations. Climactic Change. March 13. http://www.acsf.cornell.edu/Assets/ACSF/docs/attachments/Howarth-EtAl-2011.pdf

12. Levi, Michael. 2011. Rebutting the Howarth Shale Gas Study. Council on Foreign Relations. May 20. http://blogs.cfr.org/levi/2011/05/20/rebutting-the-howarth-shale-gas-study/

13. Osborn. 2011. Methane contamination of drinking water accompanying gas-well drilling and hydraulic fracturing. PNAS. April 14. https://nicholas.duke.edu/cgc/pnas2011.pdf

14. Siegel et al. 2015. Methane Concentrations in Water Wells Unrelated to Proximity to Existing Oil and Gas Wells in Northeastern Pennsylvania. Environmental Science and Technology. 49 (7), pp 4106–4112 March 12. http://pubs.acs.org/doi/abs/10.1021/es505775c

15. Annual Energy Review 2010, Energy Information Administration http://www.eia.gov/totalenergy/data/annual/archive/038410.pdf

16. Energy Information Administration 2015 - https://www.eia.gov/tools/faqs/faq.cfm?id=73&t=11

17. "The Sierra Club and Natural Gas" February 2012 - http://sierraclub.typepad.com/michaelbrune/2012/02/the-sierra-club-and-natural-gas.html

18. EPA U.S. Greenhouse Gas Inventory Report 1990-2013 - http://www3.epa.gov/climatechange/ghgemissions/usinventoryreport.html

19. Baker Hughes. 2016. North American Rotary Rig Count Pivot Table (Feb 2011 to Current). http://phx.corporate-ir.net/phoenix.zhtml?c=79687&p=irol-reportsother Accessed Jun 2016.

20. Products Made from Oil and Natural Gas. Oilandgasinfo.ca http://www.oilandgasinfo.ca/oil-gas-you/products/ Accessed February 2017.

21. World Energy Council. 2011. Global Transport Scenarios 2050. https://www.worldenergy.org/wp-content/uploads/2012/09/wec_transport_scenarios_2050.pdf

22. Brough, Kelly. 2015. President and CEO of Denver Metro Chamber of Commerce. Fracking Spurs Economic Recovery. http://www.cred.org/path-economic-recovery/ July 10.

23. American Petroleum Institute (API). Oil and Natural Gas Stimulate Colorado Economic and Job Growth. http://www.api.org/~/media/ Files/Policy/Jobs/Oil-Gas-Stimulate-Jobs-Economic-Growth/Map/ Colorado.pdf

24. Wobbekind, Richard and Brian Lewandowski. 2015. Leeds School of Business, University of Colorado at Boulder. Oil and Gas Prices – the Upside and the Downside. http://www.coga.org/wp-content/ uploads/2015/09/2012-Economic-Study-CU-Leeds-School-of-Business.pdf January 28.

25. Governor's Office of State Planning and Budgeting, State of Colorado. 2013. The Colorado Economic Outlook: Economic and Fiscal Review. https://www.colorado.gov/pacific/sites/default/files/ DecRevenueForecast.pdf December.

26. Lewandowski, Brian and Richard Wobbekind. 2013. Leeds School of Business, University of Colorado at Boulder. Assessment of Oil and Gas Industry: 2012 Industry Economic and Fiscal Contributions in Colorado. http://www.coga.org/wp-content/uploads/2015/09/2012-Economic-Study-CU-Leeds-School-of-Business.pdf July.

27. Lewandowski, Brian and Richard Wobbekind. 2013. Leeds School of Business, University of Colorado at Boulder. Assessment of Oil and Gas Industry: 2012 Industry Economic and Fiscal Contributions in Colorado.http://www.coga.org/wp-content/uploads/2015/09/2012-Economic-Study-CU-Leeds-School-of-Business.pdf July.

28 Mulvaney, Dustin. 2014. Solar Energy Isn't Always as Green as You Think. IEEE Spectrum. http://spectrum.ieee.org/green-tech/solar/ solar-energy-isnt-always-as-green-as-you-think. November 13.

29. Energy Almanac. 2015. 2014 Total System Power in Gigawatt Hours. California Energy Commission. http://energyalmanac.ca.gov/ electricity/total_system_power.html Accessed June 8, 2016.

30 Eurostat. 2015. Energy production and imports, Eurostat, Statistics Explained. http://ec.europa.eu/eurostat/statistics-explained/index. php/Energy_production_and_imports. Accessed June 8, 2016.

31. Washington Post. 2015. Mapping How the U.S. Generates its Electricity. July 31, 2015. https://www.washingtonpost.com/graphics/national/ power-plants/

32. MacKay DJC.2013. Could energy-intensive industries be powered by carbon-free electricity? Phil Trans R Soc A 371:20110560. http:// dx.doi.org/10.1098/rsta.2011.0560

33. MacKay DJC.2013. Could energy-intensive industries be powered by carbon-free electricity? Phil Trans R Soc A 371:20110560. http://dx.doi.org/10.1098/rsta.2011.0560

34. U.S. Census Bureau. 2015. Income, Poverty and Health Insurance Coverage in the United States. http://www.census.gov/newsroom/press-releases/2015/cb15-157.html September 16.

35. Chandler, Adam. 2016. Where the Poor Spend More Than 10 Percent of Their Income on Energy. The Atlantic. http://www.theatlantic.com/business/archive/2016/06/energy-poverty-low-income-households/486197/ June 8.

36. U.S. Energy Information Administration. Annual Energy Outlook 2017. Levelized Cost and Levelized Avoided Cost of New Generation Resources in the Annual Energy Outlook 2016. http://www.eia.gov/forecasts/aeo/electricity_generation.cfm August 5.

37 Wirfs-Brock, Jordan. 2015. Lost in Transmission: How Much Electricity Disappears Between a Power Plant and Your Plug? Inside Energy. http://insideenergy.org/2015/11/06/lost-in-transmission-how-much-electricity-disappears-between-a-power-plant-and-your-plug/ November 6.

38. Wirfs-Brock, Jordan. 2015. Lost in Transmission: How Much Electricity Disappears Between a Power Plant and Your Plug? Inside Energy. http://insideenergy.org/2015/11/06/lost-in-transmission-how-much-electricity-disappears-between-a-power-plant-and-your-plug/ November 6.

39. United Nations, Department of Economic and Social Affairs, World Population Prospects, the 2015 Revision. Data Query tool. http://esa.un.org/unpd/wpp/DataQuery/

40. International Energy Agency. Energy poverty web page. *About Energy Poverty* http://www.iea.org/topics/energypoverty/ – WEO 2015 Energy Access Database which utilizes 2013 numbers for electricity access and biomass use (http://www.worldenergyoutlook.org/resources/energydevelopment/energyaccessdatabase/#d.en.8609)

41. International Energy Agency. Energy poverty web page. *About Energy Poverty* http://www.iea.org/topics/energypoverty/ – WEO 2015 Energy Access Database which utilizes 2013 numbers for electricity access and biomass use (http://www.worldenergyoutlook.org/resources/energydevelopment/energyaccessdatabase/#d.en.8609)

42. CNN – Sept. 20 2012 http://www.cnn.com/2012/09/20/world/africa/kandeh-yumkella-energy-poverty/

43. The World Bank Database 2012

44. Figure "Energy Access Drives Life Expectancy": Positive correlation between access to electricity to life expectancy. Source: The World Bank 2012

45. "Burden of disease from Household Air Pollution for 2012" – World Health Organization http://www.who.int/phe/health_topics/outdoorair/databases/FINAL_HAP_AAP_BoD_24March2014.pdf?ua=1

46. Kharas, Homi. 2010. The Emerging Middle Class in Developing Countries, OECD Development Centre, Working Paper No. 285. January. https://www.oecd.org/dev/44457738.pdf

47. International Energy Outlook 2013, Energy Information Administration https://www.eia.gov/todayinenergy/detail.cfm?id=12251

48. Figure World Energy Consumption Projections. Source: International Energy Outlook 2013, Energy Information Administration

49. Worldwatch Institute. 2010. Issues of Today: Our Energy Future featuring Christopher Flavin. http://www.worldwatch.org/node/6425

50. National Petroleum Council. 2011. Prudent Development: Realizing the Potential of North America's Abundant Natural Gas and Oil Resources. http://www.npc.org/nard-execsummvol.pdf

51. COGA. 2011. Voluntary Baseline Groundwater Sampling Program. http://region8water.colostate.edu/PDFs/Factsheet%20COGA-sample-analysis-Plan.pdf

52. EIA. 2017. International Energy Outlook 2017. https://www.eia.gov/outlooks/ieo/pdf/0484(2017).pdf

53. Voosen, Paul. 2012. CONSERVATION: Myth-busting scientist pushes greens past reliance on 'horror stories'. E&E, Greenwire: Tuesday, April 3.

54. Nordhaus and Shellenberger. 2011. Love Your Monsters. http://thebreakthrough.org/index.php/programs/philosophy/love-your-monsters-ebook

55. Vaidyanathan, Gayathri. 2014. How to Determine the Scientific Consensus on Global Warming. ClimateWire. http://www.scientificamerican.com/article/how-to-determine-the-scientific-consensus-on-global-warming/ July 24.

56. Bastash, Michaeld. 2016. Top MIT Climate Scientist Trashes '97%' Consensus Claim. The Daily Caller. http://dailycaller.com/2016/02/16/propoganda-top-mit-climate-scientist-trashes-97-consensus-claim/ February.

57. Economist. 2011. The Anthropocene: A man-made world. Science is recognising humans as a geological force to be reckoned with. http://www.economist.com/node/18741749 May 26.

58. Economist. 2011. The Anthropocene: A man-made world. Science is recognising humans as a geological force to be reckoned with. http://www.economist.com/node/18741749 May 26.

59. Kolbert, Elizabeth. 2016. Climate Catastrophe, Coming Even Sooner? http://www.newyorker.com/news/daily-comment/climate-catastrophe-coming-even-sooner. March 31.

60. Sun, Y.; Gu, L.; Dickinson, R. E.; Norby, R. J.; Pallardy, S. G.; Hoffman, F. M. (13 October 2014). "Impact of mesophyll diffusion on estimated global land CO2 fertilization". *Proceedings of the National Academy of Sciences*.doi:10.1073/pnas.1418075111

61. 2013. American Red Cross. Colorado Oil & Gas Association Surpasses $2 Million in Support. http://www.redcross.org/news/article/Colorado-Oil--Gas-Association-Surpasses-2-million-in-Support

62. 2013. Denver Post. Friday, September 20. Front Range Flooding: Oil Spilling into Mix. https://pbs.twimg.com/media/BUm1IMLCEAAK52G.jpg:large

63. 2013. Denver Post. Corrections. http://www.denverpost.com/2013/09/26/corrections-281/

64. Moss, Todd and Beth Schwanke. 2014. Closing Africa's Energy Poverty Gap. http://www.gereports.com/post/94147980228/closing-africas-energy-poverty-gap/. August 8.

65. Wikipedia. Maslow's Hierarchy of Needs. https://upload.wikimedia.org/wikipedia/commons/thumb/3/33/MaslowsHierarchyOfNeeds.svg/450px-MaslowsHierarchyOfNeeds.svg.png Accessed February 4, 2017

66. GoodTherapy.org. 2011. New Research Explores Accuracy of Maslow's Hierarchy of Needs. http://www.goodtherapy.org/blog/accuracy-maslow-hierarchy-needs/ July 9.

67. Our World In Data. https://ourworldindata.org/future-world-population-growth/ Accessed February 4, 2017.

68. Kahneman, Daniel. 2013. Thinking Fast and Slow. April 2.

69. Wikipedia. Affect heuristic. https://en.wikipedia.org/wiki/Affect_heuristic Accessed February 4, 2017.
70. Wikipedia. Confirmation bias. https://en.wikipedia.org/wiki/Confirmation_bias Accessed February 4, 2017.

Made in the USA
San Bernardino, CA
12 November 2019